MAKE YOUR OWN HOT ROD

MAKE
YOUR OWN
HOT ROD

By LeRoi Smith

ILLUSTRATED WITH PHOTOGRAPHS

DODD, MEAD & COMPANY, NEW YORK

All photographs courtesy of *Rod & Custom* Magazine

ISBN 0-396-06353-5

Library of Congress Catalog Card Number: 77-156860

Printed in the United States of America
by The Cornwall Press, Cornwall, N. Y.

Introduction

Some time ago I wrote a book titled *How to Fix Up Old Cars*. Essentially for the beginner, it included a rather comprehensive investigation of older cars. Of necessity, the book covered the entire spectrum of old car renovation, with everything from restoration to hot rodding. It could not be specific. This book is. *Make Your Own Hot Rod* begins where that first book left off. It provides a detailed analysis of rod building that will be of value to old hand and beginning rodder alike.

To create a hot rod the builder should have at least a casual knowledge of American automobiles during this century. In essence, a serious hot rod builder becomes something of an automotive expert as a by-product of his hobby. No matter how limited his experience in hot rodding is, the enthusiast cannot help but be caught up in the excitement of the sport. And whether he becomes a banker, engineer, or auto mechanic, the car buff will have profited immensely from his experiences.

I've been asked hundreds of times for a definitive definition of hot rodding. I can't give one. It covers everything to do with improving performance of an old car, of course, but it goes well beyond that. A group of hot rodders were partly responsible for success in our early space program. Hot rodders are currently involved in all phases of Detroit passenger car production. Hot rodders have worked on military Jeeps and tanks, on airplanes, on boats; in fact, on everything mechanical.

Until the late 1940s, one could be more explicit. We didn't call them hot rods. They were roadsters, and coupes, and sedans. They were Gow Jobs and Lakes machines (drag racing wasn't invented until the early 1950s).

Hot rodding includes everything that has to do with high performance automobiles. Today we tend to call hot rodder anyone who works on cars in a relatively amateur way. Others are racers. The young man who builds a super-fast fuel-burning dragster is a rodder until he starts making other dragsters for sale, or he starts racing his machine in money matches. Then he is a professional, a racer. Indianapolis cars are racers, although many a hot rodder might have a hand in their construction. It's a thin line of distinction, but the best we have.

Hot rodding flourishes throughout the Americas and in several foreign lands, the foremost being Australia, England, South Africa, Germany, Sweden, and Norway. That peculiar adjunct to the sport, drag racing, is present in each of these nations and growing in popularity. Drag racing began, and remains, a simple method of testing one's automotive building prowess. But it is not the entire sport of hot rodding. Far from it. Pick a National Championship drag meet and note the thousand or so competition cars in the pits. Then count the hundred thousand spectators in the stands. Hot rodding includes everyone there, not just the tire-churning, smoke-belching quarter-mile missiles.

This book, then, is for everyone concerned with hot rodding—the serious builder, the professional, the rank amateur. It is for the enthusiastic teenager and the cautious senior citizen. Hot rodding knows no age barrier. It is also timeless. The information contained here will be as valid ten years from today as it is tomorrow. Above all, hot rodding is creative. It answers the need in every man to build something of his very own that expresses a little bit of his own philosophy. Little more could be asked of any sport or hobby.

Contents

Contents

MAKE YOUR OWN HOT ROD

1

What Is a Hot Rod, Anyway?

An old car with floppy fenders and names written on the doors? Not by a long shot. A hot rod is a piece of metal sculpture, as full of individual creativity as a bronze statue or a famous painting. It can be a 1909 Whippit roadster or a 1969 Mustang; it can be brazenly different or subtly unique.

A hot rod is any kind of car modified in some way to meet specific demands of the owner. It is a 1967 Chevrolet sedan with disc brakes and chrome wheels; it is a 1931 Model A Ford coupe, chopped and channeled and without fenders, sporting a late model V8 engine and much chrome; it is a 450-mph streamliner built exclusively for the Bonneville Salt Flats; it is a slingshot dragster with a 1000-horsepower supercharged engine. It may even be just a high performance factory-produced passenger car, with special options for better acceleration or handling. It is not, and this is emphatic, it is not a rusty old Model T body hastily wired to a creaky chassis powered by a sloppy engine.

The term hot rod has never been accepted as honestly descriptive by veterans of the sport. Sam Hanks, champion of the Indianapolis 500, got his start in rodding like so many other racing drivers and car builders. He still calls old cars that have been modified Roadsters or Coupes or Sedans. When he says it, with emphasis on the capital letter, even the automotive ignoramus knows he means some kind of very special car. Still, hot rod has come to be a universal designation for any high performance car not produced by a factory or racing garage.

The name was first applied shortly after World War II by a zealous San Francisco, California, newspaper in describing local cars that zipped and sped through downtown traffic. True, most of these cars were stripped-down Model A's and Model T's, and the majority were powered by hopped-up Ford Flathead engines. However, conscientious car clubs of the time held these imitations in great disfavor and seldom could the owner gain membership in a Roadster or Coupe association. Because of irresponsible reporting, the very great majority of enthusiasts were to suffer for the misdeeds of a very small minority. The situation remained dark for almost a decade. Then came the Drag Safari, and organized drag racing on a national scale.

But the story goes back much further. No one is sure exactly when hot rodding came into existence, or where. As soon as there were more than two cars in a community, a race was inevitable. Automotive competition was as natural as horse racing, and it took on great emphasis during the early twentieth century. While the average man might not have a huge, smoke-belching monster of a car suitable for the really serious races, practically everyone could afford a Model T. Removal of fenders, top bows, and windshield was the first step toward a Strip-Down. The basics of hot rodding were born.

Indianapolis, Indiana, became the speed capital of the United States, but only because of the great 500-mile endurance race. Weather elsewhere was much more conducive to year-round automotive competition. Southern California, with a dry, temperate climate and good roads, became the center of race car building and amateur racing. An Indianapolis race car could be built there and tested long before the annual event.

Southern California boasts a number of dry lake beds in the Mojave Desert, vast areas of hard packed alkali clay as smooth and level as the Bonneville Salt Flats. Amateur speed enthusiasts began meeting at these lakes to race each other and to test the top speed of their various creations. An individual would create special speed equipment for his particular car, and make duplicates for friends if requested. It was like a gala desert picnic, with all-night parties around giant bonfires. At best, it was mass confusion.

It was at these lakes meets, and the few oval race tracks spread through Los Angeles orange groves, that most of the famous names of modern racing were spawned. Winfield, Edelbrock, Iskenderian, Evans, Tattersfield, Meyers, Novi, Offenhauser, Kurtis, Halibrand —they were all there with Model T's and Model A's, Chevrolets and Dodges. It was a great era, with speed records available to anyone with mechanical ability and a backyard shop. Commercial speed equipment was extremely limited and would not be introduced until the very late 1930s. To go fast, you made your own equipment, and the four-banger T and A engines were running 120 mph in head-on competition with the new Ford Flathead V8.

The most famous of the early hot rod oriented race tracks were Gilmore Stadium and Ascot; the most popular dry lakes were Rosamond and Muroc. The former was not the best available, but it was convenient to a highway. The latter has since become Edwards Air Force Base, site of test flights for super-fast aircraft and space research vehicles. The hot rodders moved to more remote El Mirage dry lake, where the Southern California Timing Association (SCTA) still conducts monthly meetings during the dry season.

SCTA came into being a few years prior to World War II when

several clubs formed an association for formal timing meets on the dry lakes. That hot rodders automatically raced roadsters was an established tradition—minutes of early SCTA meetings include references to coupe and sedan owners wanting to time their cars. They were rejected, and the closed car owners (a significant minority) were forced to form their own timing associations. SCTA was soon joined by the Russetta Timing Association and the Valley Timing Association. The world war slowed activity, but it resumed with a roar in 1945.

Everywhere the Southern Californians went in the service, they showed photographs of their fenderless Fords. Fellow servicemen in New Jersey and Iowa, Montana and Florida immediately caught the fever and went home to create their own roadsters or coupes or sedans. Late model sedans and convertibles were given extensive body modifications and were recognized as customs. The sport began to boom. The great number of prewar cars, and the limited availability of new Detroit designs, only served to whet the appetite of young men for high performance machines.

With the beginnings of the speed equipment industry, which has grown in two decades from a backyard hobby to a multimillion-dollar-a-year enterprise, there came an interest in automobile shows. It was at one of these shows, sponsored by SCTA, that a young and struggling Hollywood publicity agent named Robert Petersen met SCTA secretary Wally Parks. Between them they were to create an international sport.

Bob Petersen was no stranger to dry lakes meets, so when veteran Wally Parks suggested a special program for the show, the foundation for the successful *Hot Rod* magazine was laid. On borrowed money and with tremendous enthusiasm, Petersen began *Hot Rod,* followed shortly by *Motor Trend* magazine. Now the word of hot rodding could be spread across the continent. Wally Parks became editor. From such a humble beginning, when the few dedicated staff members spent weekends hawking the new magazine at organized races, *Hot Rod* became the largest selling automotive book in the world, with an outstanding international circulation.

By 1949 it was apparent that great improvements in power were making the dry lakes too short for safe high speeds. At the same time, increasing numbers of enthusiasts crowded the pits for a run at the clocks. Something else was needed, some place where maximum speeds could be expected in complete safety. The obvious answer lay some 700 miles northeast of Los Angeles—the Bonneville Salt Flats near Salt Lake City, Utah. Timing Association officials drove to the area to investigate and gain permission from the Toole, Utah, county supervisors. They were successful and the famous Bonneville Nationals were born.

Supervised by SCTA, the annual August event was publicized by the new automotive magazines. The Salt Flats, with an amazingly hard but cool pure salt surface, were perfect. The first event in 1949 was hastily organized, but still drew a large crowd of eager competitors. A new record book was inaugurated, necessary because of the excellent track and mile-high atmosphere. By the next year Bonneville was the mecca for hot rodders everywhere, and cars were driven from every corner of the nation to compete. The new facilities allowed new emphasis on specialty vehicles, and the first hot rod streamliners and highly developed Lakesters were able to crack the 200-mph barrier.

Just going over 100 mph had seemed a great feat, and the magic double century mark was for dreams. When asked how fast he went, a hot rodder would reply, "Thirty-five." He meant one hundred and thirty-five mph. The really fast cars would come later.

Speeds of streamliners crept gradually upward, until 300 mph was within grasp during the 1950s, then a hot rod doctor from East Los Angeles revolutionized the sport. Doctor Nathan Ostich, dry lakes racer by hobby, wanted something to go really fast. He wanted a jet car. Impossible everyone said, but he prevailed, and with the help of *Hot Rod* magazine technical editor Ray Brock proceeded to build his jet car. Tires and wheels for such a large, fast car were the major stumbling blocks, but they were finally designed and built by Firestone. Hot rodding was moving well into the big leagues. The land speed record was slightly over 400 mph, set in 1947 at the same Bonneville Salt Flats by England's John Cobb. His monster had cost hundreds of thousands of dollars while the hot rodders would spend a pitiful amount by comparison. But they would get the job done.

Nathan Ostich never did claim a land speed record, but his attempts opened the door. Soon to follow were the Arfons brothers, Walt and Art, from Ohio with a 500-mph jet. Mickey Thompson, an obscure Los Angeles newspaper typesetter would break Cobb's long-standing record with passenger car engines. And a young kid named Craig Breedlove, nicknamed Craig Brave by the hot rodding fraternity, would conceive the Spirit of America.

A grand scheme, the Spirit was to be a wingless airplane, styled after a fighter plane fuselage and supported on three wheels. According to the international record keepers in Paris, France, it would be listed as a "motorcycle" because it was one wheel short of being an automobile. To hot rodders it was the pinnacle of promise.

Powered by a monstrous jet engine, the Spirit failed in its initial outing, but it showed great potential. Enough to encourage Craig to more effort. The next year he captured the land speed record at over 500 mph, and no one cared whether he was driving an automobile, motorcycle, or tricycle. He had proven a point. Hard on his heels were other jet cars, rocket cars, and cars with any number of hopped-up automobile engines. In an attempt to go over 600 mph, Breedlove experienced what few men live to relate.

Stopping of the Spirit, as with most high speed cars, is accomplished by deploying small drag chutes at high speeds. As they slow the vehicle, larger chutes are opened until the speed drops to near 200 mph when the regular disc brakes can be used. On his fateful ride, heading from north to south and toward the city of Wendover, Craig felt a slight jar as he deployed the first drag chutes. They had torn away, and he hurtled by his horror-stricken pit crew at nearly 400 mph. Now Craig was a land-locked guided missile, with very little guidance. High speed cars usually can turn the front wheel through little more than 5 degrees of travel. All Breedlove could do was hang on and hope.

Poles for the Salt Lake City and west telephone lines flashed into view and were gone. But not before the Spirit had clipped one pole with an outrigger wheel strut. The pole snapped like balsa wood, but it did swerve the car slightly more to the west, and it slowed the speed some. The brakes were long since burned useless.

A huge dike loomed ahead, paralleling the east-west highway. Breedlove hung on as the Spirit ricocheted off the piled salt, slowing the missile even more. In a great splash, the car came to rest astraddle the drainage ditch, one rear wheel on either side, the single nose wheel and fuselage sinking into the deep water. Breedlove, shaken but alive, scampered to safety. A wild ride, but he was back a year later to establish a new land speed record, over 600 mph. Current record holder is hot rodder Gary Gabelich, with the natural-gas-fueled Blue Flame. His car, similar to Breedlove, has gone over 620 mph!

Bonneville isn't as important as it used to be, for the average hot rodder, anyway. Now the emphasis is on drag racing. And that's another story. By 1951 it was apparent that Bonneville and the dry lakes were great for a few, but hot rodders nationwide needed something more local to test their mechanical ability. A few Southern California hot rodders had been gathering at the Santa Ana community airport to conduct "drags," and this seemed a logical solution. All that was needed was a small airport, and most cities or counties could provide such a facility. The original planners had no idea how popular the quarter-mile acceleration sport would become.

Spreading interest in hot rodding, evidenced by the growing speed equipment business and success of hot rod and custom car magazines prompted sport leaders to consider some kind of nation-wide organization. An initial attempt at this, the American Hot Rod Conference, failed to last. But the leaders were persistent and soon the National Hot Rod Association was formed. Wally Parks was the natural president; he remains head of the group today. Parks was wearing two hats at the time, as editor of *Hot Rod* magazine and president of NHRA. He resigned at the magazine in 1963 to devote full time to the organization.

From the very beginning NHRA recognized drag racing as the cohesive glue to solidify hot rodding, and all efforts were turned in that direction. Car club activities, including road runs and shows, were included, but drag racing would prove the most spectacular. In 1954 the NHRA board of directors established the original Drag Safari—four dedicated enthusiasts, a Plymouth station wagon, and a small travel trailer. It was enough.

The Drag Safari left Los Angeles in the late spring and didn't return until early autumn. Each succeeding weekend found the crew farther from home, helping some local hot rod club or timing association present a well-organized, safe drag meet. While the Safari carried timing clocks and the basic elements of production, the local enthusiasts supplied a place to run and the cars. Hundreds and hundreds of young rodders, having read about drag racing in the magazines, were eager to try the new sport.

In 1955 the traveling group staged again, this time known as the Safety Safari in cooperation with Mobil Oil Company, and armed with valuable experience from the past year. They would also introduce something new to drag racing following another highly successful tour across the country. The National Championship Drags were to wind up the year, and would be presented in the geographic center of the United States—a tiny town in Kansas named Great Bend.

The first Nationals were a learning experience for everyone, but they proved that such a large event was practical. And desirable. Bonneville was great, but it was just once a year. The Nationals were closer, and were just a way of crowning a champion among the thousands of local competitors. From that first event came assurance that a really big production was necessary. The Nationals moved then to Kansas City, Oklahoma City, Detroit, and finally Indianapolis. Held on Labor Day weekend each year, the event annually draws well over a hundred thousand spectators and competition is limited to fifteen hundred cars.

When NHRA moved the National Drags to Kansas City, a group of businessmen elected to continue a major race at Great Bend, thus the American Hot Rod Association (AHRA) was born. NASCAR, the stock car racing organization centered throughout the South, has sanctioned drag racing sporadically, but NHRA and AHRA remain the major guides. Presently the National Hot Rod Association is a member of the American competition committee for the Federation Internationale de l'Automobile (FIA), which elevates hot rodding to an official status as a major world automotive sport. Hot rodding has come a long, long way from those early disorganized dry lakes meets.

It was not easy to convince Detroit that the nation's drivers wanted performance options; cars that could maintain a freeway speed and still have passing power; cars that had brakes capable of stopping under all conditions; cars with suspensions that could cope with mountain curves; cars that featured advanced styling. Until the National Drags were moved to Detroit Dragway, there was hardly a murmur about performance from the Industry, other than token nods toward NASCAR racing. With major league drag racing in their backyard, Detroit planners decided to take a look. They came away impressed enough to recognize youth as a major purchasing market. Organized hot rodding had done its job again.

Volumes could be written on the fascinating history of hot rodding, but this brief recap will acquaint the reader with some of the sport's important highlights. More personal is how the present sport relates to the enthusiast. What is the modern hot rod? Are all the traditional hod rod cars gone? Does a real hot rod have to be a 1932 Ford with a 600-horsepower V8? Specifically, where does the modern rodder stand relative to the availability of hot-rod-worthy cars?

What to Buy

Many an avid hot rod enthusiast, particularly one just introduced to the sport, finds the greatest difficulty in simply picking something to make a rod from. Invariably, or so it seems, all the good cars have been taken, leaving a polyglot of offbreed brands. Apparently nothing worth considering as strong street rod or drag racing machinery is readily available. Fortunately for the sport, this lack of "duplicate" cars is also the cause of many interesting innovations in rodding.

In the "old days" you had to have a roadster to run in a Southern California Timing Association dry lakes event; coupes and sedans were discouraged. At first only the Model T was in style, and while the "nutty" rodders tried Chevy and Buick and Oldsmobile engines, everyone else stuck with the Fords. Then came the 1932 Ford (Deuce), and all else was labeled unworthy as far as body style was concerned. But even as late as 1937, the new Ford V8 was still thought of as inferior to a good strong Model T or A mill. This reluctance to be different still permeates the sport, except for a thinly spread avante garde.

If an enthusiast wants to be a follower, it is easy to build something exactly like the other fellow's, then stand back and listen as people compare his car to similar machines. On the other hand, if he wants to be one of the pacesetters, he can use his imagination and create. He can make something unusual, totally personal, imaginative, and functional. An honest hot rod. The starting point for any such project is a skull session with pencil and paper.

Countless letters cross the desks of car magazines every month from neophyte rodders wondering if their car can be made into anything. Sometimes they've been given the car by a relative, and it is all they have to work with. Sometimes they are on the right track and just want to make something distinctive. Whatever the case, editors always answer with an unqualified "yes." You can make a hot rod out of anything. However, some cars make the chore easier than others, and in many instances, the bulk of hot rodding has overlooked the obvious approach.

The first thing to do when thinking up a rod is to decide what general area you want to work in. If it's drag racing, then the problems to be considered are competition class, available money, personal building ability, etc. Far more difficult are the problems surrounding a fine street rod. If you live in an area of mild weather, a roadster may be perfect, but if it snows and blows on your block, then a closed car may be more practical.

After you've made the decision as to what you will build—street or strip—then figure out what kind of car will fill the requirements. Those who have been lucky enough to be around the sport for many years still go through this idea stage before they start actual work. As mentioned, the weather may help you decide, but don't let this be the sole guide. If a regular passenger car is available, then a roadster in the cold north country is a mighty nice "second car" when the weather is good.

Hot rod material generally lines up in three categories: Early (anything up to 1949), Late (anything from 1949 through 1956–59), and Modern (1956–59 to the present). Customs, although once a distinct entity, now are considered generally as a slim segment of hot rodding.

Each of the above categories will fulfill a particular need. For instance, an Early rod may be the most desirable, but at the same time not at all practical. A high school or college student will find a true all-out Early street rod (except possibly something from about '39 to '48) not the car for his needs. Especially if it has been hastily built and the first such car he has owned and/or built. These cars can be fraught with problems for the beginner. Better for such a person might be a Late model rod, perhaps a 1952 Chevy or Ford with ohv engine. Of course, if finances permit, a newer car would be even better. In this way, he can utilize it for mundane transportation while still enjoying an individualistic car. It's a compromise, at best, but at least workable.

In order of current popularity, the three hot rod categories line up as Late, Modern, and, finally, Early. In a typical case, the young enthusiast starts out with a 1952 Chevy, giving it the works with a new Chevy 283 engine, 4-speed transmission, and all the other goodies of an average rod. By the time he is out of school, he's ready to move up the ladder, and may buy anything from a '60 Ford to a brand new Oldsmobile. Because high performance has been such an integral part of most post-1960 automobiles there is little to do in the engine compartment, so the enthusiast at first contents himself with special wheels, a super paint job, and maybe later, engine work. For most, the transition to the more traditional hot rod, the Early type, doesn't come until the early twenties.

In the days immediately before and after World War II and Korea, a person could dream of owning little more than a rickety old Model A. A young guy just didn't have enough bucks for a new car, thus the overwhelming popularity of building rods. To-day, it's much easier to own a good passenger car (remember, a Model A in 1945 was only as old as a '51 Ford is today) because there is such a big selection of good used cars. Further, a rodder now can build up an excellent car using a stock late model engine, thereby getting sufficient power without the high cost of speed equipment.

At any rate, after the kind of car has been generally decided upon, a specialized programming starts. It's always wise to have an overall scheme in mind before launching a hot rod project. That is, what should the finished car be, look like, act like, etc. In this way, cost can be kept minimal, and the rodder can avoid some horrible pitfalls later. Nothing is more discouraging than starting on a car only to find, halfway through, that there was a much easier, and less expensive, approach.

For instance suppose a person decides to build up a car from the early fifties. He will most likely turn to either a Ford or Chevy, and then probably to the coupe or hardtop body style, simply because these cars have received so much publicity through the years. Immediately, the builder must plan on installing a late model ohv engine if he wants to keep up with traffic. Of course, someone going the full restoration route wouldn't worry about a newer engine. Anyway, such an engine swap costs dough, usually around $350.

This builder would have done better to consider a 1949 through 1956 Oldsmobile. Virtually the same body style as the Chevrolet, and already equipped with a strong V8 engine and one of the best automatic transmissions going. Half of the hot rodder's work is already done.

There are many other cars from the early fifties that can be transformed into excellent hot rods at minimal cost, while creating an entirely new "idea" platform for other rodders. Take the Chrysler Newport with the early Hemi. With an inexpensive adapter you can remove its weak spot, the transmission, and put in a manual or late-model Torque-Flite. Or a Red Ram Dodge or DeSoto Adventurer. Another good rod foundation, especially for someone who likes to build sleepers, is the '49–'54 Hudson. The Caddy is like the Olds, with lots of potential brawn built in, while the Hudson Hornet can be made to look exceptionally nice and even to run well with the inline engine.

In the mid-fifties, the Studebaker coupe is hard to beat for appearance, and runs well enough with its small V8. So do the early Plymouth Furys and Chrysler 300's. A 1957 Ford with the supercharged engine is a class winner at the drags and may be fixed up as a show winner for very few bucks. So can the '55–'56 Buick Century.

Of course, if the builder is willing to accept the problems of an engine swap, then body style becomes paramount. This means the Fords and Chevys usually. But there is one little car that looks tremendous and is a natural with a Chevy V8 or Ford 289. It is the Willys Aero sedan. Even the Willys Jeepster, a sort of modern day touring car, makes a wild rod.

Of the Modern rods, that is, the newer stockers, there are some fine-looking automobiles being overlooked by the majority. Many young drivers think of the Chevrolet as either a 1957 or 1966 product. In between, the company had some good cars, too. Like the '61 and '62 hardtops, the '64 Impalas, etc. Or what about the 1960 Ford? Once in a blue moon a manufacturer will produce a car totally unlike any other. The '60 is that car for Ford. It's a very special style, and certainly will become a classic a few short years hence. Like the '40 and '48 Fords, this one can be either a swinging custom, or brutish rod.

A 1963 Plymouth with the big wedge engine is hard to beat, and again, with the true hot rod treatment of tires, strong paint, etc., it comes on like gangbusters. So do the '59 to '66 Dodges and Chryslers. Even the post-'57 Ramblers can be made into very good Modern rods. Probably one of the most striking new cars seen lately was a '62 Ambassador running the V8 engine, beefed automatic, and fat "weenies." Painted black acrylic, it really turns 'em on at the local drive-ins. The '59–'60 Buick, with those long sweep-

ing fender lines, is another machine combining good styling possibilities with a reputable engine.

The little compacts are ideal for the low-cost hot rod treatment.
The Falcon Sprint, Dodge Dart, Mercury Comet, etc., can all be
turned into striking rods with little effort. As with their bigger
counterparts, wheels make much of this difference. However, these
smaller cars seem to really come alive with fat tires. When considering a compact, try to select one with a V8 engine to start
with, because this is invariably the first problem a rodder finds.

Foreign cars shouldn't be overlooked, either, particularly if
you're a good mechanic. Naturally, the Volkswagen is all the rage,
simply because people under twenty-five have found that the high
cost of insurance just won't permit them to easily own a sporty
type car. Even with a VW, you don't have to stick with the gang.
Ever see a VW bus or panel with the big wheels and tires, painted
a wild color, and fixed up inside? You wouldn't believe it.

The ability to make something individual is very pronounced
when you get into the pickups and station wagons, circa 1949 to
the present. Ever see a chopped '56 Chevy Nomad? Plymouth
wagons from '57 to '59 can be turned into crowd stoppers, as can
Fords for the same years. On the West Coast, the wagons have
taken over from the woodies and panels as the "in" car among the
surfers.

In the truck category, the overall favorite just has to be the 1954
through '58 Ford. Chevrolets of this vintage are also used, but not
nearly so much. The early ('57–'60) Ford Ranchero and Chevy
El Camino are good bets for someone who likes the convenience
of a pickup and the passenger car ride. Even the lowly Jeep rates
high with imaginative rodders, streamlined like a boxcar and absolutely perfect as a hot rod.

It is imperative that whatever kind of car is used in the post-1949
series, the rodder try to buy the best possible one he can find. The
engine is usually unimportant, particularly in the Late category,

but check closely the body panels, interior, upholstery, windows, etc. A little careful shopping will turn up some bargains. There are lots of these cars sitting in family driveways as second cars, that may have been driven only 30,000 miles in fifteen years. In general, try to find a car that has not been wrecked, and has good upholstery and window mechanisms. If you find these, chances are the rest of the car will be as good.

As to the money involved in these Late and Modern rod cars, the range is usually anywhere from $100 to $1000. Keep in mind that either an engine swap or rebuild will run around $350 total, tires and wheels another $200, etc. A good buy is a '57 Ford for $150. Add $500 over the span of two years, then sell the car for $400, and it has only cost $250 to own. Or roughly $10 per month, which is excellent in anybody's language.

Actually, trucks offer more of an individual approach to hot rodding than any other "body" style. The real old-timers aren't exactly closed cars, but they're not exactly open machines either. Without doors, they fall somewhere in between. From a pragmatic standpoint, they do the job—haul stuff from here to there and keep the driver relatively dry. Small trucks made before World War II were usually on modified passenger car chassis (those over one ton or more had special chassis) and were intended mostly for door-to-door delivery. In many instances, stock passenger car bodies were converted, as with the C-cab Model T. This particular truck had a cantilever roof bolted to the front portion of a Touring body (some slight panel substitution at the body rear). The accent was on just enough to do the job, no more.

This also led manufacturers to create new designs quite often. For this reason alone, there are many old trucks lying in wait around the nation, some with nameplates lost to history. Nobody has wanted the old trucks before, except the few specialty restorers, so they're going for beggar prices.

Hot rodders who have built up "restored" rods report that it is much easier to utilize the original frame than make up a special tubing support, and it cuts the cost considerably. Since only the undercarriage and powertrain must be updated, plus minimal paint and upholstery, the truck rod will usually cost less to build than a roadster or closed machine. One outstanding T truck in Southern California turns everybody's head, and it cost only $900 to build, along with after-hours for six months.

There is a good market for truck rods, too, as many automotive-oriented businesses consider them ideal shop trucks. For the wise rodder who feels a good design should grow in value rather than depreciate, and who gets a kick out of building, making up trucks can become a profitable pastime. One enthusiast in Northern California made up a 1940 Ford pickup that had been converted to a light-duty tow truck (wrecker). He sold it to a rather well-heeled midget race car campaigner for $2500 more than it cost to build. Another builder in the East made up a 1½-ton engine and under-carriage. It sold for $1200 over his cost and is used to transport a beautifully restored 1909 Ford runabout to old car meets. Of course, these prices don't reflect a reasonable payment for labor, but then, what hobby can even come close to these figures?

Helping to establish the call for trucks are the increasing number of haulers making the custom show circuit. There have been trucks at shows for years, but most have been of the Model A and later variety. The older or "classic" trucks really got started just a couple of years ago, and practically every show professional has at least one truck in the stable, often more.

Art Himsl started out with a Paddy Wagon, showing it at the National Roadster Show, and before the year was out there were a gaggle of show trucks on the circuit. Latest in the line-up, Carl Casper's eastern Paddy Wagon and George Barris' Ice Cream truck show just how different designs can be and still remain unmistakably truck.

The real beauty of the current show machine is the handmade

body. While the restorer may want to go with steel panels scrounged from countless junkyards, the serious craftsman can fabricate a body using ordinary woodworking tools and plywood paneling. Obviously, working with wood may be easier, at least for the novice, and there are always good cabinetmakers in most smaller communities. Further, this medium allows a maximum of ingenuity as to body style.

Trying to settle on an original design may be an impossible goal; easier is pouring through old library books for pictures of trucks. Anything can be turned into a winner, from pastry wagons to beer haulers. Even the old produce trucks common to American streets in the late 1920s and early '30s make fancy modern rods. All of them make great parts chasers.

You can make the truck pay for itself too. Shows are okay, but a quicker buck can be had closer to home. If you have a big food distributor in the area, then modernize the design in a nutty truck and rent it to him for special occasions. He may even want to buy it for a handsome profit. If it is an old Model T, Ford dealers might like it for a promotional campaign, and the local pizza parlor would surely consider it a crowd pleaser parked by the front door. There are all kinds of money-making possibilities, if you do a good job and make the machine eyecatching. Not necessarily loaded with chrome, but a bright color and well crafted.

It's in the Early hot rods that a person can really get twisted, especially if he hasn't had several years' background in rodding. All of these cars were used by hot rodders in their day, but there wasn't widespread publicity about them then.

Take an early Pontiac for instance. Here is a car with an excellent body style, good handling characteristics, hydraulic brakes, and an engine compartment big enough for a diesel. You can stuff something like a '57 Pontiac engine and automatic in there without even touching the fender panels. Or how about the '32 Chevy roadster, as fine a piece of rod material as ever was built, and very rare? In all instances with these unusual Early rods, it is economically wise to go the restoration route. That is, keep the body and exterior components as nearly stock as possible, even down to the bumpers. Use a big late-model ohv engine, better transmission, and new rear end; but by all means keep the removed parts stored somewhere. Chances are that the car can be sold in the future not as a rod, but as restoration material. The author has a buddy who did this with an early Buick sedan and had a fine car for three years, then sold it for $2500, exactly $1350 more than he had invested! Even a Model A, as apparently plentiful as they are (it is estimated that over 40 percent of all A's produced are still around), will soon be consumed by restorers.

Of the Early type rods, the 1936 through 1948 styles are the least demanding, and are most practical for someone not overly mechanically inclined. They also offer a chance at distinct individuality. Who can deny that the 1939 and '40 Buicks are formidable machines, on the street as well as drag strip? A '39 to '48 Chevy with GMC 6 engine is a sparkler, as is a '41 to '48 Ford with Olds power. The combinations are endless.

Of cars produced earlier than '34, all are about the same. That is, they all need good late-model engines and powertrains, and all border on the realm of antiques. Nevertheless, they are the foundations for most current custom show stoppers. The fiberglass body has seen to that.

Even the fully restored automobile is basically a hot rod. In fact, for the young enthusiast, it is often wisest to start with this kind of car. Of course, planning ahead doesn't hurt. Suppose a thirteen-year-old boy wants to own a rod. Finances and parents seem to stand in the way, but if he suggests buying an old Model A and fixing it up, until the day he can legally drive, he meets little opposition. Mom thinks it's a safe way to learn about mechanics, and Dad remembers his first A-bone.

The enthusiast buys not just any old Model A, but a coupe or roadster (something that can be turned into a wild rod later). Then he goes the route of disassembly, cleaning, painting, and reassembly. Maybe it will be purely restored right from the start, but maybe it'll have hydraulic brakes as a safety measure. Later on, after he has been driving for a year or so, he adds an ohv engine, modern running gear, and so on. Little by little the car is transformed into a true hot rod, but this transformation has been gentle and deceptive. And, most important, unlike the hastily built rod, it is well constructed and has cost little. Further, the enthusiast has grown to understand what a car really is. He recognizes the responsibilities of driving, and isn't about to be foolish and wreck all that hard work!

It really isn't important what kind of car is selected. The important thing is good planning and careful work.

2

The Economics of Hot Rodding

"Speed Costs Money. How Fast Do You Want To Go?" These prophetic words are emblazoned across the front of a speed shop counter in Los Angeles, placed there not in 1967, or '57, but way back before World War II. The cost of hot rodding has always been a sore point with enthusiasts, particularly those unwilling to reduce the price by personal labor. The economics of this sport have a way of putting the damper on unbridled enthusiasm. It need not happen, if you are fully aware of what it really costs to have a personalized automobile.

What Does a Car Really Cost?

Most of us have a problem of seeing well when we spy *the* car. There it sits all shiny and gleaming and the very epitome of hot rodding—a veritable jewel in the rough. Rose-colored glasses tend to overlook the bent rear fender, broken door glass, pitted chrome, sagging upholstery, and tired, tired engine. We see only the finished dream. It's a malady that strikes all enthusiasts, not just the beginner. The experienced builder learns to go home and sleep on it a night, so he can evaluate what the car will *really* cost in the long run, and whether or not it will be an economically feasible project. There is far more to the cost of a car than the price painted on the windshield. Consider.

Suppose you have $500 to spend for a neat '61 Chevy hardtop. The car is in excellent shape to begin with. So, your total cost will be (for one year's driving):

1. Initial cost, including taxes, etc. .... $ 500
2. Insurance, liability only .... $ 150
   (under 25 years of age)
3. Petroleum (gas and oil, with one tank of gas a week) .. $ 300
4. Upkeep (tune-ups, minor repairs) .... $ 100
5. License and registration .... $ 15
6. Depreciation .... $ 100

                                            total: $1165

Now, assume you only pay a small down payment on that car. The expense is going to go up drastically.

1. Down payment .... $ 150
2. First-year payments, including interest .... $ 410
   (24-month loan)
3. Insurance .... $ 515
   (minimum liability plus lender coverage, city costs)
4. Petroleum .... $ 300
5. Upkeep .... $ 100
6. License and registration .... $ 15
7. Depreciation .... $ 100

                                            total: $1590

These are generalized figures, but remember they are for a car in excellent used condition. If a major repair job is required, or new tires are necessary, add from $100 to $200. The second year will be about $200 less, because you may be able to pay the car off early and get rid of some of that insurance, but don't plan on it.

In essence, you must look at car ownership as a sort of rental figure, or roughly, how much it costs per mile for transportation. In the case of the suburban car, it will run approximately $100 a month for the privilege of driving, or an average of 10 cents a mile.

The greatest single mistake many hot rodders make is buying an "in" car. That is, the machine they think automatically makes them one step higher in the hot rod hierarchy. This can be disastrous, and must be avoided at all costs (pun intended). Remember the '57 Chevy hardtop. Great little car, and very popular with the "in" group. Up until 1965, such a car in premium condition would bring as much as $1200 in the larger cities. Jazzed up with chrome wheels and a floor shift conversion, the same car could command $1500. Taking advantage of this popularity, many a hip used-car dealer would add $100 worth of goodies to make an additional $200 profit.

The "in" car is the one that looks good! Popularity and fad enthusiasm are the product of car owners who have imagination. A '57 Chevy 4-door station wagon can be made to look just as tough as the hardtop, and it will cost perhaps half as much. At the same time, shopping for the used car *must* include the powertrain. It is wise to buy a car already equipped with the basic goodies, such as V8 engine, 4-speed transmission, limited slip differential, etc. Unless you plan on setting up shop on the drag strip, a 4-speed manual transmission can become the biggest pain in your life. You'll end up skipping one of the gears during normal street driving anyway.

So, the "in" car may not be as in as you think. And what about our '57 hardtop. You can get one anywhere in the country now for under $500. Depreciation on the order of $500 to $1000 is pretty strong. That same $500 might buy a car three or four or five years newer. Buying for style alone can be a bottomless trap.

What About Financing?

One of the big reasons car magazines are so successful is their adherence to the principle that the younger car enthusiast cannot afford to lay out $3000 or $4000 for a new car every year. For that matter, neither can the older married man. If the car is to be the basis for a personalized machine, then initial cost must be within reason, leaving money for modifications.

To this end, it is wise to pay cash for any car that will see use on a drag strip or in shows, or that will receive a lot of modification. As already shown, the privilege of buying a car on time can actually cost as much as your desired "changes." When the amount involved is quite low, it is possible to obtain a personal bank loan, at a low rate. Usually, however, financing must be handled for sums as large as $500 or more.

There is nothing wrong with financing a car that is to be used for transportation, provided the buyer can really pay out the car. But there have been many instances where the "super swift" enthusiast has figured out a sure-fire way to win the big drag meet. He goes to the new car agency, makes the minimum $300 down payment ("The monthly payments are *only* $175 for five years!"), and throttles straight to the speed shop. The engine is pulled down and blueprinted, new tires with rear slicks installed, the transmission reworked, and in general, a loan of over $1000 is poured into the new "stocker." Now he runs at the drag strip, but seldom fast enough to win a $30 trophy. All this has happened in the short span of two or three months, during which time he has failed to keep up his car payments.

Swifty had figured he could "rent" the new car for a few bucks, laying in the speed equipment, then remove the goodies after the race and let the agency repossess the car. What he didn't plan on was the sales contract conditions. The repossessed car can end up costing him a bundle of dough. For instance, suppose he still owes

$3000 on the car, and the company can only sell it for $2000 (after all, it is now a used car). Then Swifty is stuck for the remaining $1000. Simple as that.

Is Insurance Necessary?

Assume the car is paid for. In that case, all you need is PL and PD (public liability and public damage), unless you wish to insure car value. That is, you may value your car at $3000 although it only cost you $500. Insurance companies don't mind, as long as you're willing to pay the premium on $3000.

In this respect, many older hot rodders figure it costs them less in the long run to maintain PL and PD only as major coverage, plus other insurance for fire and theft. Their reasoning is that if the car is damaged in a wreck, they have lost only their own personal time, and that most of the pieces can be inexpensively rebuilt by them.

Such does not hold true for fire and theft. The first needs no amplification, but theft should be considered from all angles. After all, a front end collision may bend some metal, but it won't ruin the bucket seats or dual 4-barrel intake manifold or genuine Isky cam. Theft wipes it all out.

In cases where the car is financed, the lending institution will require insurance to cover collision, fire, theft, etc. But in some cases, it is possible to get financing that does not cover all the bases. This was the case of an owner who financed his car through a well-known company and assumed he had adequate insurance coverage. Until his car was stolen one night and he found there was no fire or theft in his contract. He was out the cost of the remaining balance due on the car unless it was recovered. Fortunately it was, minus front fenders, hood, grille, etc. That little lesson cost him $327, or the price of replacement parts.

If a car has been equipped with specialty parts, such as wheels, stereo, engine equipment, etc., then theft insurance is an absolute must. At the same time, the owner should still take pains to protect his investment by keeping it garaged securely at night and never parked in a questionable area. The cost of insurance is one place you can't cut corners.

The Cost of Customizing

That sign about speed holds true in all aspects of hot rodding or customizing, so some careful planing is in store for the wise enthusiast. Again, the cost involved will be a direct reflection of the owner's desire and ability to do his own work. Remember, you are paying someone else a fancy fee for every hour he works on your car, and that is as it should be. After all, the customizer is a craftsman and is about as much like an ordinary body man as a house painter is like Picasso.

The following is what a professional might charge to customize a '55 Ford or Chevy.

Top chop	$ 800–$1000
Channel	$ 800–$1000
Section	$2000–$2500
Wheel Radius	$ 125 each
Grille Change	$ 500–$1000
Taillight Change	$ 30–$ 200 each
French Headlight	$ 100 each
Electric Doors	$ 100 each
French Antennae	$ 30 each
Rolled Pans	$ 175 each
Chrome for Engine	$ 150–$ 250
Chrome for Exterior	$ 100–$ 500

These prices will vary, but they give an idea of just how expensive customizing can be, and why it is vital to learn the process personally. It is easy to understand how $3000 or $4000 can be tied up in customizing an early car, and unfortunately the customizer can seldom expect to get a fraction of the expense back upon sale.

The Hot Rod Approach

Far less expensive is the hot rod approach, making minor changes to body style and concentrating on brute power appearance. This is the foundation of most of the current popularity of wheels, wheel radius, fancy paints, and good interiors on all cars, old or new.

There are really two distinct ways of building a hot rod: from scratch, or starting with a good basis. The scratch car, usually referred to as a "Fad" machine, will invariably be a fiberglass-bodied roadster. As such, it utilizes the minimum number of parts and is by far the most inexpensive of hot street machines providing you do the majority of the work. This car can be built from one of several commercial kits available, the kit costing roughly $700, or it can be constructed piecemeal. If it is built of pieces scrounged locally, you can put a completed car on the road for less than $1000.

Starting with an old Model A coupe or a '55 Chevy sedan, the final cost will vary widely. If you just want to clean up the A, this can be done for around $150. An engine and transmission swap will run at least $250 more, etc. The same figures hold fairly true for the later car, although materials cost will be slightly more, offset by mechanical parts costs.

Generally speaking, to get a car chassis set up in hot rod tradition (whether adding hydraulic brakes to that A-bone or traction bars to the Chevy) will cost about $200. Most of this will be spent on brakes and shock absorbers, but it is money that must be sacrificed. The body will run another $100, assuming you prepare it for paint and don't have lots of repair. The engine will cost at least $100 if you do the rebuilding yourself and much more if farmed out, while transmissions can cost from $75 to $300. Tires and wheels will add at least $200, so the original purchase price of $500 has now swelled past $900 (at least). However, much of the equipment added in the hot rod approach may be removed when the car is sold, thereby saving money. At the same time, a car tastefully prepared in this manner will bring several hundred dollars more at resale if the seller advertises among the enthusiast society.

How to Buy a Hot Car

If you can't scrape together the bucks for a new car, how about looking over the used performance car market. With a little know-how, you can probably find just what you're looking for at a substantial saving.

How do you go about finding a good deal, without getting stabbed? The first thing is to know exactly what kind of car you're looking for. Do you want a custom, hot rod, or just dependable transportation? Suppose you've got a drag machine tucked away in the garage, and you're in the market for a good tow car. Whatever you need, know exactly what you're after before you start your search.

Used cars exist only because former owners, for various reasons, decided to get rid of them. You can bet that many of them have passed the point of no return, and would only represent headaches for the new owner. However, there are still used cars with plenty of serviceable, carefree miles left in them. When considering a used machine, keep in mind that age, condition, cost, and resale are four factors that determine the overall value of a car. Be wary of the "fly-by-night" used-car lot. Buying trade-ins from a new-car dealer almost guarantees you someone to fall back on if (and when) things go haywire.

The first things that grab your eye while inspecting used cars are the extra goodies and overall appearance. Accessories such as mag wheels, tires, custom paint, gauges, tach, engine accessories, and custom interiors are instant attention-getters. It's a good idea to get as much as you can along the accessory line, since later purchase can be expensive.

If you know that bucket seats, a four-speed transmission, and a 327 fuel-injected Corvette engine with a 4:56 positraction is what it takes to make you happy, don't settle for less with the intention of adding to it later. When you start buying parts separately, you're talking dollars—many more than you planned.

On these street hot rods, there are two points of view you can take. You might feel that a fellow hot rodder has enough horse sense to take decent care of the car. This is true for some hot rodders. On the other hand, there are the street cruisers that hop on it at every stop light, wind out through the gears, and in general whip a car. Both types of owners exist, so you have to be smart enough to separate them. Either of these types generally take excellent care of the car, appearance wise. Appearance, mechanical condition, and running condition should all be carefully inspected.

For appearance, check to see that body panels line up. See if the paint job is even. Different shades of the same color may be hiding a repaired accident. Look for dents, chips, and nicks. Candy, pearl, and metalflake cannot be touched up successfully— they must have all new paint. Does the car look as if somebody has kept it clean? If upholstery is stained, rotted, or odd smelling, it is a pretty good indication of the care received. The headliner is a telltale way to spot any water leaks. Make sure you're considering a car that has windows that roll up and down (including power windows). There is nothing cheap about replacing power window mechanisms.

If anything about the car's appearance displeases you or makes you uneasy, think twice before signing. The additional cost of repair or replacement will fall on your shoulders in most instances.

Even if the dealer agrees to altar the car to suit you, he will probably tack the expense onto your purchase price.

Ready for a test drive? Here is where major problems show themselves. The car should start readily. If it doesn't, don't believe the salesman when he tells you it's been sitting a long time. The car should perform, period! With the car running, look at the exhaust smoke.

A white smoke (steam) that rapidly diminishes is caused by condensation. It usually stops as soon as the car is warm, but if it continues, it may mean that water is entering the engine system (possibly a blown head gasket). Blue-white smoke is the most ominous, usually indicating excessive oil usage. Bad ring clearances, seals, and valve seats all are problems here. Black smoke distinguishes a carburetion problem.

Note how the car responds to the throttle. Does it accelerate smoothly? If it is equipped with multiple carbs, see if all respond. A steady howling noise is most often caused by the rear end or a possible differential, transmission, or wheel bearing failure. A squealing noise that increases or decreases in relation to your speed rate can be wheel bearings. Grinding noises and low pedal pressure are all signs of brake trouble. If the car you're considering has a standard transmission, (either 3- or 4-speed) make sure it operates smoothly.

Find a handy freeway or highway to try the car. High speed has a way of showing steering and handling difficulties. You can also learn if the car has enough power to make it into the flow of traffic without blubbering and falling on its face. Any wandering should be noted. Take the car to a front end shop and have them run it up on a rack. Let them check to see how the suspension (ball joints, idler arm, shocks) and frame are. It is hard to disguise a bent or reworked frame. Uneven tire wear indicating poor alignment of frame, and steering damage from an accident, can also be spotted.

If the car is still in your ball park, give it a few more tests to pass. Check under the hood again. Excessive rust stains in the engine compartment or radiator itself may indicate a leaking cooling system, or a car that overheats and boils habitually. Clean engine compartments are big selling points, and dealers know this. Look beyond the paint and chrome. Check the oil dip stick. Filthy, black oil rarely means that the car has been given the million-dollar treatment. If it's low, possibly you're looking at an oil burner.

Check the area where the car is parked. If you notice stains (either water or oil) this would suggest leakage from the radiator, hoses, engine, transmission, or differential. If you can take a look at the exhaust pipes without standing on your head, here is another way to pick up a clue as to what you're getting. White or light gray residue can show leanness; black indicates excessive fuel or oil burning.

Don't forget the little things such as cigarette lighter, radio, interior lights, wipers, heater, horn, spare tire, jack, and lug wrench. Again, they all total up to dollars. It might be wise to check around and see what the car you're considering is selling for elsewhere. If you're still in the ball park, be careful and read the fine print before signing. Don't sign until you are completely satisfied. Once you put your name on the dotted line you own the car.

With the recent introduction of transferable new-car warranties, buying a used car is greatly simplified. You can save the fantastic amount of depreciation suffered by the new-car owner, while still getting an excellent (and identical) warranty.

If you have a car that you yourself want to dispose of, your best bet is to sell privately. Car dealers will insult you. No matter if you have a 427 Ford wedge engine equipped with custom pistons, roller camshaft, and ram log manifold the dealer is going to overlook this. In fact, a dealer is instantly on guard when a car with racing equipment pulls up to his door. He's apt to tell you it's worth less because you tampered with it; yet if he were selling the same car, it would be worth plenty!

Lately, with the increase of young buyers in the market for hot machinery, used-car lots catering strictly to the hot rod type of car have sprung up. These lots can definitely supply you with something along the line you want. They also can give you a better deal on your machine when it comes to trading.

Treat the matter of buying a used car as a system, and you stand far less chance of being burned. All you have to do is get out there and "deal."

Upholstery—Rags to Riches

Although it is a subtle distinction, nothing so sets a car apart from the norm as upholstery. And in the economic scheme of things, it is vital. If that $500 car has good upholstery to begin with, it costs less than $50 to make new rugs and recover the worn arm rests. But complete reupholstery can cost from $150 to $500.

Selection of materials has a great deal to do with vehicle upholstery costs. A top-grade Naugahyde may run as much as $10 per yard more than good fabric, and it may be unnecessary. In a closed car, any modern upholstery material will be good for at least four years (much more with care) and if carefully selected will produce a far richer appearance than cold Naugahyde. Since the fabrics are easier to work with, the overall cost will be much less, too.

Upholstery cost is one way to measure the cost of building different types of cars. A roadster will cost about $200, a touring about $375, a sedan about $425, a coupe about $275, etc. The more material yardage involved, the more labor, and thus the higher prices. The same holds true of paint, chrome, and all the rest of the car.

Upkeep

Here's where the cost of a car can get under the skin. When a new car is purchased, the owner thinks it will surely run forever, without his having to lift the hood. For some strange reason, this doesn't happen. Instead, after two or three years, that little squeak in back becomes a clank and then a clunk. And then it needs fixing, which costs $30. So before long it's $30 here and $30 there, until you own the national mint.

Serious hot rodders tend to look after their machines much better than the average driver, so the problem of upkeep is not nearly so great. However, it is terribly easy to say, "Oh well, I've got to repaint the car anyway, so that little fender ding doesn't need fixing right away." Pretty soon there are two dings, then four.

The annual cost of upkeep, including two very good yearly tune-ups, should be right around $100—if you do the work yourself. It's a discouraging fact that a single good tune-up alone now runs $60 or more, so learning the function of points and plugs is plain good sense. Like insurance, upkeep must be considered one of those necessary costs that cannot be circumvented.

When It's Time to Sell

The art of selling a hot rod or customized car is special unto itself, and it usually takes two or three experiences before the facts are learned. In hot rodding as in everything else, the laws of supply and demand are much in evidence, and adherance to the principles will make you either richer or wiser, or both.

Because a resale should always be considered possible, it is vital the car be kept in top appearance at all times. It may run like a top, but if the paint is scurvy, it's a dog in general opinion. Or it may run terribly, and as long as the paint and upholstery is good, it's popular. That's human nature.

Too, it pays to advertise the car in full dress. That is, put it up for sale with the mag wheels in place and the supercharger on the engine, etc. Then when the buyer is interested, you tell him that the price does not include these costly items ("Of course, you can add another $500 if you want them!"), but that he will get the stock wheels with baby moons and the original 4-barrel intake system. This is fair, and wise.

Never sell a specialty car with any kind of guarantee, because you don't know how the new owner will treat it. And if he comes back with a little problem, next time it will be bigger. Do give him the full information on what is in the car, all the little eccentricities, so he will be fully acquainted with the machine from the beginning.

It is possible to make a living fixing up old cars and reselling them as specialty machines, if the cost of materials is kept down. High school and college enthusiasts have been doing this for years, and they've learned excellent trades in the meantime. They spend two or three hours each afternoon plus all day Saturday fixing up cars they've bought for under $200. A paint job, repaired and cleaned upholstery, repaired mechanical parts, and the car is ready for the new owner. They keep a close eye on used custom/speed equipment and add this as necessary. They can gross over $10,000 a year! Right in their own backyards.

But What About Drag Racing and Show Cars?

Talk about shoveling money down the drain, here's the place to do it. In all the phases of hot rodding, there is nothing to compare with racing or showing as a drain on the finances. Consider show cars first.

Face it. The only reason rodders build cars is to be a little different from the norm, whether they want the extra excitement of better performance, or the ego salve of congratulations. When a show car is built, it usually starts out as a challenge to curiosity. But right away, the bills skyrocket. Where chrome plating had been figured at $150, it costs $1500. Body work is tenfold, and so on. If you have plenty of money and need the trophies, then build a show car. If not, better stay away. That is not to say a good street machine can't be show-worthy, far from it. It's just that a car that does nothing more than sit in the garage 330 days out of the year is economically unfeasible.

There are ways to make a show car pay for itself, and if this is considered at the beginning, then the car takes on meaning. For instance, if your car is selected by a model company for a kit, you may gain from $2000 to $5000 on the deal. Or if it is so outstanding that a show promoter would like to put it on tour, you may pick up around $3000. Or you may be able to rent it to specific shows for $200 to $300 a shot. Or it is possible you can rent it out to new-car agencies and similar businesses for $25 a day. There are lots of maybe's to be investigated.

The actual cost of building a show car is really small when compared to the cost of *owning* it. Of major interest is the insurance, which is an absolute must. And because you have a car worth the price of a new Cadillac, you must pay that kind of premium. Then too, when it is being transported between shows you want insurance for that, and some kind of insurance against the little kid who likes to scratch the paint during the show, ad infinitum. In the end, a show car costing $3000 to build will cost approximately $75 a month just to own (notice; own, not to drive).

In racing, the situation is even more severe. Unlike the show car, where some kind of duality of purpose is possible, the race car is *not* a street machine. If it is, then it doesn't win trophies, and that's the unvarnished truth.

A championship stock car may never be driven on the street, and a topnotch drag street roadster must be radically detuned for any kind of cruising. So . . . any thought of serious racing must include the reminder that some form of ordinary transportation is necessary.

An AA/Fueler dragster will cost at least $10,000 to build, breaking down to over $3000 for the chassis, the same or more for an engine, $1500 for body, etc. Add to this the cost of a trailer and tow car; then figure in what each weekend visit to a drag strip will cost, and the figure is staggering—over $40,000. A good funny car will run about the same, and a topflight Super Stocker is only slightly less.

Professional Race Cars

The cash outlay it takes to bring a competitive car to the Indianapolis 500 is beyond the imagination of the average citizen. How does a base nut of at least $100,000 sound? For one car. That's what it costs to go back to Indiana and live it up and race it up with the fastest guys. You can go for less, but you won't even be a dark horse threat.

The Indy fraternity were long considered denizens of the stone age. The big, heavy, front-engined cars they fiddled with every year had bloodlines as far back as the roaring twenties. Apart from coachwork they were painfully out of date compared to the open wheel, open cockpit, European road racing rigs. If the cars were old-fashioned, they were also easy to build and take care of, they were hardy and durable, and they didn't get obsolete overnight. Most car owners could figure on total expenditures of roughly $50,000 for the month of May.

Now consider the Lotus. The car is built in three pieces; the nose cone, the tail cone, and the main fuselage in which the fuel tanks are located. These three parts are held together by bulkheads. The tab on this engineless body/frame is over $25,000. This includes $250 for rack and pinion steering, and a suspension system that has a replacement value (coil/shock, disc brake, and hardware) of over $1200 *per wheel*. This package might be expensive, even overpriced, but it's a winner, and that's what counts.

The next thing is the engine. Staying with the winning precedent, Ford racing mills are needed. Other engines are available of course; the old faithful Offenhauser, which comes supercharged for $16,000 or injected for $10,000. Also, there are certain high-grade American stock block engines, such as the Chevy V-8's that are so popular in Sprint Cars. In dry-sump, fuel-injected, fuel-burning form, they go for about $9000. The Ford however, is the champion, and it rates top billing. It costs $31,000.

Now, with the addition of a Colotti, Halibrand, or Hewland rear end and other needed pieces, another $3000 gets used up.

Following a $300 paint and numbering job, plus chroming certain pieces and magnafluxing and X-raying others, installing shoulder harnesses and upholstery, adding fire-preventive fuel tank bladders . . . the new owner has spent at least $50,000 for his very classy, very competitive, and very expensive race car.

He will then find that a first-rate driver can't be touched for anything less than a $10,000 seasonal contract. The contract will not be just for Indy, but for the full championship trail. In addition to the ten-grand retainer, the driver will receive expenses, plus 40 percent of all prize money. It's a hard bargain, but Indy is tough, and for that kind of money the driver is expected to win . . . nothing less.

With the driver in his pocket, the car owner next goes about seeking a mechanic. Mechanics are like drivers. There are few really top-grade wrench twisters, and their services come high. The chief mechanic will bank on a yearly salary of something like $12,000, and receive a 15 percent cut of all prize money.

Add all the spare parts costs, etc., and this all comes to the big-league figure of $115,650 minimum. Of course there will be some saving grace for the owner if he is able to line up a sponsor who will pay to have his name or product advertised on the side of the car. Sponsorship deals of $30,000 are common, but certainly this figure is paltry compared to the costs. Admittedly there are a few small compensations. Fuel, oil, piston rings, spark plugs, and other assorted services are free at the Speedway.

One year, when a record Indy purse of $500,000 was paid out, $168,500 was handed over to the winner. Taking out the driver's 40 percent, and the mechanic's 15, that leaves about $76,000 for the owner. Subtract this from the cost figure, and you'll see that this little excursion set him back almost forty grand. And he won!

3

Cutting Corners on Cost

You don't have to be filthy rich to build award-winning hot rods. In fact, penny squeezing can often produce results far superior to buck tossing. All you need do is learn the Technique of Scrounging.

Learning not to completely copy other ideas is the first step. Just because most of the roadsters, coupes, and sedans are made from Ford products does not exclude other makes of cars from being excellent hot rod material. The greatest advantage a rodder can have is the ability to think creatively.

After you have the general idea of what you want, take a heavy dose of patience pills and start looking. The key to making up an inexpensive car is time. Take time to round up all the important pieces. As the price of any object depends largely on demand, the less immediate the demand, the lower the cost.

Begin gathering parts for a project well ahead of starting actual work. Preplanning and patience, again. Tubing front ends are nice, but the cost of a new one is sometimes unhandy, perhaps as much as $150 for a commercial unit. Old '37 Ford tubes are at least $35 when you can find them. So, a substitute is in order.

These axles aren't new, really, and some good examples were made before World War II. Like the ones under prewar Chrysler products.

The best place to begin scrounging is the small-town garage, where old parts tend to pile up out back. The garage owner will usually sell such pieces at a giveaway price. Same goes for the blacksmith shop. Small wrecking yards often have usable items tossed in a bin, but in this case you'll have to put on the dickering hat to get a reasonable deal. If it isn't for a Ford, chances are it'll go for pennies.

There is a certain air of nonchalance necessary to being a good scrounger. Never make a beeline for that old touring over in the junkyard, but just casually whistle by, as if uninterested. "How much for that old car front end. Not very sturdy-looking, but I want to make a little trailer to haul trash in. . . ." Crossed fingers can save bundles of dough.

The abandoned car is a serious scrounger's delight, but the law must be carefully observed here. Everything belongs to someone! And in the case of abandoned cars, the local government is the ultimate authority. Suppose you notice an old coupe parked on a vacant lot. It has obviously been there for a few years, and the wheels are missing, along with a few other minor parts. Why it is there you don't know, but the V8 engine and transmission are enough for interest.

First, check with neighboring homes and businesses. Chances are this will unearth the owner, who will probably give you the hulk. If no owner can be found, then locate the property owner. He, too, will probably want to get rid of the car. Next, check with the city, taking in the car serial number and license plate number. If the car has truly been abandoned, and the property owner consents, the city will usually turn it over to you. Never just haul such a car home, assuming it is abandoned. You may spend months building up a nice rod, only to have the car's owner stake a legal (and binding) claim to it.

It is wise to get a bill of sale for everything you scrounge, even if it's for free. This is not so important for a frame, body, or small parts, but it is vital for an engine, transmission, or rear end.

A good scrounger also keeps a sharp eye out for giveaways, or low-priced cars and parts advertised in the local newspapers. The small neighborhood papers are best for this. Then, there is the swap meet where bargains are rampant.

As a stockpile of parts grows, much of the preliminary work can be taken care of in spare time. For instance, if a fad roadster is planned, using a fiberglass body, you can virtually construct the entire chassis and powertrain before every buying the body.

First, get the measurements of the body. When you know that the new frame will be so wide across the front crossmember, so wide at the rear, and the engine will be about so, you can draw rough plans and go to work. When you haul in old, dirty, or rusty pieces, try and keep them dry, either in a garage or covered outside. If the parts are greasy, chances are rust has not set in. Incidentally, if rust remover is not available at the time of disassembly, ordinary water will sometimes soak rust loose. Then, there is the use of heat. Turn the torch on a rusty bolt, and when heated the nut will often spin right off.

Assume you have gathered an old channel frame of some kind, a 1948 Ford front end and steering, and a 1949 Olds rear end. Using the general measurements of the body, you know what the frame must be. Cut the frame rails from the crossmembers, put on the rear pickup if one is involved, then make up tubing front and rear crossmembers. (Old Ford driveshaft torque tubes make ideal crossmembers. If the crossmember doesn't need to be extra strong, ordinary driveshafts work well.) While this is going on, the bolts on the front and rear ends are soaking free, and you'll be keeping an eye out for an engine and transmission. By scrounging parts and working in stages like this, you can keep busy and cut the cost of building to the bone.

There are certain things that just can't be scrounged, such as chrome plating and upholstery. But, you can get other items, such as paint for the car. Unless you're going for a way-out custom color, you can check the local body shops and get enough leftover paint for a freight train. These shops invariably have pints and quarts of unused paint just taking up shelf space. Ask for some, and the painter will probably end up helping you select or mix a color. He'll probably even give you pointers on painting your car.

The body shop is also an excellent source of other parts you may need. Take tires for instance. Did you know that if a tire sidewall is even slightly gouged most insurance companies replace it? The old tire is perfectly good, so, again, check with the body shop. Same goes for batteries, and steering wheels, and suspension parts. Then, too, if you want some bits of sheet metal to make a floorboard or firewall—yep, they've got that, too.

The final place to scrounge is the new-car dealer (assuming you've already started scrounging from all the neighbors and relatives). Just because he sells new Dodges doesn't mean he has no older parts. Check with the parts manager, explaining what you want, and he'll usually allow you to inspect the parts bin where older parts are kept. In this instance, don't overlook the basement or attic, where such parts gather dust for years. When you find something, the salesman will probably put a low blanket price on it, as his books won't show a cost, and the parts won't be on the dealership inventory.

Used Parts Are Less Expensive

The sharp hot rodder considers the automotive wrecking yard his most invaluable ally. Even the knowledgeable car tinkerer has long since learned what values lie beyond those high tin fences.

There are three basic types who visit the wrecking yard; the person who is only bumbling around looking for a part and doesn't know a junkyard from a new-car dealer, the fellow intent on buying the best used equipment available at the lowest possible price, and the scrounger. Most hot rodders belong to the last group.

A junkyard is an automotive secondhand store, where you can buy slightly used (or maybe abused) merchandise. It's a place where cost and availability are the predominant factors; cost because the price asked and/or paid is much lower than for a similar new item, and availability because so many automotive parts for cars three or more years old are hard to find anywhere else.

The junkyard operates like any other business, with a wholesale and retail price structure. The retail price of a used-car part may be one-half new-part cost, but a further saving is passed along to bonafide garages.

Wrecking yards come in all shapes and sizes, from the one-man postage stamp operation to great bustling warehouses covering acres of ground. The former is likely to be a lackadaisical affair, with little attempt at organization, whereas the latter is almost always terribly efficient. In either case, it behooves the hot rodder to introduce himself to the owner, explaining that for his parts sleuthing he needs to know exactly what the yard has in stock. It is not the general policy of junkyards to allow browsers, but when the owner knows you're a solid customer interested in finding an unknown quantity, the barrier is usually dropped. For example, how do you know exactly which steering gear you will need for that new deuce coupe if you've never had a chance to look at all the gearboxes available? This is why it is so important to wander around through a wrecking yard occasionally, getting a firsthand look at Detroit's finest.

As any experienced hot rod builder will verify, not every part can be purchased used, if dependability is necessary. But at the same time, a really wide selection of used equipment is well suited for reuse in building a hot rod. Learning what parts to buy new and what to buy used is the real problem for a beginning rodder. Don't assume that just because a piece comes from a running car it is good. Mechanical things like pistons and crankshafts and clutch discs obviously will have wear, but the beginner may think a carburetor or fuel pump never fails. Unfortunately, the opposite is true. Just because a carburetor has few moving parts doesn't mean it will last indefinitely. As a rule, a carburetor will need a rebuild after 15,000 to 20,000 miles, and this kind of consideration must be included when buying used parts.

So you must know whether a used part will do the job. As mentioned, buying a used carburetor is not always the answer, since a new unit may be available for a very few dollars more. Although rebuilt carburetors (especially for a high performance engine) are not the best bet, they may prove even less expensive than a used carburetor.

No matter where you buy a used part, you probably won't get a guarantee other than the promise of an exchange if the unit proves faulty within a couple of weeks of purchase. If you are going to buy an electrical-system component, such as a generator or starter, it's up to you to check the condition. Look at the general external appearance first, but keep in mind that caked grease on the outside does not mean the unit is bad. But a bent pulley or cracked housing is a pretty good indication of how severe a wreck the car was in, and may point to some internal damage. If there is any sign of an impact, look the working parts over very carefully before you buy.

The internal condition of an electrical unit is a function of hours of use, so you'll want to check the brushes and commutator closely. If the brushes are worn more than half their width, for instance, it shows a starter or generator has been used in normal service for about 30,000 miles or more since new (or the last rebuild). If the commutator is not bright, it may be worn. If little spots or streaks of solder are on the housing inspection band or end plate, there is a good chance the unit has been excessively hot and should not be purchased.

The wrecking yard operator normally will let you check an electrical item before you buy it. In fact, he would prefer that you do this, as it will keep you from coming back in a black mood. Check the generator by installing it on a running engine. A booster battery is used to check a starter motor. If you don't check the electrical item at the yard before you buy, get an agreement that you may return it promptly for another should the unit be inoperative.

Never install used brake equipment! The exception would be parts that are not subject to wear, such as the backing plates. Brake shoes, wheel cylinders, and flexible hydraulic hose should always be purchased new (usually these are sold on an exchange basis, so use the used parts for trade-in). A used brake drum should be carefully inspected, and a drum that has gouges in the shoe surface should be turned down by the local garage. Careful here! Brake drums can only be turned down a certain percentage of their original thickness, and you'll have to rely on the machine shop operator or brake shop to tell you whether or not the used drums can be saved. Again, the wrecking yard will usually let you get other drums if yours prove too bad. Although it is best to use new wheel cylinders and flex line, used items can be installed during the building process to check fit, but should be replaced by new pieces before driving.

It may prove hard to find specific parts for the older car, especially anything older than fifteen years, and a car with a low original production run will not be common in wrecking yards. The answer to securing parts under such conditions is to look into parts interchangeability. Most wrecking yards have a special "interchange" book, produced by either Chilton or Hollander. These books will usually carry data for up to fifteen years, and most yards will have books that go back twenty or thirty years. Because automobile manufacturers must keep production costs low, they will tend to use identical mechanical parts for a number of years. In many cases, two or three manufacturers will buy parts from a single outside source, so these parts will interchange between all the cars. Examples are bearings and rear-end gears. Ford and Chevrolet rear ends made by Spicer will interchange with each other, and also with Jaguar, although the latter is an imported car. Sometimes, engineers working within certain limits will design parts that will interchange by accident, such as connecting rods and pistons.

Chances of getting parts for an older car are especially slim if the wrecking yard does not cater to vehicles more than five years old. Wrecking yards have a very definite clientele, so you'll have to search out one that carries the older cars. In some cities, there are even yards that specialize in one type of car only, such as Chevrolet, and others that will keep only the very old cars, such as Model A Fords, etc. Often, it is possible to find parts for older cars in very small towns.

Most modern wrecking yards maintain a close contact with other yards through a cooperative telephone or telegraph system. Thus, if the yard you stop at doesn't have a certain item, they can send out an immediate call to all the other yards, and whoever has the piece will reply right away.

Before you go shopping for a used part, it is wise to know what a good price is. You should check what a new part will cost, and if possible, what a rebuilt part will cost. For instance, if you're going to buy a manual transmission, you should know exactly what that particular transmission will sell for new or rebuilt. The yard operator will probably quote you a blanket price, but if you know that particular unit sells cheaper rebuilt, you can advise him and the price will be lower.

If a part is rare, or in high demand, the price will be listed accordingly. Hot rodders like to use the XKE Jaguar full independent rear end for instance, and in certain areas these units go for upward of $250 complete. But the same pieces in other areas where there is little or no demand may cost $100 complete. It pays to shop around. It is also possible to get a small additional discount if you buy through an established garage, since most yards offer a discount rate to a business (from 10 to 30 percent).

As a general rule in figuring the cost of used parts, allow about 60 percent of the new list price on body panels. Mechanical and electrical items will be from 50 to 75 percent less than new units, while major mechanical components (like a complete engine or rear end) will be even less.

When buying parts from a wrecking yard, always get a receipt. This is necessary if you want to return a part, of course, but it also is a legal requirement with the state motor vehicle department. When you apply for a license on that hot-rodded Model T, you must show a sales receipt for the engine, transmission, and rear end. In any case, do not buy anything from anyone if you suspect it might be stolen.

There is a great amount of automobile theft in the nation, with special attention to high-performance equipment. Cars are stolen, stripped, and the parts shipped out of the area for a quick resale. If stolen parts are identified in your possession, you must legally return them to the original owner. And you're out the purchase price.

You can save lots of money repairing your own car if it has been in a collision. Most body and fender work is of the "remove and replace" type, and you can do this as well as anyone. You can buy the used parts at about half-price. Incidentally, just because a radiator has been twisted or bent in a wreck, it is not necessarily ruined. Take the damaged radiator to a radiator shop and ask for their opinion. It is a way to save as much as $150.

Many hot rodders buy an engine through a wrecking yard, but it is up to the buyer to get the right engine. If you explain what you want, the wrecking yard owner will try and help you select the best engine available. However, don't go shopping for an obviously expensive engine—more on this subject later. Transmissions should be checked carefully, because they are subject to direct driver abuse. On a manual transmission, turn the input and output shafts and feel for bearing damage. It will show as binding of the shaft, or a grating noise. If seals in the transmission are gone, there will be oil around the input or output shaft (on the housing). If the transmission has been "hot rodded" to death, it may include some cracks in the housing, especially around the shifting-fork cover plate. To check the tailshaft, slide a universal yoke onto the shaft. If the tailshaft splines are good and have not been twisted due to "drag racing," the yoke will slide in freely to "bottom." Also move the shifting levers, since they should move freely with no catches or binding. Always pull the shifter coverplate and look at gear teeth and synchromesh gear condition. Any indication of wear here is bad news.

You'll probably have a hard time checking an automatic transmission. The obvious thing to look for is a cracked case, since most late automatics are made with an aluminum housing. Remove the inspection coverplate (oil-pan cover) and check for caked oil around the pump pickup screen. The oil should have that peculiar odor of automatic transmission fluid; if it doesn't, chances are the automatic has been run too hot and internal parts may be damaged badly. Finally, take the unit to a mechanic acquaintance and ask for his opinion before installing it in a rod. If the seals should be replaced (they sometimes harden from disuse), do it before installing in the car. Do not rely on the quick cure promised by some oils sold in gas stations.

Picking out a rear end is usually a matter of trying to find something that will fit the car. Most wrecking yards have a complete variety of rear ends to choose from, but don't go in looking for the drag racing units that feature very low gear ratios (high numerically, meaning a 4.11, 4.32, 5.21.1 and so on). These are for drag racing only and bad on the road. As a rule, the average street hot rod can do very well with a rear-end ratio of 3.90:1 or less (toward 3:1).

When selecting a rear end, try and get one that can be installed with the least amount of work. That means one that will have the same wheel-bolt pattern as the front end, if possible, and will mount to the existing car springs easily. It is not difficult to make special spring attachments for the rear-end housing, however.

When buying a used rear end, check the axle bearings (they'll grind and feel coarse when you turn the wheel if bad) and the axles (for twist). Check the ring and pinion gear if you suspect they might be bad. Put some white grease on the ring gear and rotate the pinion gear several times. The pinion-gear teeth will remove grease from the ring-gear teeth where they come in contact. If the wear is correct, the wiped pattern will be in the middle of the ring gear rather than at either end. The pattern will be constant on all teeth, also.

You can do a lot of trading with a wrecking yard, sometimes much to your advantage, but this must be set up on an individual basis with the owner. Also, while some yards don't want what you have to trade, others are happy to get the items, especially the smaller yards. Learning to buy from a junkyard is a talent, but one you'll find quite rewarding.

Tips on Used Speed Equipment

The modern speed equipment business in the United States and Canada is a multimillion-dollar-a-year operation. Tons of raw aluminum and magnesium alloy are consumed daily by specialty manufacturers; special wheels are produced in the tens of thousands weekly; camshaft grinders can hardly keep up with the demand. In short, a booming business continues to boom.

One might think that all this production would soon fill the coffers to overflowing; that demand would begin to taper off as the supply increased; that the amount of used speed equipment would quickly fill the after-market. Not so. A visit to any established speed shop proves just the opposite. Used speed equipment is indeed readily available, most of it in excellent shape, yet it serves more as an appetizer than an appeaser. It is the introduction to a fascinating hobby.

Used speed equipment generally is bought by the younger rodder, high on enthusiasm and ideas, low on capital. But a goodly portion is absorbed by veterans, builders who have learned from long experience that the total cost of their hobby can be cut considerably by careful shopping. In many instances, the cost of a used piece of equipment is less than half that of a new part. With equal results!

Of course, speed equipment is like anything else. The longer and harder it is used, the more wear it will show. Learning to shop wisely is the keynote to success in buying used speed equipment.

Perhaps the most common piece of speed equipment is the intake manifold. Usually made of an aluminum alloy, but often of cast iron, the multiple carburetor setup is one of the first pieces of special material added to an individualized automobile. Even Detroit sets its performance car apart by adding two or three carburetors. With literally thousands of used manifolds on the market, finding a good one is not difficult.

Generally, a big quad or dual/triple manifold will be sold with carburetors. This is most often the best way to purchase it, as you will be saving a considerable amount on the carbs. But first, minute inspection of the manifold itself is paramount. Always remove the carburetors for a really thorough look. Using a straight edge of some sort, check the manifold-to-head mating surface. It is not uncommon to find that an aluminum manifold will warp after initial use. This warpage is not bad in itself. However, if the manifold has warped several times in the past, and been machined to straighten out the surfaces, the bolt flange area will be rather thin. The thinner this area, the harder it is to get a good seal.

The same holds true for the carburetor mounting surface. Many times the engine has been mounted in a boat, drag car, or some other vehicle wherein the engine mount angle is more than your particular need. In order to keep the carbs level, the manifold may have been machined (the proper method here is to use special wedges under the carbs). Check the mounting angle before you buy.

Look closely at the water transfer area if the manifold is so equipped. Water will raise havoc with aluminum, tending to eat great gouges in the most unlikely places. Also, pay particular attention to any threaded holes in the aluminum. Sometimes, a previous owner will use a bigger than normal stud or bolt to compensate for stripped threads.

Finally, check for breaks or cracks in the casting, and/or casting irregularities. It is very unusual for a bad casting to get by a manufacturing inspector, but it does happen occasionally. In this respect, the pattern core will sometimes shift during casting, offsetting the interior passages. If this has occurred, the manifold will still probably be usable but may require extra effort in fitting. Also, if the interior passage comes too close to the outside wall, it can break through under the slightest pressure.

One of the normal causes of premature manifold discard is for a broken-boltdown flange. Most manifolds have a small ear sticking out in at least one place where a manifold bolt is used. If the manifold is installed incorrectly, or the bolt is torqued too much, this small flange is likely to break off.

None of the above problems are severe enough to throw the manifold in the trash heap. They are, however, serious enough to allow the potential buyer some bargaining ground. A veteran rodder spots these things quickly, can assess the probable repair cost closely, and can buy the manifold at real basement prices.

If the manifold is warped or the carburetor mounting angle is incorrect, a simple machine shop operation will suffice. If water has eaten severely at the transfer tubes and passages, the area can be cleaned with a rotary wire brush. If this "cancer" has eaten across a mating surface or through a wall, a professional welder can repair the damage. Stripped threads or too-large holes can be repaired with Heli-Coils. In fact, it is wise to install Heli-Coils in all aluminum threads. Breaks, cracks, and broken flange pieces must be welded by a professional. After the welding, the area may be ground smooth and all mating surfaces remachined for trueness.

As a final gesture, the aluminum manifold may be polished, lightly sandblasted, or soaked in acid cleaner to restore that new appearance. A cast-iron manifold can really be made to look "right from the shelf" it it is thoroughly cleaned in solvent and painted with a heat-resistant enamel.

What should you pay for a used manifold? That depends entirely on the situation. Since it's usually a buyer's market, you will probably be able to bargain somewhat. A typical dual quad manifold, aluminum, for a Chevy 283 will go from $25 to $50 minus carbs. It should cost less if it needs repairs.

The purchase of a used carburetor is simply a matter of never assuming anything. No matter what the seller claims, always inspect the unit yourself. Better yet, try and observe the unit in actual operation if possible.

A good used carburetor (probably a four-barrel) should cost about one-half new cost. A typical Carter AFB, for example, goes on the used market for $15 to $25, depending entirely upon condition. A brand-new AFB for most of the smaller cubic-inch engines can be purchased from almost any speed shop for less than $35. Of course, the cost of a used carb is in direct proportion to availability and popularity. If the new Holley is being used by the winners at the local drag strip, chances are you will have to pay $10 more than normal.

The most common type of two-throat carburetor used in hot rodding is the Stromberg 97. This is a relatively big and trouble-free unit, and it is easily distinguished by the needle valve assembly mounted in the left side of the bowl. It is also usually quickly discernible by the many nicks and scratches on the bowl and top casting around the needle valve area. This particular carburetor is prone to have the needle valve stick open, with resulting flooding. Pounding on the carb housing usually relieves the situation. Be suspicious of a battered housing.

Properly set up, a good dual 4-barrel arrangement will run rings around four two-throats. But be cautious. It is common practice to remove the choke from a four-barrel, but some inexpert backyard tuners also remove the secondary dampeners too. If the carburetor is on a running engine, this will quickly show up as a stumbling falter just as the secondaries are opening.

On any carburetor, the assembly screws are the giveaway to probable condition. If the screw slots are rather smooth, chances are the carb has not been tinkered with much. If the slots are all torn up from repeated screwdriver wear, the carb is probably sick.

It is easy to overhaul a carburetor, and inexpensive. But not if the basic body must be replaced due to broken castings or grooves worn in the throats by the butterflies. Should an overhaul be necessary, use the best overhaul kit you can buy. Also install extra-good needle seats. Naturally, the cost of an overhaul should be considered when talking purchase price.

One final note. The outside cleanliness of a carburetor does not necessarily indicate interior condition. A new-looking carb can have filthy insides, and vice-versa. Just look into the venturi area, for a quick way to make them look like new is to use a solution of one part Mr. Clean to three parts warm water. Spray or dip the parts, let set for a few moments, and then hose off. This cleaner works on almost any greasy part, but do not get it on a painted surface as it will spot.

Because of the intricacy of a fuel injector, there is little one can do to insure good condition. If you don't know the past history of the unit in question, you'll have to go on the assumption that at least minor repair or adjustment will be necessary. Especially if the injector is off a street driven car.

An Algon, Enderle, or Hilborn competition constant flow injector is rather uncomplicated and consists primarily of a fuel pump, metering system, and control housing. The fuel pump itself can be tested by spinning it with an electric motor and checking the apparent flow of fluid. The metering unit can't be checked without proper tools. The housing is a matter of broken flanges or cracks. In all instances, a used competition injector should be sent directly to the manufacturer for a complete inspection and overhaul if necessary. This isn't an expensive thing, and an absolute must if serious competition is considered.

For street use, the Corvette and Pontiac injectors are available for just about any price in the book. The early injectors, which are considerably narrower than the newer units, are going for prices between $75 and $125. The newer injector units, which are much more flexible especially in cold climates, are selling upwards of $350.

The sharp buyer knows that the injector is one unit that can be purchased for a song if the time is right. In many instances, the owner knows little or nothing of the mechanical parts on his car. If the injector starts to act up, and there are no good service facilities available, he will often want to trade the injector for a good carburetion system. Service of the Chevrolet injector is really quite easy, especially using some inexpensive servicing tools and instructions available through any Chevrolet parts department.

As with the competition injector, there is precious little that can be checked on a street injection system. With the entire system on a narrow table, so that the injector nozzles are free to squirt gas, the feeding operation can be checked. Fill the fuel meter with gasoline, then spin the pump with an electric drill motor. A constant spray from all the nozzles indicates the unit is probably working all right. By removing the line from the diaphragm and sucking on the open line, the nozzle flow can be varied as in actual use. If these two checks work, chances are the unit is good.

Buying special pistons and rods is like buying a pig in a poke. Be sure to check. Arbitrary inspection of a piston or rod (aluminum) will reveal any major cracks or defects. However, for a complete check, the items should be magnafluxed, the rods checked on an alignment machine, and the pistons checked to make sure they have not collapsed. All this can be done by any mechanic anywhere. If the rods are factory steel, check the casting numbers against factory specifications to insure proper type. In other words, don't just take someone's word that you're buying genuine Stage Three Chrysler rods.

There is probably more minor bilking done in the used camshaft business than in the entire sport. Cams supposedly made by a well-known grinder often turn out to be stock units, or bogus grinds, with the popular name stamped on.

When buying a used cam, first of all try and learn its history personally. Secondly, be familiar enough with hot versus stock cams to identify the cam profile of a hot cam. In essence, a hot cam will have a flatter top on the lobe. A stock camshaft has a fairly pointed lobe. Third, find out from some local expert or write to the factory about how that particular manufacturer marks his cams. Each grinder uses a slightly different form of identification. All grinders keep a close tab on their cams by serial numbers. Using this number from a used cam, you can discover the original owner, what the specs on the cam are, and the original sale date.

Condition of a camshaft and related lifters (either roller or flat tappet) is indicated by the wear pattern on the lobes. Flat tappets that have gouges and pits on the base are on their way out. A cam lobe with a slight discoloration just below the peak is beginning normal wear. If this area becomes galled, the cam will need to be reground. The simplest way to check wear is to check each lobe against the others. Usually, several lobes will remain okay.

If possible, also have a qualified mechanic check the cam to see if it is bent, twisted, etc., and have a magnaflux run. To check a Dontov Chevrolet cam, look for the numbers between the lobes. The early cams, '57–'63, are relatively mild and have the numbers ending with 098. The '64 and later cams are quite hot, with the numbers ending in 347.

Many times, excellent cams and kits can be purchased from racers, who are constantly changing combinations in the search for more power. Use only a cam suited to your purpose. A big supercharger camshaft is not right for a normally aspirated, street driven car!

As with cams, stroked crankshafts built by reputable manufacturers are stamped. Always have the crankshaft thoroughly checked by magnaflux for cracks; check each journal for size and wear, and the entire unit for alignment.

Special tubing headers are beginning to show up on the used-part shelves, and rightly so. About the only things a prospective buyer will be concerned with are condition and whether or not the items will fit his particular engine/body style. Check the header flange for warps (which can be removed by machining) and cracks around welds. Good used headers are selling from $25.

Strange as it may seem, there is much traffic in used heads, especially high performance items. Generally speaking, a head should be inspected for cracks; the cylinder surface should be checked for warpage and enlarged ports should be checked for cracks or break-through. In the latter instance, some home-grown porting experts often fall into the water jacket and then don't know that the area can be brazed.

If you'll be paying a stiff price for a supposedly competition head, have each cylinder c.c'd. If they don't come within two to three c.c's of each other, be suspicious.

On late model Chrysler Corporation heads, the standard head is used on almost all standard blocks, no matter what the cubic inches. The special heads have much larger porting and are readily apparent. The same holds true for Ford heads, and some high performance heads are available. However, check each head for absolute fit before you pay your bucks.

Chevrolet heads are a regular din of confusion for used-equipment sharpies. The ends of the head are marked with a special form, while certain design characteristics of each are definitive.

It is important to get a basically sound head, expecting to do a complete service job on the valves. If aluminum heads for a flathead are being considered, definitely check them for warpage, cracks in the combustion chamber, gouges above the valve area indicating valve/head interference, and water damage. As with an aluminum manifold, water will react with the aluminum, eating away at the metal around all water passage openings. On Ford flatheads, this is most prevalant in the water openings at each end of the head, and the passage right in the middle. Minor "cancer" can be repaired. By adding a small amount of soluble oil to the water, or by using an antifreeze, this water/aluminum reaction can be circumvented.

It's easy to check an ignition—merely take it to the nearest ignition shop and have it run up on their machine. The common cause of special high-performance distributor failure is the driving shaft and point plate. A magneto usually loses magnet force. In either case, the units may be bought at prices ranging from $25 to $75 and should be returned to the builder for overhaul if possible.

Be very careful when buying a used flywheel/clutch assembly. An aluminum flywheel should be checked for a perfectly flat surface and cracks. The steel surface on either aluminum or steel flywheels will show severe checking (small irregular cracks) if the plate has run very hot, such as from a slipped clutch, etc. These cracks will not be of consequence unless they are very deep and run to the inside of the flywheel. If a minor resurfacing will not take out most of the checks, the flywheel should not be used in competition.

You must use top caution with custom wheels. Closely check each wheel thoroughly for cracks around rivets, welds, and bolt holes. Check the rims for breaks and alignment. If it is an alloy wheel, make sure the previous owner has used the correct lug bolts. It is rather common to use standard lug nuts (tapered) on a wheel requiring shoulder lug bolts. If the wheels are magnesium or aluminum, they should be magnafluxed before you buy them. Steer clear if cracks of any kind show up!

Always assume that there is something wrong with the equipment. Inspect it closely, and deal wisely. You'll fast become an expert, and have lots more rodding pleasure in the process.

Used Engines

If you've been interested in cars for more than a month, you've had the experience of checking out prices for a good used ohv V8 engine. And most likely, you've come away from the local engine dealer a little confused. The average person seldom knows all the intricacies of buying a good used engine. After all, it isn't much like horse trading, where you can get on the critter and see how he rides.

Before making the decision to buy a used engine, you should always first have a reasonable knowledge of the product. If you're set on a Chevy V8, know beforehand what V8's are available, some of their general characteristics, and an average per-unit cost. Next, utilizing some of the information in this chapter, thoroughly inspect the engine, making sure it is exactly the engine the seller claims it to be. It is this particular step that will give you a dud or a real bargain.

After you are sure you have located the kind of engine you need, continue the inspection to determine the engine condition. It's always nice to hear an engine run, and it is preferable to drive the car, although this is seldom possible. You can, however, get an excellent idea of overall condition merely by spending an hour looking at the mechanical innards.

The first clue to how good or bad an engine is will be the general overall appearance, which will vary according to miles of use. Just because the assembly is covered from one end to the other with a thick cake of dirty grease, don't discard it as bad. Indeed, it may just prove to be in better shape than an outwardly clean unit. If the engine is caked with grease, it primarily indicates the unit has been used on dirt or gravel roads, or around construction, or has never been cleaned since it was installed in the car.

It is common practice to steam-clean a used engine, the assumption being that a customer will consider a clean engine a good indication of interior condition. Some engine dealers go so far as to paint the cleaned engine. Right here a novice can get in trouble. The unscrupulous seller, and the country is full of them, will sometimes take an engine in only reasonably good shape, paint it up, and sell it as a new unit. Of course, the dead giveaway of such a cheat is gasket appearance. Since these engines are not disassembled, the original gaskets will still be in place and dirty. New engine gaskets will be virtually spotless. A further check is removal of a valve cover. If the cover sticks to or breaks a gasket, the engine is probably bogus. Further, the rocker arm area will appear very clean on new engines, with only a thin film of clean oil, much like a polished piece of furniture. The entire insides of a new or very recently rebuilt engine will appear the same way.

Naturally, an engine formerly owned by a serious hot rodder will often appear as new on the used engine shelf. Inspection of such an engine should include removal of one head, the intake manifold and valley cover, and the pan.

General condition of engine accessories will also indicate whether or not you're getting a good buy. Look at the generator brushes and ignition points, the ignition wire and plugs, the water pump inlet and outlet, the starter. All will show excessive wear and abuse.

While still just looking at the overall engine, try and find an engine rebuilder's plate. This will normally be riveted to the bell housing (transmission rebuilders use similar markings on a rebuilt trans) and will tell the date of rebuild and size of cylinder bore/ crankshaft journals. Production rebuild shops usually tag their engines this way (smaller shops don't) and from the tag you get an idea of how long the engine might have run. In addition, if one throw on the crankshaft has been turned down .030-inch while all others are stock or .10, you may plan on your own rebuild.

Next, always take the engine partially apart. The dealer will seldom do this for you, as it costs him money in labor, and his phrase is invariably, "We don't know what it's like on the inside." Indeed, that would be an absurd requirement for anything other than a new engine. The dealer will, however, usually let you do a partial disassembly. If you find the engine not what it would appear, you have done him a service. And you've kept him from having a dissatisfied customer.

First, remove a rocker arm cover and look for excessive sludge build-up. If the sludge is really thick and gooey or hard, the engine has been run a long time. Sludge, though, can be the result of a little old lady only driving the car three blocks to church on Sunday. Next, remove the intake manifold and valley cover, also looking for sludge. While the intake manifold is off, check the ports for any indication of excessive carbon build-up on the walls, which would indicate poor intake valves.

Remove one of the heads and check cylinder wall taper with

an inside micrometer. This taper, or wear, will be an almost direct reading of engine use. For normal use, anything less than .008-inch taper won't require a bore job. Rotate the crankshaft and inspect each cylinder wall. If there are streaks of black running well down the bore, there is excessive ring blow-by. If the walls are scratched or gouged anywhere, a piston or ring has failed. If the wall lower ends look as if they have been hot, they have, due to inadequate lubrication. The lip, or ledge, around the top of the cylinder bore will indicate bore wear if you don't have a micrometer handy.

The top and edges of the piston can tell a story too. If the piston surface looks like overheated tinfoil, beware. If the edge of the crown is broken or irregular, replacement will also be necessary.

Normally you won't have anything handy to compress the valve springs so you can look at the seats. If the valves look perfectly round, even though discolored, they're probably usable. The exhaust valve is the big problem, as it gets all of the heat, and will normally show failure first as an irregular edge on the head. A badly burned valve does not mean, however, that the rest of the engine is in bad shape. Check the combustion chambers carefully for small hairline cracks, and the surface of the head with a straight edge for warpage. Broken rocker arms and bad valve springs are immediately apparent, and do not necessarily reflect the overall engine condition.

Remove several of the pushrod lifters and check the lifter cam face. If it is smooth, even though slightly discolored, wear is minimal. Wear will show as small or large pits on the lifter face. While you're looking, check each and every lobe of the camshaft. If there is any difference in the apparent shape of the lobes, the cam may be worn. In addition, look closely on the cam lobe opening side for pits, extreme discoloration, etc., which also indicates excessive wear.

Finally, remove the pan. If the oil pickup screen is covered and plugged with sludge, it's a good bet the engine wasn't getting enough oil. Try and move the crankshaft fore and aft. If there is more than a slight amount of movement, there is excessive thrust bearing wear.

Now check each connecting rod individually. With the throw halfway between BDC and TDC, wrap the thumb and forefinger around the journal next to the rod. With the other hand rotate the crank slightly. You should *feel* only the barest vertical movement between rod and crank. You will also feel rod sideplay, but this is irrelevant at the moment.

Place a pry bar over the pan bolt face and beneath the crank. Feeling around the main bearing journals on the crank, as with the rods, move the pry bar up and down. Only a very slight (if any) movement should be felt.

If after all this lower end checking you're still in doubt, pick two different rod caps to remove and at least the rear main cap. Expect to find some scuffing of the bearings, with some small metal particles embedded in the bearing face. If the bearing or journal is discolored from heat, rebuilding or replacement will be necessary.

There are many additional condition characteristics that are used to distinguish good engines from bad. The above are general, do not take a lot of time or effort, and will save the buyer from a bad mistake. Keep in mind that you are looking mostly for excessive metal-to-metal wear.

Deciding what kind of ohv V8 you want to buy is as much of the purchasing procedure as the actual selection. Number one on any engine buyers list should be ultimate use of the product. Will it be entirely rebuilt for all-out racing of some kind; will it go into a boat; will it just be cleaned up and dropped in a street machine? The ultimate use dictates what type of engine will be bought, what kind of general condition is required, and what kind of cost factor is reasonable.

For racing engines, it is always advisable to select a particular year and design most closely suited to racing use. A person building a big supercharged dragster would use a 327, 396, or 425 Chevrolet to much better advantage than a 265 or 283. In addition, a person building up a class Gasser would certainly want to get an initial design better suited to his purposes, say a Chevy 283 with large port fuel injection heads rather than a stock 283 with small port heads. Again, a double A fueler would go for a 352 or 392 early Chrysler hemi as a basic start rather than a 375-inch Packard. You must always start with the best possible beginning, so as to have the least amount of building trouble and expenditure. If the engine is to be entirely rebuilt for racing, only the basic assemblies are important: block, heads, crank.

If the engine is going to be used "as-is," then you want to get one in as good original condition as possible. Always try and buy an engine from a running car if possible. When scouring the junk yards, look for the typical high performance car. It is always a fair bet the old Pontiac hardtop convertible will have the top horsepower engine of its line, while a station wagon or four-door sedan of the same year will probably have an economy model. A four-barrel or multicarburetor setup also indicates the engine is reasonably powerful.

The cost of your engine will depend mainly upon current local popularity, condition, and the salesman. Because it is in high demand, the Corvette engine, complete and ready to run, costs about $350. A standard passenger car 327 will average $250. Both will give similar performance, at least for street use. At the same time, a good Rambler 327 only costs about $200. Very similar to the Chevrolet design, but with small intake ports, this is an excellent possibility. A Chevy 265, which can very easily be made into a 283, will cost only about $60.

Naturally, if you're only buying an engine for the basic foundation of a racing powerhouse, condition is much less important. Take that Chevy 327 for instance. You're going to install a stroker along with all the other goodies, so you'll be able to buy a good core assembly for about $50. Sometimes, if you are buying an older engine, like a '57 Olds or Chrysler, the price will be nearly the same. A 392 Chrysler will cost in the neighborhood of $125.

Many hot rodders who have been playing with cars, both racing and street, for a long time often buy an entire car just for the engine. You have a '54 Ford and you want to put in a better Ford engine. If you watch the newspapers and local car lots, sometimes you can find a very good late model Ford for a low price, from $200 to $300. These cars can always be driven and the exact engine condition assessed. Remove the engine, transmission, and rear end. The remaining hulk is then either sold for junk iron for $15 or $25, or the various pieces are sold. The rear end, for instance, can bring up to $50, the radio might be worth $15, the radiator $10, etc.

Other good places to seek used engines are dealer garages, body and fender shops, and automotive insurance agencies. The dealer often has used engines available. The body and fender shops are a good source, especially for good racing cores. Since most of those wrecked late model stockers you see in the wrecking yards were once insured, the insurance agency is a natural. When a client totals out a car (that is, the cost of fixing it up is greater than the current market value of the car), the agency puts the remains up for bid. Highest bid takes, with the price directly relative to original value and current market price. A wrecked 1969 Corvette will go for a big bundle, but a standard '69 Chevy passenger car will often move for as little as $200.

Last of all, the price you pay depends upon you and the fellow selling the engine. Don't be afraid to bargain. You have nothing to lose, especially if you find something wrong with the engine.

Learning to spot various models of a particular engine design will help you to get a good, reasonable buy. However, don't expect to learn all the little characteristics, unless you intend to make ohv engine buying a profession.

Before starting on your ohv engine shopping tour, it is best to check with local dealers and mechanics for basic year serial numbers. When you have located what you believe is a good purchase, record the serial number and double-check it with the dealer before laying out the cash. A prudent buyer will be able to save himself many, many dollars by shopping with his brain instead of his heart.

One last thing. It will prove ultimately beneficial if you begin your engine search well in advance of the actual purchase time, in order to have a thorough knowledge of engines available, what may become available, and *exactly* what each possible engine really is.

TYPICAL ENGINE WEIGHTS
OHV–V8

Engine	Displacement	Weight
Buick	401	640
Cadillac	390	645
Chevrolet	327	540
Chevrolet	409	640
Chrysler	413	670
Chrysler	392	765
Ford Fairlane	289	470
Ford	292	625
Ford	406	660
Olds	394	715
Plymouth	318	580
Pontiac	421	675
Pontiac	327	580
Rambler	327	600
Studebaker	289	650
Buick, small V8, Aluminum	215	266

Note: These weights are given as a guide, and do not include clutch flywheel, or bell housing.

TYPICAL RETAIL PRICES—Used OHV V8 engines

Engine	Price (complete good)	Price (core)
Buick, all big V8's	$ 75–$450	$ 30–$125
Special small V8	$150–$400	$ 30–$ 75
Cadillac	$ 50–$400	$ 30–$125
Chevrolet 265	$ 50–$200	$ 20–$ 75
283	$100–$250	$ 50–$130
327	$175–$350	$ 85–$175
348	$ 50–$200	$ 20–$ 75
409	$ 85–$250	$ 50–$150
427	$350–$550	$125–$200
Chrysler (includes all Chrysler Corporation engines)		
331–392		
241–335 '51–'58 Hemi's	$ 50–$250	$ 25–$100
276–341		
'A' series	$ 75–$250	$ 25–$ 90
'B' series	$ 75–$250	$ 40–$100
426 Hemi	$500–$600	$100–$150
Ford (includes all Ford Company engines)		
239–312	$ 5–$100	$ 0–$ 50
332–428	$200–$400	$ 75–$150
221–289	$100–$350	$ 50–$150
Oldsmobile		
303–324	$ 5 $100	$ 0–$ 50
371–394	$ 15–$150	$ 10–$ 50
371–394	$ 15–$150	$ 10–$ 50
400–427	$250–$450	$125–$200
330–up (new series)	$225–$400	$ 50–$125
Pontiac		
287–389	$ 5–$400	$ 0–$125
421	$300–$450	$140–$200

Note: Only the more popular engines are listed here. Naturally, they will cost more than the not-so-popular engines, such as Lincoln, Packard, Studebaker, Rambler, etc. Core prices shown are average for bare block, crankshaft, and heads. Prices quoted by dealers invariably are based upon manufacture year, and will vary either well above or below our average.

This has been a lengthly chapter, but it contains the very heart of economical hot rodding. When the enthusiast, new and veteran, learns to apply these rules, he is well on his way to an outstanding future in the personalized automotive sport. Hot rodding becomes more fun than ever, because more of it is possible.

4

All About Engines

For as long as there have been cars, there have been hot rodders. And for the same time, most of the rodder's attention has been focused on the automobile engine. Trying to get just an ounce more performance from Ol' Betsy intrigued grandpa just as much as it now interests junior. The only difference has been in the foundation for experimentation—grandpa worked on a four-cylinder Model T, junior is absorbed by a modern V8 or inline 6. While total performance has skyrocketed in a few short decades, the methods of achieving performance have not.

Essentially there are two basic requirements in improving the performance of any engine—increasing the engine's breathing ability (it can then convert greater quantities of fuel and air to mechanical energy during a given period of time), and improving the relationship of moving parts (reducing friction to gain a greater percentage of mechanical energy at the flywheel).

The majority of speed equipment produced for modern engines is aimed at helping the engine breathe better, or to increase the volumetric efficiency. While commercial speed equipment is di-

rected toward helping the engine breathe, the individual hot
rodder is always instructed to make the mechanical changes in
the basic engine to help it live. That is, he must be very concerned
with cylinder block preparation, careful selection of components,
modifications to the cylinder head, and so on. A piece of equipment from the speed shop shelf may have a bolt-on power increase
of ten percent, but if the rodder builds his engine correctly, the
horsepower addition may double. And this, specifically, is where
the amateur is separated from the professional.

Things done to engines for normal reworking jobs are many
and varied. Some of them are concerned directly with making it
easier for the engines to induct more mixture but others are to
help the engines withstand the greater pressures that will be
created in the cylinders and to run efficiently at crankshaft speeds
much higher than normal.

The basic method of increasing the amount of fuel and air
mixture an engine can induct is by making the cylinder displacement larger. This is the method used by automobile manufacturers and it is also one of the methods used by hot rodders. No
matter how large an engine's standard displacement may be, a
hot rodder is always ready to make it even larger. This makes
good sense when the aim is additional power.

An engine's displacement can be made larger by increasing the
diameter of the cylinders or lengthening the crankshaft stroke.
Most rodders use a combination of both methods.

Although boring is an accepted procedure involving an operation to enlarge the diameter of engine cylinders by removing
material from the walls of the cylinders, it can result in the
scrapping of a perfectly good engine block because of improper
sizing and piston fit. It is a fairly simple matter if one has the
proper equipment; however, there are limitations on the amount
of material that can be removed from the cylinder walls of a particular engine block and, if this limitation is exceeded, it is pos-

sible that a portion or all of the walls will be bored away. Sometimes a cylinder may appear to be sound after it has been bored to a large oversize, but after the engine is reassembled and fired up, the wall may crack or a section may be blown out of it. Sleeving may save the block, but usually such an engine should no longer be used for competition purposes.

A rule of thumb for cylinder blocks of most late-model engines is that they have adequate cylinder wall thickness for an overbore of ⅛ inch. Almost without exception, to make a larger cut than this is taking a chance on ruining a block. Before boring a particular block, be on the safe side and check with someone who has had experience with that block. Another method to check maximum bore size is to find out what sizes of special pistons are available for the engine; this, however, is not a positive rule because some piston manufacturers deliberately make and sell pistons for cylinder bores of extremely risky diameters. Stock replacement oversize pistons cannot be used as a gauge of how much a block can be bored because the maximum diameter of pistons made for this purpose is only .060 inch greater than that of the stock cylinders. Most engine manufacturers recommend that a block with cylinders that must be bored larger than .060 inch be discarded and replaced with a new one.

When boring oversize, the last cut made by the boring machine should always remove only a small amount of material from the wall, assuring a clean, straight cylinder. Often, the machinist will take large cuts causing the boring bar to deflect and chatter, producing a rough, uneven finish which results in ring failure and additional friction loss.

Occasionally, when price is no object and a definite cubic inch classification is causing a restriction in bore increase, it may be desirable to increase the bore and reduce the stroke, retaining the necessary cubic inches but resulting in a more efficient bore to stroke ratio.

Sleeving, except as a method for decreasing cubic inches, produces no advantages in performance for an engine builder and should be avoided whenever possible. It is accomplished by installing a cylinder liner in the existing cylinder bore, reducing the area by the wall measurement of the liner. It is sometimes done when de-stroking is too expensive or impossible due to obstacles within the engine block, and it is used, of course, as a method of repairing engine blocks which have had a wall failure. Usually, it isn't satisfactory for engines used in conjunction with supercharging or nitrated fuels.

Stroking is a subject of considerable controversy among the experts. The actual advantages of stroking, for instance, may be questioned by the individual who de-stroked his engine and obtained greater power; this all proves that there are many and varied modifications and, in the proper combinations, one can obtain the desired results.

Stroke is the measurement the piston assembly travels up and down the cylinder. The term stroking is associated with lengthening this movement, causing the piston to travel a greater distance from the top of the cylinder to the bottom during each cycle of operation, while de-stroking is the term associated with shortening this piston travel. Each has its definite advantage.

The advantage of additional stroke is derived mainly from the increase in cubic inch displacement which proportionately increases the low- and mid-range torque characteristics. When the port area and camshaft timing are increased proportionately, maximum horsepower will also increase in direct relationship until the ability of the engine to breathe reaches its limit. At this point, the horsepower-per-cubic-inch ratio becomes less, and the functional operative rpm limited. Torque, however, continues to increase, and, to take advantage of this low rpm torque, higher gear ratios should be used.

The disadvantage in increasing the stroke is in the additional wall friction created because of the longer travel of the piston.

This may rob the engine of a relatively small amount of power, and it also creates an increase in cylinder temperature, an undesirable factor in high-performance engines due to the preheated expanding air-fuel mixtures. Although these factors are measurable, they remain small compared to the cubic inch increase.

De-stroking, or shortening the stroke, is a method used mainly for decreasing the cubic inch displacement in the engine block when a specific competition class requirement is to be met. When a specific engine displacement is held, demanding a decrease in cubic inches, it is always more desirable to retain the bore size and decrease the stroke, due to the advantage of combustion surface area which helps chamber cooling. The reduced stroke decreases wall friction and in turn produces much more effective combustion control. A distinct advantage of the short stroke is that it functions more efficiently at higher rpms, due to the decreased piston speed. The one disadvantage of torque loss relative to cubic inch reduction is overcome when the engine is equipped with radical valve timing, high compression, and lower gear ratios, keeping the rpm well into the power range; the engine actually produces very high horsepower relative to cubic inch displacement.

In recent years, the popularity of stroking has made it possible for many shops specializing in high performance equipment to manufacture complete "stroker" kits. Contained in these kits are all the parts needed to stroke an engine. All that is required is to have the cylinders bored, grind whatever clearance notches are necessary in the lower ends of the cylinders, and install the kit parts in the block.

Stroker kits contain a crankshaft with the desired stroke length; pistons for the desired cylinder bore diameter to match the stroke; piston pins; piston rings; connecting rods; connecting rod bearing inserts; and main bearing inserts. All the parts are balanced as an assembly. As a rule, crankshafts in kits are also purchased; connecting rods are generally used but completely reconditioned, sometimes new; all other parts are new. The customer often has the choice of makes of pistons available. There is usually a trade-in allowance for the customer's crankshaft and connecting rods if they can meet certain specifications. This makes it possible for an engine builder to save some money on the modification and still take advantage of the convenience it offers.

The item which undoubtedly takes more punishment than any other part of the crank assembly is the piston. This component travels a fantastic number of feet per second at high rpm at temperatures exceeding 2200 degrees. Therefore, the choice of special pistons (which must be used with stroked crankshafts) should not be governed by price but by structure. The best for competition purposes is the forged piston. A forged piston is made from an aluminum extrusion. This assures that all areas of the piston have 100 percent wrought or solid structure and, after completion of machining, the pistons are thoroughly tested and checked to specifications by the manufacturer. All ring groove depths are held to exact clearances, and specific wall depths may be ordered on demand, assuring a perfect component.

The reason for use of special pistons with stroked crankshaft is that piston pin bores in the connecting rods of a stroked crankshaft rise to a higher position in the cylinders when the shaft rotates than they did originally. The distance the rods travel up the cylinders above stroke position is equal to one-half the amount the shaft was stroked. Thus, if a shaft had been stroked ½ inch, the rods would rise ¼ inch higher in the cylinders than they did with a stock crankshaft.

Balancing the Engine

All internal combustion engines, regardless of type or use for which they are designed, are balanced to certain standards before they are assembled at the factory. It is easy to take factory procedures for granted and assume that the products released by them are as near perfection as modern machines and methods can make them. Unfortunately, such is not always the case. With the exception of most high performance engines, which are special order, the average engine leaves a lot to be desired in the way of balancing. Objectionable vibrations caused by imbalance in the crankshaft assembly of modern engines is isolated by highly engineered rubber engine mounts. Though they do dampen out a large percentage of the engine vibration before it reaches the frame, the imbalanced forces in the engine nevertheless continue their destructive and power-absorbing pounding.

The primary cause of vibration in an automobile engine is the state of balance of the rotating and reciprocating parts of crankshaft, connecting rods, pistons, and flywheel assembly. These parts are balanced at the factory during the course of manufacture but the final success of the balancing job for a specific engine is, in most cases, dependent on a lucky selection of the parts used in the engine. This is because the parts are not balanced to perfect weights, but to mass production "tolerances" specified for the respective parts.

Unbalance, or imbalance, is simply the uneven distribution of weight. In motion, that unbalance becomes power . . . uncontrolled, wasted, on the loose! Even so small an amount of unbalance as one ounce an inch away from the center of the rotational axis is multiplied forty times—it becomes a two-pound, ten-ounce weight at only 1200 rpm. At 5000 rpm this same unbalance, one inch-ounce, creates a force of forty-five pounds, ten ounces. That dynamic balancing plays a vital role in engine performance, part longevity, etc., needs little emphasis by now.

Factory tolerances are greater than those established by balancing shops catering to high performance enthusiasts. Such firms use a tolerance of .01 ounce-inch for piston and connecting rod assemblies, and .05 ounce-inch for crankshafts and flywheels.

Balancing operations are of two types, static or dynamic. Static unbalance of appreciable magnitude is observed when the unbalanced part is mounted on horizontal knife edges. The part will roll until its heavy or unbalanced point reaches the lowermost position. The presence of dynamic unbalance is shown only when the part is rotating. This type of unbalance is caused by two weights located on opposite sides and opposite ends of the rotating part. Static balance is accomplished by adding material to light sections or removing material from heavy sections. Corrections are made without regard to the location of unbalance along the axis of rotation. Dynamic balancing is accomplished by rotating the part to be balanced at sufficient speed to bring into play centrifugal forces caused by the unequal distribution of weight along the axis. The amount of unbalance can be directly located and measured on special dynamic balancing machines.

A crankshaft can be checked for static balance by placing each of the outer main bearing journals on parallel knife-edged supports positioned in a horizontal plane. Flywheels must be mounted on a mandrel that can be placed between these same supports. In this manner an object may rotate on its axis with a minimum of friction.

Objects of the short-axis group, such as flywheels, are generally in dynamic balance when they are in static balance. Such is not the case with all objects and dynamic balance becomes more important as the length of an object increases.

Assume that a crankshaft is in a condition of static unbalance, and that the heavy spot is toward the front end of the shaft. Perhaps the front counterweight is too large. Any time the crank is rotated and released this counterweight will pendulum the crank until its heavy spot is at the bottom. A weight equal to that causing the unbalance can be placed 180 degrees, or diametrically opposite this heavy spot. With the balancing weight in position, the crank is now in static balance.

But suppose the weight added to the crankshaft to place it in static balance were added to the rear end of the crankshaft, or the end opposite the original unbalance. In these positions the two weights, although they are directly opposite each other, are widely separated from each other by the crank length. When placed in motion, centrifugal force acts on the statically balanced weights at each end, causing the ends of the crank to be pulled away from their normal axis. Since the heavy points of the crank are opposite each other, and at opposite ends, the ends of the axis are being forced in two directions at once, resulting in a wobble or rocking motion.

By merely moving the balancing weight from the rear of the crankshaft to a position in the same plane as the unbalanced force, and exactly opposite, the crank can be placed in a condition of dynamic balance. With the balancing weight in this position, centrifugal force acting on it and the previously unbalanced weight would be directly opposite in direction and equal in magnitude and the crankshaft would rotate without any tendency to move from normal position.

Balancing an in-line engine is simply a matter of equalizing the weights of all its pistons and connecting rods, and dynamically balancing the crankshaft, flywheel, clutch pressure plate assembly, and vibration dampener. The procedure for balancing 90-degree V8 engines becomes more complicated in that the crank is balanced to specified rotating and reciprocating weights of the piston and connecting rod assemblies. Rotating weight is the weight that revolves, and recriprocating weight is the weight that moves up and down in the cylinders. Pistons, pins and locks, rings and upper ends of the connecting rods are reciprocating weight; the lower ends of the rods and bearing inserts are rotating weight.

Conventional 90-degree or two-plane V8 crankshafts require that weight equivalent to all of the rotating weight and one-half the reciprocating weight normally connected to the crankpins be added to the journals before the shaft can be dynamically balanced. Since it is impractical to attach the pistons, rods, etc., to the two-plane crank being spun in the balancing machine, master weights (bob weights) are instead attached to each throw. These bob weights exert a force on the rotating crank equivalent to that exerted by the piston-rod assembly.

To equalize the respective weights of an engine's rotating and reciprocating parts, it is necessary that all piston and pin assemblies be of equal total weight. Also, the connecting rods must be balanced end for end, so that all the upper ends are of the same weight and their lower ends are the same. This is essential because the lower ends are rotating weight whereas the upper ends are reciprocating weight.

Pistons and their respective pins are weighed individually to find the lightest pair. Weights of the other pistons are then reduced by machining until they are the same as the lightest within prescribed tolerances. As with the pistons, the heavier rods are ground at the bosses or along the sides of the I-beam until the two ends of each rod match the weights of the light rod.

Compression Ratios

Anyone who has been around hot rodding for very long has seen the effects of too-drastic increases in compression ratio. Not only does a mistake cost the hot rodder a lot of the power he has worked so hard to get, but it may cost him an engine. Push the compression ratio too high and suddenly holes begin to appear in pistons—and sometimes even in the side of the cylinder block. Of course, the factor that makes it all so difficult is that there is such a thin line between "just right" and "too high." It is significant that professional engine builders find it worth while to push past the limit, when developing an unfamiliar engine, simply to determine what the limit is. This is costly, and if getting the highest possible compression ratio were not so important, these professionals would not be so willing to sacrifice a set of pistons.

Most people think that the power from an engine is derived from the force of a burning air/fuel mixture pushing against the top of the piston. That is almost correct; unfortunately, it is just far enough from the truth to lead one astray. Power, in a piston-type internal combustion engine, is derived from the expansion of superheated air.

Fuel burning, and the temperature and pressure increases, all occur before the expansion (power) stroke. The greater the difference between the volume of the heated air before and after the expansion stroke, the greater will be the power output. If expanding the heated air to twice its original volume will deliver to the piston X-amount of power, then expanding the air to four times the original volume will deliver power in the order of 2X. Thus, at the same amount of heat input, an engine will always have a higher power output as the expansion ratio (which is to say, compression ratio) increases. All other things being equal, an engine's power output (and under "output" we group both horsepower and torque) will always rise with increases in compression ratio.

Unfortunately, at this point a lot of side effects begin to creep into the picture. It is not possible to keep increasing compression ratio without causing a mechanical disaster. It is interesting that the point of disaster varies from engine to engine, and with the fuel used.

In the normal combustion process, the spark starts a tiny flame which then quickly spreads outward until it reaches the ends of the chamber and the entire mixture charge is ignited. Detonation occurs when parts of the mixture—usually those in pockets at the greatest distance from the spark plug—are heated by rising pressure and heat radiated from that part of the mixture already burning. When this preheating raises the temperature of the mixture (ahead of the normal flame-front) to the ignition point, the entire remainder of the charge fires spontaneously, or detonates, and this sets off a pressure wave of such intensity that when it strikes the walls of the combustion chamber, it actually makes them ring. This ringing is what one hears when detonation occurs.

Pre-ignition is much less a problem. Hot-spots usually do exist in a combustion chamber, and their temperature is usually above the ignition point of the mixture, but the mixture swirls about so violently that it tends to cool the hot-spots without actually igniting. After an engine is shut off, there may be some evidence of pre-ignition, which appears as a tendency to keep running even though there is no spark. This happens because the throttle is closed, and the engine speed drops so low that the mixture turbulence all but disappears. Under these conditions, with the mixture nearly stagnant, and the hot-spots remaining hot, the engine will sometimes run raggedly for a few moments after the ignition system is switched off. In a few rare cases, the running-on may continue. The driver can end this embarrassing business by banging open the throttle, which will admit enough cool mixture to quench the hot-spots and stop the process.

Due to the fact that it is mixture trapped in the corners of a combustion chamber that is so prone to cause detonation, it follows that good combustion chamber design-practice is to eliminate those corners. Ideally, the combustion chamber would be a perfect sphere, with the spark gap located exactly in its center. Practical considerations make this impossible.

Combustion Chambers

Combustion chambers in modern engines can be divided into three basic groups: hemispherical, bathtub, and wedge. The first of these is typified by combustion chambers in the "hemi" Chryslers. The second, the "bathtub" chamber, is not commonly employed in this country, but is often seen in British or European engines. The third, or wedge, chamber has become the standard for most engines made in America.

Except for economic considerations, it is probable that we would only have to deal with the hemispherical combustion chamber. This layout is definitely best, with regard to valve sizes, and that provides good breathing characteristics and, hence, high power output. Unfortunately, the hemispherical chamber is not particularly adaptable to high compression ratios. It is true that the shape is right, but it is also true that at modern bore/stroke ratios, compression ratios with such chambers cannot be made very high without considerably distorting the shape away from a true hemisphere. To get compression ratios much above 10-to-1 it is necessary to provide a very high dome on the piston, and that brings us right back to the heavy piston and an inconveniently large area of the piston exposed to flame. In racing engines, we have learned to live with these problems, but piston cooling and high inertia loads remain to cause occasional failures. Also, as the piston dome is pushed upward, the shape of the combustion chamber begins to lose its pure, hemispherical form, and it acquires pocketed areas around its edges. These pockets can create more problems with detonation than the original shape of the chamber had cured. It has been found, however, that by shaping the piston crown so that squish areas are created up in the hemisphere, somewhat higher compression ratios than were at first considered possible can be used. But, the cutouts needed to allow clearance under the valve heads (to accommodate "overlap") must remain, and in a racing engine with a 12-to-1 compression ratio, the combustion chamber usually comes out looking more like a bent pancake than a hemisphere. As a result, wedge or bathtub chambers will often tolerage a higher compression ratio (on any given fuel) than the classic hemisphere, and for that reason, if no other, the hemispherical form does not have quite so much of an advantage as is commonly supposed.

The wedge and the bathtub chamber were clearly creatures of necessity—at least in the beginning. When the engine designer angles the valves apart, he enormously complicates the valve actuating mechanism, and such complications are always expensive. The only completely satisfactory means of valve actuation in the hemispherical layout is to use an overhead camshaft—and it is better to have a pair of them. The hemispherical-chamber Chryslers use a single camshaft located in the block, with long, heavy rockers reaching over to operate the exhaust valves. That is obviously not the best of all possible methods. Such a system has too much reciprocating weight, and that inevitably imposes limits on operating speed. To avoid the complications outlined, most designers prefer to place all of the valves in line, or nearly so, as this permits the use of short, light rockers and an uncomplicated valve gear. With all of the valves in a row, a wedge or a bathtub combustion chamber is what we get.

With the bathtub configuration, the combustion chamber is compact, and it is probable that this form will allow the highest compression ratios of all. In England, where the type is common, this is extremely important, as their economic situation forces most car owners to use low-octane fuels. But, the manner in which the valves are pocketed up into the bathtub chamber must limit the engine's breathing. For that reason, American rodders do not expect to see the adoption, on a significant scale, of the bathtub chamber in this country.

In all but a few rare cases, boosting the compression ratio will be done either by removing material from the under surface of the cylinder head or by adding material to the piston crown. In most instances, the latter method is best. High-dome pistons may add to the inertia loads on the crank, bearings and connecting rod; removing material, by milling, from the cylinder head will often weaken it to such an extent that it will never again hold a head gasket.

Chronic head gasket failures are usually blamed on a too-high compression ratio, but the cause may be too-enthusiastic milling of the cylinder head. A head gasket will blow, immediately, unless it is gripped firmly between the cylinder head and the block. In a stock head, the designers have provided enough metal along the lower surface of the head to insure that it remains flat even when subjected to fairly high combustion pressures. The head will usually withstand pressures substantially above those it was designed for—if it is otherwise left intact. When the cylinder heads on an overhead valve V8 are milled, the intake port faces are moved down and inward, relative to each other, and the intake manifold will no longer fit. This will require that the intake manifold be remachined to fit the altered setup, or that a new manifold be made. Also, it will be necessary to shorten the valve pushrods by the same amount as was removed from the cylinder heads or it may not be possible to obtain proper valve clearances.

Yet another problem in milling a cylinder head is that of losing the working clearances between piston crown and the various bits in and around the combustion chamber. Most cams, especially those intended for high-speed operation, give a valve timing that has the exhaust valve hanging partway open and the intake valve starting to open as the piston comes up to top center between the exhaust and intake strokes. Consequently, there must be enough clearance between these partly opened valves and the piston crown to prevent contact.

In many engines there is just enough clearance with the stock cylinder head thickness, and when this is reduced by indiscriminate milling, the valves will bind against the piston. Moreover, many hot rodders fall into the double error of simultaneously milling the head and installing a high-lift, long-duration camshaft—which virtually guarantees that there will be trouble. All too often, the error is only discovered when the engine is assembled.

On a few engines, the valve heads overhang the sides of the cylinder bores slightly, and in such engines head milling can bring the valves down low enough so that when fully open, the valve heads will bind against the sides of the bores. The cure is to trim away enough material from the block to restore the working clearance.

The amount of compression increase that may safely be obtained by milling is limited, and as stock pistons are not usually suitable for racing engines, and are not often available in the oversizes that interest the hot rodder, special pistons are often installed. Under no circumstances should more than 90-thousandths be removed from modern heads, and most engines are happier about a 30- to 50-thousandths surgery.

Checking clearances is not very complicated, but a lot of time is required and some people will try to find short cuts. They will be sorry. Simply measuring the various parts will give a good idea of the approximate clearances, but to be safe—at least when domed pistons are involved—assemble the engine block, up to the cylinder head face, and then drop a cylinder head into place with the head bolts in place but not pulled tight. After this, crank the engine over. If all has gone well, nothing will hit the cylinder head. Incidentally, do not forget to drop in an old, compressed cylinder head gasket.

Assuming that all has gone well up to this point, it will then be time to check the valve-head clearances. Follow roughly the same procedure; but this time all of the valve gear will be installed and timed, the cylinder heads bolted down (not too tightly) and the valve-lash set as specified. Crank the engine over very gently. If there is any sign of binding, stop; if all goes well again, remove the heads and prepare for the "claying-in" procedure.

Hot rods are really where you find them. This was once a 1927 Model T Ford body, but Ak Miller rebuilt it with a homemade frame and Oldsmobile V8 engine. It beat many expensive sports cars in the old Mexican Road Race.

This is also a hot rod, created by stripping a Volkswagen sedan frame and cutting away the flooring. It is used for dune buggy competition and general off-road driving.

Still another hot rod, this one a highly modified Jeep. With its V8 engine and high flotation tires, this car will go anywhere.

A pair of homemade Volkswagen dune buggies have at each other in organized sand drag racing.

Top: *Hot rodding isn't all huge engine displacement. Here is a fiberglass-bodied 1923 Model T on homemade frame with VW engine in rear. Bottom: Assembled, the VW rod gives no clue as to power. It weighs less than 900 pounds, will out-run most Corvettes in a drag race.*

More traditional in rodding is the 1932 Ford. This is a five-window coupe that has been restored to look original, although a better chassis and engine have been fitted in.

Another 1932 Ford (Deuce) coupe, this one with a three-window body by Murray Company.

Above: *A very special car for a very special purpose. The dragster has the engine as near rear wheels as possible. Speeds are over 225 mph in quarter-mile acceleration, with elapsed times under 7 seconds.* Below: *Old trucks are finding great favor with hot rodders. This one has a homemade wooden body.*

Some modern hot rods can be used for long road cruises. This one is a chopped 1934 Ford sedan.

Perhaps the most popular of modern hot rods is the touring car, such as this clean 1927 Model T.

A customized Thunderbird. Customs are losing popularity.

The latest idea, and smallest displacement. Volkswagen and Porsche engines and transaxles are now being fitted to super-lightweight fiberglass T bodies to give an outstanding power-to-weight ratio.

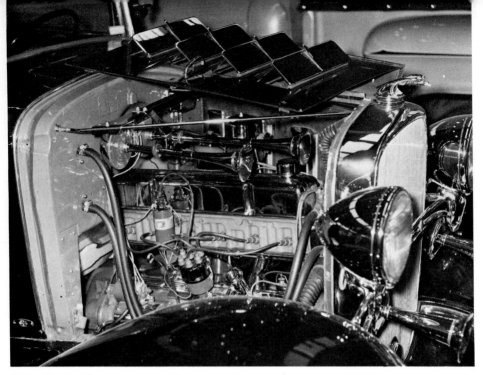

It is wise to select an engine that is compatible with the car. Here a late Chevy six-cylinder engine is installed in a rodded and restored early Chevrolet chassis.

Late Chevrolet V8 engines are particularly suited to early cars, since the engine is narrow, lightweight, powerful, and inexpensive. Single quad carburetor is most popular for street rods.

Different, and more expensive, type of carburetion is shown on Chrysler slant 6 engine. The Webers, imported from Italy, work like carburetors, but meter gas like fuel injectors.

Fuel injectors for all-out racing on a Chevrolet inline six engine. These are set for a very narrow rpm range, are not suited to street.

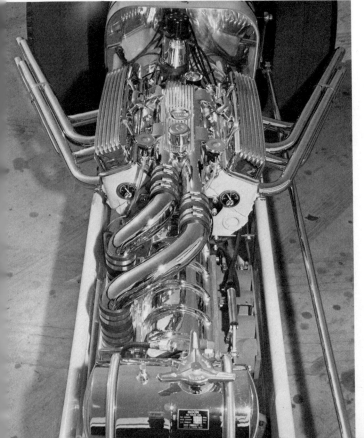

Above: *Another Chevrolet engine, here in an early Model T coupe body, is set up with a GMC 4-71 Rootes type supercharger.*

Larger 6-71 GMC supercharger (from diesel truck engine) is mounted ahead of Chevy engine in a dragster.

Headers are especially important to any engine hop-up. Such an exhaust system can often account for over 50 additional horsepower.

Graphic difference between stock head (top) and modified head for hot rod engine. Modified unit has larger valves, polished combustion chambers, polished intake and exhaust ports.

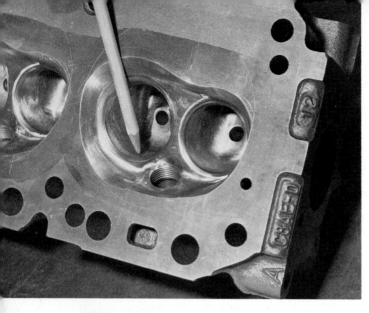

Valve seats in high performance engine are minimum possible width; shape of chamber and ports is supercritical to power production.

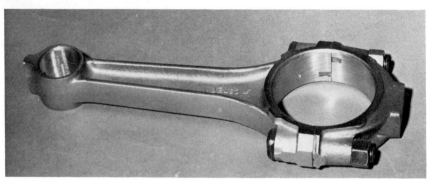

Connecting rods for most factory high performance engines are sufficient for street rodding. Special units are sold for very strong racing engines.

Special pistons are essential to best performance. Shape of the top is determined by compression ratios, valve interference.

Good hot rod mechanics leave nothing to chance, insist on absolute cleanliness, quality tools. Here engine main bearings are being torqued.

The automatic transmission is the favorite for all forms of hot rodding. Not really very complicated, automatics can be hopped-up to take over 1000 horsepower dependably.

Internal hop-up goodies for an automatic are many. Typical are the double-wrap bands for TorqueFlite (right) as compared to a stock one-piece factory band. Special parts often find their way into stock passenger cars after two or three years' testing on drag strips.

The typical hot rod chassis may be a completely homemade unit, such as this rectangular tubing frame. A fiberglass body is used, but without the body the chassis is a showpiece.

Most rod makers use the frame that comes with the body and install special suspension members such as a dropped front axle.

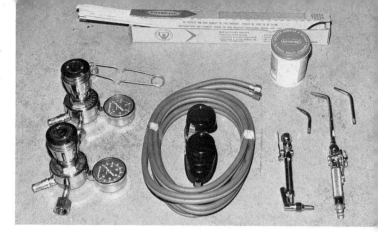

Basic welding outfit includes gauges, hose, tips. Acetylene and oxygen bottles are extra.

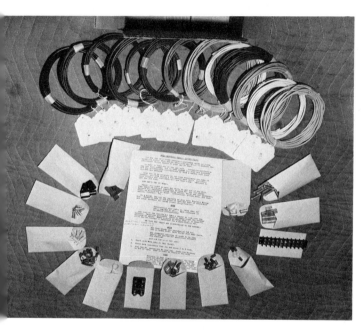

Electrical kits for special jobs are available through speed shops.

Correct method of holding torch tip and welding rod.

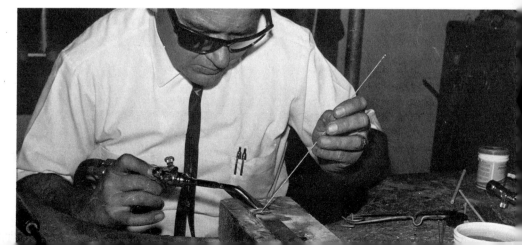

A hot rod often starts life as a pile of junk pieces scrounged from some farmer's field. This is a 1916 Oldsmobile touring.

Gathering of the clans. Hot rodding is gaining in popularity as the sport begins to include highway cruises. There are over 150,000 early (pre-1948) hot rods in the United States, many times the number of late-model rods.

Claying-in is done by placing thin, flat strips of clay over the top of the piston under the squish area, and any place the valve heads might make contact. With the clay in place, and the engine assembled, ease the engine over one complete turn. Then, pull the heads again, and take a look at the clay. There will be a flattened piece of clay under the squish section of the combustion chamber, and a couple of dents in the piece under the valves. With a razor blade, slice across the thin places to see what kind of clearances you have obtained. Comparing the thin spots with the thicknesses of feeler gauges will give a fairly close reading on the clearances involved. Allow at least .040 inch under the squish area, and at least .060 inch under the valve heads.

If an engine's compression ratio is to be raised much above 10-to-1, special preparation of the combustion chambers is necessary. Any sharp corners should be rounded and any rough spots in the chamber polished. Also, the threads in the plug holes should be ground away right down to the nose of the plug. This will insure that none of the threads are exposed—which is very important, as these threads will become red hot when the engine is pulling hard and can be a source of pre-ignition. Doing this will require that you select and retain some particular make of plug; although all plugs of the same basic diameter and reach have threaded portions that are nominally the same, there are small variations between makes that can upset things.

It is sometimes wise to install oversize valves in the cylinder heads. Larger intake valves will make it easier for greater quantities of fresh mixture to flow into the cylinders and larger exhaust valves will make it easier for the exhaust gases to flow out of the cylinders. Combustion chambers are sometimes enlarged around the seats to increase the area between the valve heads and the chamber walls so that greater quantities of fresh mixture or exhaust gases can flow between the walls and the valves.

Oversize valves in some cylinder heads can't do the job they should unless the port passages are enlarged and irregularities removed. Porting is a job that requires a basic knowledge of the mechanical design of the heads and experience with the tools used. It is better, if at all possible, to have this done by an expert.

Porting would, by itself, be a waste of effort if intake and exhaust passages were handicapped by small-capacity intake and exhaust manifolds. Ample flow capacity can be provided on the intake side of the cylinders by installing any one of many makes and types of special intake manifolds. These manifolds accommodate different types and sizes of carburetors, making it possible to provide the correct amount of carburetion for practically any type of engine. Special manifolds are also available to accommodate superchargers. For an all-out competition engine it may be desirable to install a fuel injection setup.

Modifications made to allow free flow of exhaust gases from the cylinder heads depend on how the engine is to be used. For a passenger car, standard exhaust manifolds, if they are correctly designed and have adequate capacity, can sometimes be used satisfactorily. Special headers can be installed on an engine for normal driving and some types of competition. For all-out competition, most rodders prefer an individual exhaust pipe for each cylinder.

Action of the valves has much to do with the quantity of fuel and air mixture an engine will induct on intake strokes and the amount of exhaust gases that will flow from cylinders on exhaust strokes.

The Camshaft

At the bottom of the valve action in any engine is the camshaft. The cam determines when the valves will open and close in relation to piston position in the cylinders. It also has complete control over the speeds at which the valves open and close and the distances they are lifted off the seats. These factors combine to determine the amount of torque the engine can deliver at high crankshaft speed at which the valve action will function correctly.

High performance camshafts usually require valve lifters made of a specific material, and as light in weight as practicable to keep to a minimum the weight of the moving parts in the valve-actuating mechanism. Keeping the total weight of the actuating parts as low as possible helps control valve float.

Special tubular pushrods that are usually lighter in weight than standard pushrods are used to transmit tappet movement to the rocker arms. Some pushrods are fitted with devices that enable their length to be varied for making lash adjustments between the rocker arms and the valve stems. These are for engines that were fitted originally with hydraulic valve lifters and on which nonadjustable rocker arms will be used. Some engines that had hydraulic tappets as standard equipment are fitted with special rocker arms of this type that are lighter in weight than the standard ones they replace.

A camshaft and its related mechanism opens valves but the valves are closed by springs. If the valves are to follow the cams correctly at high crankshaft speeds, the springs must be well designed and considerably stronger than stock. Special springs for this purpose are provided by the companies that grind camshafts. For most installations two springs are used on each valve stem.

There are two current methods in use to check valve timing. The first is to check timing at the valve with the valve train solid (zero clearance). This is the only method for an L-head engine, but it creates accuracy problems with overhead valves and should be used only as a field spot check.

The second and best method is to check timing at the lifter. Three items are essential: a dial indicator, a degree wheel, and a rigid pointer or tab on the engine made to correspond with the degree wheel. A fully degreed crankshaft pulley, vibration damper, or flywheel will prove useful.

First, find exact top dead center of number one piston by using the dial indicator and rotating the crankshaft slowly and smoothly by hand in the normal direction. When the indicator shows TDC, the pointer or "O" mark on the tab must be exactly lined up with the top center mark of the degree wheel.

Next, place the top of the indicator stem in contact with the lifter of the intake valve of number one cylinder. Be sure the lifter is contacting the heel of the cam lobe, not the nose or flank. Because the indicator stem should bear on a smooth, flat surface, the lifter button can be removed from the lifter, or a flat disc inserted in the lifter body for the required flat surface. Do not locate the indicator stem in the radiused pushrod seat; there may be damage to the indicator. Move the indicator stem until it is parallel to the sides of the lifter body in both longitudinal and lateral planes. At this point, the indicator should have a preload of .010 inch or slightly more.

With the indicator in position and slightly preloaded, rotate the crank slowly in normal direction until the indicator shows that the lifter is at maximum lift. Mark on the degree wheel with chalk to coincide with the pointer on the tab. Identify the mark "IN" for intake. Rotate the crank exactly one turn, until the mark is again exactly lined up with the pointer. This rotates the cam exactly one half revolution, and places the lifter in contact with the cam lobe in the center of the clearance sector of the lobe. Carefully rotate the dial of the indicator until its needle is exactly lined up with the zero mark on the dial, without changing the preload of the indicator.

Now rotate the crank slowly in normal direction until the indicator shows that the lifter has been raised an amount exactly equal to the cam's checking clearance or checking height. Read the degree wheel from the pointer to the top center mark on the wheel. This corresponds to the point of intake valve opening be-fore top center, using the prescribed checking clearance. Write this figure down. Next, continue to rotate the crank as the lifter rides up the opening flank of the cam lobe, across the nose and down the closing flank of the lobe, until the indicator needle shows the checking clearance has been reached on the closing side. Count the number of degrees from the pointer to the bottom center mark on the degree wheel. This corresponds to the point of intake valve closing after bottom center. This figure must be added to the first, plus 180 degrees, to obtain the duration with the prescribed clearance.

Repeat the process several times for accuracy, starting at the "IN" line on the degree wheel with indicator needle at zero. Dirt can give false readings. Clean the cam lobes and journals plus lifters and bores, oil them lightly for easy action. With everything right, the indicator should reach the zero point and stay there before and after the mark on the degree wheel is reached.

After this procedure on the intake lifter of number one cylinder, the indicator must be transferred to the exhaust lifter on the same cylinder and the entire operation repeated. In this case, the exhaust opening checking clearance will be reached at a point before bottom center. As with the intake, the number of degrees from the bottom center mark on the degree wheel to the point at which the checking height is reached must be counted and noted. Again, rotate the engine as the lifter rides up the opening flank, across the nose and down the closing flank, until checking height has been reached. This will occur at some point past top center. Count the number of degrees from this point to top center, add this to the first (opening) figure, plus 180 degrees. The sum of these three figures will be equal to the duration of the exhaust at the specified checking height.

Under ideal conditions the timing points found by the above method will coincide with the points on the timing card that comes with the cam. A generally accepted tolerance is plus or minus two degrees, but closer is better. If the timing check shows 10 or 20 crank degrees off, the timing chain and sprockets (or gears) are mislocated by one or more teeth. Correct the condition and recheck. Do not run an engine in this condition. The results will be disastrous.

If valve timing is off, correction is usually best accomplished at the crankshaft. Here is one method, using Woodruff or square key stock. Measure the diameter of the crank nose where the sprocket or gear fits. Multiply this diameter by pi (3.1416) to obtain the circumference, then divide by 360 to obtain the linear distance of each degree. Have a key machined to the proper offset corresponding to the required degree distance. If the cam is advanced, the offset segment of the key must be to the left of the crank keyway centerline with a chain-driven camshaft, to the right with a gear-driven cam when facing the engine. This will retard the camshaft an amount equal to the offset in the key. For a retarded cam, the opposite applies.

Strong, well-timed discharges at the spark plugs are required to fire the highly compressed fuel and air mixture in a reworked engine. Fulfilling these requirements is beyond the scope of many ignition systems. The strain on the system becomes even more pronounced as crankshaft speed goes up. For these reasons, a special ignition system of some sort must be installed on a re-worked engine. This can be either a good dual-point distributor or a magneto.

Modifications made to internal parts are not as numerous as the modifications made to improve the engine torque output, but they are just as important. It doesn't matter how much torque and horsepower an engine is capable of creating if it comes apart the first time the throttle is opened.

Pistons

Among the most critical parts of a reworked engine are the pistons. For many years pistons were a constant source of trouble, especially in blown engines, but modern racing pistons are so much stronger than earlier types that they seldom fail. About the only things that cause them to fail are severe detonation or excessively lean fuel mixtures. Detonation creates extremely high pressures and lean mixtures can cause temperatures of combustion chamber surfaces to rise to the danger point. Pressure and vibration caused by detonation can crack a piston head. High temperatures resulting from lean fuel mixtures can lower the strength of the material in pistons to the point where the heads can't withstand combustion pressures and temperatures. The usual type of failure resulting from lean mixtures is a hole burned through the head.

The first type of piston commonly seen in class racing is the sand-cast piston. This is manufactured in a way ideally suited to low volume production and reasonable cost to the buyer. The critical points in this type are possible blowholes and cracks and faults caused by the temperature imbalances that sometimes occur when pouring low volume molten aluminum. This type of piston is ideal for compression ratio changes (in place of milling the cylinder head) in engines up to the four-inch-bore class. They will withstand abuse well within reason, although they were never intended for large supercharged engines.

The next type, the permanent mold piston, is common in factory stock cars. Because of its more precise molding methods, it reduces machining costs. Many of the aluminum pouring heat control problems, such as core shift and shrinkage, are eliminated in this process. It is rarely used for racing pistons, however, because of the high cost in setting up production for individual orders. Venolia Piston Company in Long Beach, California, is one of the few manufacturers to offer this type of piston, pioneering it in the speed equipment field.

The forged piston will not produce any more power than the other types, but it will absorb more abuse. It can tolerate cracked and flexing cylinder walls, floating valves, and a fair amount of detonation and resulting heat, due to its forged molecular structure.

The higher cost of this type of piston is caused by the amount of machine work necessary for each individual order at different bores and compressions. Because it begins as a rough blank, pounded into a semifinished lump that is not dimensionally anywhere near the finished product, it requires machine work on every surface, except for the internal ribbing. From a reliability standpoint, forged pistons have been known to last in drag racing from one run to six months of 85 and 90 percent nito. It all depends on the engine's operating conditions plus fuel mixture and rpm range.

Today's piston has become a second line of defense in the war against engine failure. Often, because of the driver's difficulty in shutting off the engine past the traps, mixture conditions cannot be properly read from the plugs. If the engine is running too rich no internal damage has been done and the car will indicate this condition by its drop in performance; if the engine is too lean and possibly does not show it on an old fouled plug, the piston will spray molten aluminum on the plug and inside of the exhaust pipes before it fails, giving fair warning of its condition. The engine tuner has no right to ask any more from a properly engineered and manufactured piston. Its failure is a warning that he should question his own particular methods to find the answer to his tuning difficulties.

Connecting Rods

The stock connecting rods in most engines on the market are built to do the job—and little more. While the factories build a considerably safety margin into their products, it's usually exceeded by the average car owner—and greatly exceeded in high-revving, hard-pounding competition engines.

The standard stock connecting rod is an I-beam structure, the strongest possible configuration for the job. However, only average steel is used and tolerances aren't as close as they could be. Thus, under very demanding conditions, stock rods are prone to failure.

The aluminum rod is best suited for short sprints, such as drag racing. Since most of the drag crowd is extremely weight conscious, the aluminum rod is appealing. It is not a great deal lighter than a stock rod (about 530 grams, or one pound, four ounces), but when eight are used, the saving is about four pounds. This four pounds can be used elsewhere in the chasis for safety.

Naturally, the reciprocating weight is cut down, allowing higher engine rpm's if the cam train will allow. Also, not as much weight is acting upon the crankshaft throws.

The aluminum rod is considerably bigger than a stock rod, because aluminum needs more mass to get the job done. But, an aluminum rod is also 2½ times as strong as a stock rod! This is extremely important in a strong engine, especially one that is supercharged.

Dissipating heat much faster than steel rods, aluminum rods draw the heat away from the crank bearing and wrist pin bushing. This is important since, for example, a blown Chevy will have a bearing temperature of around 200 degrees at the end of a quarter-mile blast.

Aluminum rods, however, aren't always just a bolt-in part. Usually, a builder seeking maximum performance via an alloy rod will also use a stroker crank. Since the aluminum rod is bulkier, rod-to-block clearance can easily become a problem. This is normally cured by lightly grinding the block or the rod, or both. Such grinding must be kept to an absolute minimum.

Blocks are usually ground at the bottom edges of the cylinders, sometimes on the pan bolt face. Usually a small amount of metal can be removed from the edges of the aluminum rod, but this must be minimal, especially if the material removed is around the cap bolt. Don't cut away too much of the thread area!

Forged steel rods were developed because aluminum rods aren't particularly suited for extended hard use. Long boat enduros, the Indy 500, etc., take a tremendous toll in rods.

A forged steel rod is heavier by about five ounces than an aluminum one, but it is far stronger. Made of 4340 aircraft steel, it has a tensile strength of 218,000 psi, about three times the strength of a stock rod.

This strength is gained partly through quality steel, and partly through special design. The rod beam is wider than a stock rod and has a very deep I-beam cross section. It's also stronger around the pin boss area. Manganese-bronze pin bushings are recommended because they have twice the strength of stock bushings and good compression and expansion characteristics. Also, they will not gall.

Welded or boxed rods are also extremely popular, but the application is again very important. They are generally used in combination engines, where street work is the primary use, with an occasional fling at the drags. Often they're used in all-out competition engines with acceptable results.

Easy to build for virtually any engine and/or stroke, boxed rods are about twice as strong as stock rods and their cost isn't too great. A boxed rod normally has a piece of 4330 steel welded to the I-beam edges. Since the rod is usually mild steel, the two different steels can't be heat treated the same way. Likely problems with boxed rods are stud breakage and pin loss (break).

Even with the very finest equipment, failures sometimes occur. If the rod breaks either next to the big end or adjacent to the wrist pin boss, suspect detonation. Bearing loss usually results in a rod broken through the small lower part. Excessive side loading normally causes a rod to give way either right in the center or in the bolt area. Piston seizure stretches the rod, breaking it at the weakest point, usually the pin boss or the bottom of the cap.

Actually, spun bearings probably account for 90 percent of all rod failures, with pin failure responsible for five percent and metal fatigue for the remaining five percent. Common causes of bearing loss are poor lubrication, too tight clearance, and heat.

Engine bearings are made to take punishment and to reduce wear. In the long run, they have to be expendable. It's theoretically possible to make bearings that won't wear at all, but these would wear out the journals and crank pins instead. A set of bearings can be replaced at much less cost than a crankshaft or camshaft.

Wearing surfaces (bearings, journals, pins, pistons, cylinders, and valve guides) take more attention in a performance overhaul than the rest of an engine, which often needs only a thorough cleaning, plus alignment.

Three factors are the key to good bearing replacement: cleanliness, care, and accuracy. Cleanliness, because dirt is the number-one enemy of all internal combustion engines; by far the leading cause of wear and failure. Care, because misalignment of bearings can cause serious and expensive damage. Accuracy, because it's so important to efficiency and top performance.

When disassembling the connecting rods, be sure caps and blades are marked and kept together so they won't get mixed up in reassembly. Caps and blades were matched when the engine was built.

Now sort out all parts for reuse, parts that have to be cleaned and inspected for possible rework, and parts that definitely have to be replaced. Parts to be reused must have a thorough cleaning. Best cleaning practices include boiling, descaling, and cleaning out all parts (including the water jackets). This should be followed by thorough rinse with clean solvent. Be sure to get all the dirt out of the webbing and cylinder block recesses. Oil passages must be cleaned out with a brush and hydrostatic pressure, or with filtered demoisturized air. Keep clean parts covered when blowing air. The dirt flies. After parts are reworked, clean everything again to make sure.

Pre-Assembly

Next measure (with a micrometer) minimum and maximum diameters of crankshaft journals of about ¼ inch from each end— enough to clear the fillet radius. Record these dimensions on a chart so that size, out-of-roundness, and taper can be determined. Start with the front journal. In a rebuilt engine with any journal more than .001 inch out of round, rough or rigid, the crankshaft should be reground to a standard undersize.

Take and record measurements of the crankpins. If any are out of round more than .001 inch, the crankpins should be reground. A perfectly round, nontapered crankshaft ground to an accurate finish is best for good bearing performance.

Measure the camshaft the same way, and if there's much wear on the lobes, the cam should be replaced or reconditioned. Examine the camshaft bearings. If they're damaged, replace them. If the crankcase has been boiled to clean it, cam bearings usually need replacement, because in some cases the chemical cleaner will destroy them. If the camshaft bearing bore has a sharp edge, deburr or chamfer it with a scraper or file.

Connecting rods must be checked to be sure the large end bore is round and the rod straight. To check roundness of the big end, assemble number-one cap to number-one rod, without the bearing. Do this with each rod in the set, making sure each cap goes on its original rod the right way. Tighten the nuts lightly, tap the cap with a plastic mallet and then tighten the nuts to your recommended torque specifications. Check each bore with an out-of-roundness indicator, or with an inside micrometer. If any rod bore is out of round more than .001 inch, the rod should be replaced.

Measure each rod for parallelism. A suitable fixture makes this easier, but with care it can be done on a surface plate. Correct or replace rods that are twisted or bent. Examine the backs of the rod bearing that you've removed for signs indicating any rod bored to oversize or otherwise unfit for reuse.

Check the main bearings you remove. If they are warped, scored, damaged, or show signs of overheating, suspect that one (or more) of the crankcase saddles is warped or out of round.

The best way to check saddle bore alignment is to place a properly ground arbor, about .001 inch less in diameter than the smallest saddle bore specification, and as long as the crankcase, into the saddles. Install and tighten the caps to specification, making sure they're in correct relation to the front of the engine. Turn the arbor with a 10-inch handle. If you can't turn the arbor, the saddle bores may be out of round or the crankcase warped.

If you don't have an arbor, place a straightedge in three alternate (but parallel) positions in the saddles. Use a feeler gauge whose thickness is equal to the mean specified oil clearance. If you can get the feeler anywhere under the straightedge, the bores may be out of round or the crankcase warped. The preferred method of bringing saddles into alignment is to rebore the crankcase. You can also install semiundersized bearings, but this is tricky. Better let a reputable mechanic handle this job in either case.

Check your camshaft housing bore sizes. If they're not within specifications, get undersized cam bearings and bore them in place. Using a shoulder arbor of proper size and a cam bearing assembly tool, line up the oil hole and press each bearing in place. Using a small pin or piece of wire, make sure all oil holes in the camshaft bearings align exactly with those in the crankcase. After checking to make sure all parts are perfectly clean, assemble camshaft.

If the crankshaft has been reground, check both journal and crankpin sizes, recording the maximum size of each. Accuracy is important. At the same time check each fillet radius gauge to be sure it's right. A radius gauge is a handy tool for this.

Buy main bearings of the proper size according to your recorded measurements. Then check new bearings against old to be sure holes, grooves, locking lips, and other features are the same.

Remove bearing caps. Wipe off each case bore and the back of each bearing with a clean cloth. Lay the upper half of each main bearing half into the crankcase and snap it into its seat, making sure each locking lip nests into the recess provided. Put two or three drops of clean oil on the surface of each bearing; smear in with a clean finger. Using a small drift pin, check bearing oil holes for register with holes in the case.

Wipe the crankshaft journals again, and position the shaft on the bearings. Lower it into position gently (keeping it parallel with the bores). Thrust surfaces are easily damaged.

Now wipe each main bearing cap bore, then the lower bearing. Snap bearings into place, check the lip in the recess. Smear the insides of the bearing with oil. Install the caps, each in its original position and facing in the proper direction. After tightening the screws finger tight, tap each cap with a plastic mallet. This helps it find its natural position.

Push the crankshaft forward until the rear faces of the thrust flanges are aligned properly. Tighten the main bearing cap screws or stud nuts alternately until snug. Finally tighten each to proper torque specification. Using a suitable tool, rotate the crankshaft by hand. It should turn with reasonable freedom.

Next check crankshaft end play. Proper end play is built in unless a semiundersized thrust bearing was used. But to be sure it's within specified limits, check it with the feeler gauge.

As a final inspection of the main bearing installation, recheck cap markings and the torque on the cap nuts, then be sure the crankshaft doesn't bind. If everything checks out, install cotter pins or lock nuts.

Get a complete set of connecting rod bearings of the proper size to fit the pins. In some cases it may be wise to replace the wrist pin bushings. These should be examined for wear and checked with the piston pins. Before installing the con rod bearings, check the new bearings to make sure that oil holes, grooves, and locking lips are identical.

After wiping out the con rod cap bores and the backs of the lower bearing halves, snap them in place, making sure that locking lips nest properly into their recesses. Follow the same routine with the blade half bores and the upper bearing halves.

Installation of the rod assembly is a matter of making sure each is in the right cylinder. With the bearing in place, seal the rod on its crankpin. A word of caution: Don't let the rod studs touch or bump the crankpin. They can damage it. Now install the rod caps and turn the nuts down finger tight. Tap each cap with a mallet to seat it in natural position, then tighten the nuts to the recommended torque specifications. Rotate the crankshaft by hand to check for possible binding. If you can't turn it, find out what's binding and fix it.

One more precaution. Recheck the reference markings to be sure all parts are in correct position. Recheck the tightness of cap screws and nuts. Install lock nuts (if provided).

A quality bearing must have three important characteristics: fatigue strength, conformability, and embeddability.

Fatigue strength measures ability to stand up under bearing

loads. Modern practice in engine design has gone to shorter engines with less room for bearings—higher speeds and higher compression ratios, all of which demand higher fatigue strength. None of the babbitt bearings withstand much more than 1800 psi, while aluminum alloys stand up to 6000 psi.

Conformability denotes ability of bearings to act as a cushion during break-in . . . to move and compensate for any minute high spots on the shaft during run-in. Stronger metals are deficient in conformability, so it is supplied by adding a lead-tin overplate.

Embeddability is a quality that would be unnecessary if engines could be kept absolutely clean. It is a measure of ability to absorb a normal amount of abrasive dirt caused by engine wear, which sinks below the surface of the bearing metal and causes no more trouble.

In tests determining the various ratings of bearing alloys, it was found that tin-base babbitts scored low in fatigue strength, medium to high in conformability, and medium to high in embeddability. Copper-lead was very high in fatigue strength, medium in conformability and low in embeddability. The steel-backed aluminum alloy scored very high in fatigue strength, high in conformability and low in embeddability.

Obviously no single bearing material can have a maximum of all desirable qualities, because some qualities are in mutual opposition. For example, stronger metals which have more fatigue strength will be deficient in embeddability or conformability.

With improved filtration of air and oil, embeddability becomes somewhat less important. However, the wear of pistons, cylinders, crankpins, and journals generates some dirt, so as much embeddability as possible is built into bearings.

Lubrication

You can assemble a racing engine from a pile of junk and get by with the deception. But never ever think you can rely on an oiling system anything less than perfect.

All too often, the hot rodder places maximum emphasis upon this or that segment of the modified engine, forgetting entirely that the *real* heart of the engine is lubrication. Without lubrication, an engine would last but seconds.

In a typical oiling system, oil from a sump (the pan) is picked up by the pump, pressurized, and sent through various cylinder block passages to the crankshaft/camshaft bearings and (in the case of an overhead valve engine) the rocker arm shafts. Following other passages, the oil is pulled by gravity back down over the pushrods, lifters, cam lobes, and timing gears/chains to the sump. Half the journey, then, is done under pressure.

The average person seldom thinks of oil as a cooling agent for an engine, yet it is this precise additional duty of oil that helps an engine keep running hour after fatiguing hour. The radiator water carries off part of the internally generated heat, but the oil returning to the sump (from the time it leaves the pump) is responsible for a share of the chore. Although this percentage of cooling is one of those extremely difficult things to determine, it is generally estimated that the oil is responsible for approximately 15 percent of the cooling in an average engine. In a high performance drag engine, where water cooling is drastically limited, this percentage of oil cooling is considerably higher and infinitely more important.

The oiling cycle begins in the sump, as indicated, and it is here that many modified engines meet their doom. All too often, an engine builder approaches the heart of this oiling system—the pump—with inadequate knowledge of what is involved.

Oil pumps generally can be categorized in two different types:

the gear pump (Chevy, Olds, etc.) and the Hobourn Eaton rotor pump (Chrysler, etc.). The gear pump consists of two straight-cut gears, one free-moving as an idler, the other driven at half engine speed off the camshaft. The meshing gears pump the oil much as a GMC supercharger pumps air, trapping the oil between the gear cavities and the pump wall until the outlet port is reached. The bigger these gears, in any respect, the more oil the pump can move. The early Ford flathead is an example of this, as the stock pump was just barely adequate. In this case replacement with a truck pump, which had longer gears, was a necessary procedure of most hop-ups.

With a gear pump, it is vital that the gears fit closely within the pump body (just as with an all-out supercharger). Any end-float of either gear above factory specifications (which can be as low as .001 inch) may result in a loss of oil pressure, especially at low speeds.

The rotor pump is much more efficient and wears less than the gear pump, and may be driven off the crankshaft or cam. The moving parts consist of an externally lobed inner rotor mounted on the driveshaft, and an internally lobed outer rotor. The inner rotor has one lobe less than the outer rotor, necessitated by their operating relationship. The outer rotor revolves in the large circular bore of the oil pump body, this bore being offset from the inner lobe driveshaft. As the inner rotor turns, it contacts the outer motor lobes near the close side of the pump bore. As rotation continues, the two rotors begin to separate. A large inlet port in the pump housing allows oil to enter this widening area, which is at its greatest 180 degrees from the nearest contact point. Then as the rotors begin to close again, the oil exits under pressure through another hole in the pump body.

Whatever kind of pump is used, all moving parts must fit precisely and move freely. The gears or rotors must be perfectly free of burrs and nicks, which may cause binding. There must be no appreciable driveshaft-to-pump body wear that would allow the gears or rotors to misalign or wobble. This particular problem is a rather common type of wear in a gear pump, and shows up as an uneven wear pattern on the gears and the end plate. To facilitate uninterrupted oil flow, the gears and rotors may be polished if minute detailing is desired; in any case, nicks should be smoothed as the flow of oil is impaired by irregularities. In no event should a pump that has an obvious bind be installed in an engine, racing or stock.

The average oil pump is more than adequate for even the most stringent competition conditions, capable of pumping far more pressure pounds than the engine will ever use. However, it is flow rather than pressure that a high performance engine demands. That is, how much volume, or quantity, of oil can be passed through the pressure portion of the system.

Pressure ensures lubrication of hard-to-reach places, volume reduces operating temperatures of these lubricated areas. The higher the rate of flow through bearings, the lower the running temperature. With true lubrication (as distinct from boundary lubrication), the bearing and the journal are held apart by a film of oil in continual shear. This shearing action between the adjacent layers of oil film creates the viscous drag that ultimately produces heat. Just as with the flow of water through engine openings, the flow of oil through this bearing area helps dissipate heat.

Even with such attention to proper lubrication, the average modern engine will have a friction loss equal to about 55 bhp at just over 4000 rpm. About half of this figure is due to ring and piston drag, the remainder is split between rod/main bearings, valve gear, water pump, etc. To reduce this friction, increase flow of oil, and increase the load-carrying capacity, competition engines include increased running clearances. Bearing clearances are usually from the stock .001-.0015 inch to .003-.005, while cylinder wall clearance is increased a minimum of .002 (this figure is dependent upon the particular builder's policy, but is a vital part of any performance engine). Of course, increasing the bearing clearances means they take a severe pounding relative to stock bearings, but this is of little consequence to a serious dragster owner. Even so, many fuel-burning Chrysler hemi's are noted for retaining the same bearings for nearly a hundred all-out runs.

The typical engine uses a sump in the oil pan as the main oil storage chamber, the crankshaft and connecting rods take up the rest of the pan area. In a dry sump system, used quite successfully by road racing cars, the pan is little more than a cover for the lower part of the engine. After the oil returns to the pan area of a dry sump design, a pump forces it outside the block to a cooler, filter, and storage tank before returning it to the engine. Location of these various parts will change with particular dry sump systems, but the main idea is to do away with the large sump in the pan, so that the engine can sit much closer to the ground, sometimes as much as five inches closer, and for closer control over oil temperature and pressure variation.

For the normal engine the pan sump is many things: a settling basin where large foreign matter can drop to the bottom and out of circulation; a ready reservoir of oil for the pump; and most important of all, a place where the thoroughly agitated and aerated oil can resume its natural state before being reused. This last problem can become a source of major headaches in a high rpm engine where the revolving crankshaft is really churning the oil.

The oiling cycle actually starts at the pump, consequently it is vital that when oil reaches the gears or rotors, it be as stable as possible. Remember, the pump is a pressure device, not a suction pump, so the ideal is to keep the pump saturated with nonfoamed, calm oil at all times. To reach such a goal, attention must be paid to the sump, pan baffles and the pump pickup tube.

If the car is subject to violent forces, which all racing vehicles are, additional baffles will be required in a stock pan to keep the oil around the pump pickup. However, caution must be observed as to the design and number of these baffles. Sometimes a maze of baffles so restricts the oil that the rotating crankshaft cannot adequately splash oil on the cylinder walls, pistons, and rods. This is one place where a three-dollar phone call can save a three-thousand-dollar engine. Any well-known engine builder will give pointers as to baffle design for a particular engine.

In dragsters, where the engines are often placed extremely low to the ground (a design trend now being reversed by commercial chassis builders, primarily because of the oiling problem), the oil pans have been so pancaked that the sump has all but disappeared. The problems with such a situation are obvious; the crankshaft continually flails the oil to a froth and it has no place to calm down before being hurled back into action. A sump around the pump pickup is always desirable.

Sadly, it is the pump pickup that causes the majority of trouble. A typical pump has a tube running from the pump body to an inverted pan, the pan opening covered by a screen to keep the larger nuts and bolts from entering the pump. This inverted pan is a quieting chamber where the thrashed oil can calm down. Theoretically, oil will lose most of its foaminess before entering the chamber. Unfortunately, even as calm oil flows up the small-diameter tube to the pump, the resulting vortex and "stretching" actions stirs it up again and foam is again possible.

To make matters worse, some rodders take off the stock quieting chamber and cover the exposed end of the pickup tube with a piece of screen wire. This merely agitates an already undesirable situation in really strong engines. This problem of oil foam control is a major one, and should never be overlooked.

Current practice among racing engine builders to solve the pump pickup problem is merely to add one of the Milodon pump pickups, items designed to supply the pump mechanism with quiet oil at all times. These covers are cast from 356-T6 heat-treated aluminum. They are hard anodized a minimum of .002 inch, and the friction face (where the gears or rotors may touch) is baked with a dri-lube process.

The covers replace the end plate of the stock pump, with a screen-covered quieting chamber immediately adjacent to the pump. In some cars, such as the Ford and late Chrysler, basic engine design requires the initial screened chamber to be remote from the pump. If so, the transfer galley or tube is quite large and designed to reduce vortex and "stretching" (stretching is caused by the frictional properties of oil flowed through a pipe) to a minimum. In this type of design, a secondary quieting chamber is also located on the pump.

From the pump, the oil is pressurized in the cylinder block passages. An average passenger car engine will run about 40 pounds oil pressure, and average dragster engine will run from 60 to 90 pounds at mid-rpm. An average of 75 to 80 pounds is considered good. Normally, doing nothing more than adding one of the special pump covers to a good pump increases oil pressure 15 pounds!

Pressure can be further increased by adding washers beneath the pressure relief spring, or by using factory heavy duty springs. Don't add more than three number 8 washers or coil bind may result. Washers should be used, as spacers without center holes will restrict the oil that bleeds around the relief valve from escaping.

More important than increased pressure, however, is a 35 percent increase in oil flow by using a special pump cover. In a high performance engine, this is superb insurance. It is interesting to note that the large percentage of oil passing through the pump is not sent through the engine at all. Most of it is channeled through the pump bypass, a necessary procedure to make sure pressure to all points of the engine is constant and does not pulsate. A dragster engine will only turn over about 600 times during a quarter-mile run. Of the resulting 300 revolutions of the oil pump, perhaps 280 revolutions pass oil through the bypass. In an actual test, it was found that such an engine passed little more than a quart of oil through the engine. The remaining oil was bypassed. With a restricted system, then, this small total of used oil would be even less.

Getting the oil under way is only part of the chore. Using it effectively at the destination is the other part. And this is where the men are separated from the boys. It's also one of the places where a true speed secret exists as far as successful engine builders are concerned.

Grooved bearings (or crank mains) tend to allow oil to escape from the high load areas of the bearing. This disadvantage, however, is more than offset by the fact that these grooves allow oil to be passed to the crankshaft passages during 360 degrees of crank rotation. This means that the oil galleys to the connecting rods are always pressurized. Enter one of the "secrets." The edges of these grooves, whether in the bearing or crankshaft, may be very carefully rounded. This will allow oil to escape outward onto the main bearing surfaces more readily, the increased controlled flow meaning lower bearing temperatures. Maximum temperatures should not exceed 275 degrees, so this increased oil flow will help keep main bearing temperatures within reason in competition engines.

Another little known oiling trick is to completely chamfer the oil holes in the crankshaft. This procedure is partially completed by crankshaft regrinders, but all too often the hot rodder will install a new crank with these oil hole outlets left with sharp edges. If they are sharp, they act as an effective seal to oil flowing outward onto the bearings. If these oil hole outlets are very carefully radiused, with the opening tuliped outward, greater oil flow is facilitated. This helps oil to flow to all parts of the bearing surface.

Although seldom expressed in terms of oil flow, it is generally agreed that a racing engine must have increased rod side clearance to prevent rod seizure. Oil flowing from the crank to the bearings must escape somewhere, which is out the sides of the bearing. If the normal rise in temperature causes the rods to expand and drastically reduce this escape opening, flow is naturally impaired. Overheating follows, and eventual failure. Not because the materials involved just became too big to fit their working area, but because the lubrication path was clogged.

The mist created by the churning crankshaft assembly oils the cylinder walls, pistons, and rods. At the same time, it is continually cooling these areas. Oiling of the top of the engine must be adequate, but is not nearly so critical as the lower end bearings.

On the subject of the oil itself, engine builders recommend that a special racing oil not be tampered with by adding a defoaming agent. In the first place, the oil engineers created the special formula for a specific reason, and any modification may ruin the formula. As to the brand of oil to use, that's strictly a matter of personal preference. The weight to use will depend upon the car, a gas dragster taking 40–50 weight, while fuel cars and oval trackers will need 60 weight.

Space does not permit a blow-by-blow description of high performance engine assembly or construction of specific parts. That information is usually available from speed shops and monthly hot rod magazines. We have covered the important areas often overlooked, with special emphasis on the subjects essential to long high performance engine life.

5

Clutches, Transmissions, and Rear Ends

While the initial interest of the beginning hot rod enthusiast is directed almost entirely to the high performance engine, it doesn't take long to learn that getting power to the ground is paramount in winning trophies. It is common to hear of an engine developing a fantastic amount of flywheel horsepower, but serious enthusiasts tend to discount this. Especially with stock bodied street machines. They are more interested in rear wheel horsepower—just exactly how much of that great power curve is being sent to the asphalt.

It is not at all uncommon for a 450-horsepower Detroit super car to deliver less than 200 horsepower at the rear wheels, as measured on a chasis dynamometer. This figure will vary in direct proportion to how well the engine is tuned, but for the most part the power losses are between the flywheel and rear tires. They occur somewhere within the transmission, rear-end third member, and axles. Important to the competition-minded enthusiast, then, is keeping the power transfer system in perfect working order. In this way, horsepower loss will be kept to a bare minimum.

A gasoline engine must run freely and attain sufficient rpm to supply the torque needed to overcome all resistance (vehicle weight and drivetrain) before it can be used to drive the vehicle. The engine must be able to continue to run when the car is stopped, and because the internal combustion engine develops its most useful power over a comparatively short rpm range, a transmission with three or four different gear ratios is necessary to maintain this effective rpm range. A clutch accomplishes all these things.

The clutch must be able to transmit maximum engine torque without any loss of power due to slippage. As the clutch takes hold, torque must be transmitted to the drive train in a gradual and uniform manner or the resulting "shock" on the drivetrain components can break the transmission gears, universal joints and/or rear axles. When the clutch is released, it is imperative that it positively disengage so there is no continued rotation of the transmission input shaft.

A conventional automotive clutch has three main components: the flywheel, which forms one of the friction surfaces and is referred to as a "driving" member; the disc, which is referred to as the "driven" member and is splined to the input shaft; and the pressure plate, which can also be called a driving member because it is bolted to the flywheel. A throwout bearing operates the clutch but is not a part of the clutch assembly.

The action of these three components is quite simple. The flywheel is bolted to the engine crankshaft and revolves with it. The pressure plate is attached to a cover or housing which is bolted to the flywheel. Inside the clutch cover there are a series of small springs or a circular diaphragm spring which presses the pressure plate forward. The disc is squeezed between the flywheel and pressure plate, splined to the input shaft, and only revolves when the clutch is engaged. In addition, the splined input shaft is supported on the transmission end by a ball bearing and on the crankshaft end by either an Oilite bronze bushing or ball bearing.

The design of the driven member or disc is a little more complicated than it appears. It is actually made of many parts but the two main components are the inner splined hub and the outer ring to which the friction material is either riveted or bonded in some manner.

While the splined inner hub is riveted to the outer ring and can't pull away, it can rotate about ¼ inch. An integral part of the hub is a ring of five or six stiff coil springs (some have inner springs as well) that absorb the shock of engagement. They also absorb engine vibrations (uneven pulsation regardless of flywheel weight) and very slight misalignment. The hub rivets act as "stops" for the rotational movement; however, coil bind (full compression of the springs) will result before the outer disc hits the stops. If this were to happen on a hard start, the disc would be ruined.

The outer ring is a series of stamped steel wafers bent slightly to which the friction lining is riveted. These wafers also provide a cushioning effect when the clutch is engaged and will be squeezed flat at full engagement. The crimping helps prevent the disc from sticking to either flywheel or pressure plate when the clutch is disengaged.

When the disc is squeezed between the pressure plate and flywheel (engaged position), torque is transmitted to the rear wheels. To disengage the pressure plate (against the spring pressure), there are several release levers that pivot on the clutch cover and pull the pressure plate back. The release levers are pushed in by a throwout bearing that rides on a collar which extends about halfway up the transmission input shaft. The bearing is moved by a clutch release fork. The clutch fork, or release fork, pivots on a simple ball/socket arrangement at the edge of the bellhousing. The bellhousing is referred to as the cover housing. It runs from the rear of the engine block to the front of the transmission case and houses the flywheel and clutch mechanism. Since the clutch release fork is mounted to the bellhousing but pivots front to back, and the pressure plate with its release levers is rotated when the engine is running, the throwout bearing must accommodate both of these movements at the same time. The throwout bearing looks like an ordinary ball bearing except that one side (the side that contacts the clutch levers) has has a hardened steel surface which is backed by a ball race. It is this ball race which turns when it comes in contact with the rotating levers. The inner part of the bearing housing is pressed onto a collar which is in contact with the release fork.

Actual control of the release fork may be accomplished by one of two means: a fully mechanical linkage of levers and rods which extends to the clutch pedal in the car, or by a hydraulic clutch. A hydraulically operated clutch has a master cylinder (similar to the brake master cylinder) which is connected by linkage to the clutch pedal. When the clutch pedal is depressed or released, the clutch master cylinder operates a "slave cylinder" connected to the clutch release fork with a short adjustable rod. When pressure is applied to the slave cylinder, it in turn operates the release fork.

There are three basic clutch patterns or designs in use on American automobiles: Borg & Beck, Long, and diaphragm.

The Borg & Beck pressure plate design has been in use for about twenty years and is used mainly in Chrysler Corporation cars and some GM models. Conventionally, this is a 12-spring pressure plate assembly and is currently available in 10½- and 11-inch sizes (as measured across the friction face). It can be identified by its three "wide" release levers which do not have an end adjusting nut.

The Borg & Beck plate gets its total pressure from "spring pressure"—about 2800 to 3300 pounds face pressure at lockup. The levers give some centrifugal assist, not much, but some—spring pressure is what this unit is based on. This makes the Borg & Beck tiring on your left leg because of the stiff spring pressure against the clutch pedal, but it affords a "clean release" at high rpm for smooth shifts.

To gain some additional centrifugal action, Borg & Beck installed needle bearing rollers on some plates which forced out against the pressure plate during rotation. They are housed in special machined grooves on the back side of the pressure plate, and centrifugal action wedges them between the pressure plate and the cover. In principle this works well, but these roller weights prevent shifting at high rpm because there is nothing to return the free-floating weights to a neutral position. While this is a distinct disadvantage in shifting, another drawback or weak point is the three eyebolts which must hold the high spring pressure. The spring pressure contained in the pressure plate housing isn't all exerted against the flywheel—an equal amount is also pushing back out against the cover. Thus, the need for a strong cover and bolts, especially if you're going to use this on the Long-type unit on a hot street machine or for all-out drag racing.

The long type of pressure plate has been around for over thirty-five years and is an offshoot of the early Ford style made popular by the V-8.

The Long is available in 10- and 11-inch sizes and is a nine-spring unit. This one gets its effective pressure from springs and a centrifugal assist. The release levers protrude through the cover plate. It is this weight at the end of the lever which exerts centrifugal force against the pressure plate for positive lockup. Other advantages are that this type is impossible to overcenter—you just can't push the levers far enough forward. For around-town driving, spring pressure on the clutch pedal is much easier than that of the

Borg & Beck plate. However, at high rpm the weighted levers exert a high centrifugal loading and shifting is difficult. At 7000 rpm the weight exerts some 4500 to 5500 or more pounds of spring pressure.

The Rockford diaphragm type has been around for about fifteen years or more. It is used mainly on GM cars and comes on 10½- and 11-inch sizes.

There are two pressures associated with a diaphragm clutch in stock form—holding pressure (about 1800 pounds, pedal IN), and peak pressure (about 2500 pounds, pedal OUT). These of course can be changed by varying the length, width, and thickness of the diaphragm plate.

The diaphragm type is popular for stock and street machines because of the easy pedal pressure and smooth shifting qualities. In racing use, it has a quick lockup action that can break axles and U-joints—so be careful with this one.

This type of pressure plate is not recommended for use in cars where the engine will be turned at over 7000 rpm because centrifugal force tends to hold the levers in after a power-on shift. When the levers are pressed in, they are very near "center" position so centrifugal force holds them in this position until rpm's fall off enough to allow them to come back out. If this happens you can over-rev your engine very quickly. The diaphragm plate only moves about .075 to .100-inch at the edge, so wear on the disc is critical. Keep checking it often and your assembly will last a long time.

While the three styles of pressure plates—Borg & Beck, Long, and diaphragm—do not outwardly resemble each other, the Borg & Beck and diaphragm type have exactly the same mounting bolt pattern (providing they are of the same diameter). The Long type has a narrower pattern which is called "three sets of two's." If you want to change pressure plates it's possible to redrill your flywheel to accommodate both mounting bolt patterns. Most speed equipment manufacturers sell their special flywheels with this dual pattern already drilled and tapped.

Fundamentally, there are four types of discs available: damped (with springs around center hub), undamped (without springs, solid center section), and riveted or bonded linings. Add to this a variety of friction materials available and you can just about design your own disc.

The reason for the damped disc is because an internal combustion engine is a pulse-making machine regardless of flywheel and it needs a means of smoothing the pulse out before it gets to the drivetrain. At the start of engagement, the springs take up this pulsing and smooth out the shock. At lockup, the complete drivetrain—transmission, drive shaft, rear end, and wheels—all become in effect a flywheel which further smooths things out. The springs in the disc are very important also—too little spring pressure will not dampen the shock sufficiently and tear out the hub. Additionally, too stiff a spring will make things too rigid and also tear out the hub. Spring pressure has to be just right according to the usage for which it was designed.

The solid or rigid disc, as it is sometimes called, is not recommended for street use. There is nothing to absorb the shock and it's difficult to slip for a smooth start. In operation it seems as if no matter how you try working the clutch pedal, the solid disc is either engaged or it isn't. It's definitely best for the drags.

As for rivets or a bonded lining, it is up to intended usage as to which is best. A riveted lining is used with the wafer design outer ring. The Marcel or pitch angle of the wafers gives the disc compressability for further smooth engagement. However, at 7500 to 8000 rpm, a riveted disc becomes marginal and is quite apt to start chunking off pieces of material from between the rivet heads.

While the bonded disc has no compressability, it is superior to a riveted disc in the high rpm range. With increased contact area it is very doubtful that a bonded disc will ever chunk off its lining.

In conjunction with describing the various types of clutch components, it may be worth while to mention here that while throwout bearings are similar, they are not interchangeable; that is, from a lever-type pressure plate to a diaphragm-type, and vice versa. Size is all-important and the face of the throwout bearing must contact the release levers at exactly the right spot. Obviously, if they don't meet just right things will be chewed up since the release levers are rotating and the throwout bearings won't be at contact point.

In the early days the theory was to beef-up stock clutch components—heavy springs in the pressure plate, as heavy as you could find, and lighten the flywheel as much as possible to bring up rpm quickly. But with the big cubic inches available today this has all changed—it's no problem for big cubes to bring up rpm quickly with a heavy flywheel, and it's now necessary to have the weight to maintain momentum when a shift is made.

Today, you can't get away with just beefing-up stock parts. Engines are too powerful and high rpm makes centrifugal force a potential time bomb. Special metals, sophisticated machinery, and careful assembly are now all part of the scene. Crower, BID, Hays, Schiefer, and Weber are manufacturers who build complete matched and engineered assemblies. These special assemblies are the only parts that should be considered for use on a high performance car—competitiveness and safety depends on it. Equipment manufacturers need to know what type car you have, the weight, tire make and size, engine horsepower and rpm, gear ratio, etc., to recommend the best type of pressure plate, disc, and flywheel to get the job done for you. It is as important as matching any other piece of speed equipment to your engine for total performance.

Specialty manufacturers have adapted the Borg & Beck-type pressure plate to racing by increasing the thickness of the cover.

This enables the cover to withstand high rpm and the additional heavy spring pressure required to transmit torque.

Since this pressure plate doesn't have a centrifugal assist, shifting is smooth at high rpm. The only disadvantage is that you wouldn't want to use it for street driving due to the high spring pressures. Your left leg would soon be numb if you had to drive through traffic.

BID, Hays, Schiefer, and Weber offer this type of unit. BID and Weber both have forged steel facings, while Hays offers it in forged steel or with a rivet-on heat-shield facing of sintered bronze. Schiefer uses forged aluminum with a special patented metal-sprayed surface of copper and steel which is finished by Blanchard grinding.

While the Borg & Beck type units aren't totally suited for racing, they do have a place and are particularly adaptable to the smaller bellhousings. The Borg & Beck has smaller overall dimensions than the Long, so it's particularly suited where space limitations are a problem.

The diaphragm-type pressure plate has received similar beefing-up with a thicker cover plate and heavier diaphragm spring. The diaphragm plate utilizes the Belleville washer principle. Besides giving equal pressure around the entire 360 degrees, it permits light clutch-pedal holding pressure. It works this way: pressure applied to the diaphragm fingers increases as they are depressed until an "over center" position is reached. After this point is passed, very little foot pressure is required to hold the pedal down. This feature alone makes the diaphragm popular for street use. The only disadvantage is that at very high rpm, centrifugal force tends to hold the fingers in. Schiefer uses helper springs to help eliminate this undesirable problem.

The Long is probably the most widely used pressure plate, as it can be used with a single disc or dual or triple disc assembly.

Spring pressure is not objectionable for street use and where power shifts must be made, the plate is provided with a standard type of lever without the big barrel weight at the end. By increasing or decreasing the weight at the end of the levers you can control the amount of centrifugal assist. When ordering the Long unit be sure to specify the kind of intended use, and the manufacturer will supply you with the proper levers on your pressure plate. This is particularly important on competition cars where no shift is made and lockup is required about three quarters of the way down the strip. By varying the amount of centrifugal assist (lockup) you can control the initial slip coming off the starting line. This slipping clutch idea has been in drag racing for several years now and it has caused considerable change in dragster thinking. The problem is simple: If the tires are getting maximum traction, and the engine is putting out maximum torque and horsepower, something, somewhere, has to give. In this case it's the clutch.

The idea is to never let the tires break traction, which means keeping wheelspin completely out of the picture, which in turn means that under current dragster construction practices, the clutch must be slipped. Clutch slippage is the only way to get a direct-drive machine off the starting line without bogging the engine. With a 3.23 rear end ratio and the engine idling up around 1000 rpm, the car would be traveling around 40 mph with the clutch engaged. To get out of the hole at over 4000 rpm, therefore, the clutch is allowed to slip and then lockup at a point that won't break tire traction. Setting up a clutch to slip to the precise point and then to lockup is no amateur process; it must be left to professionals.

In the flywheel department, Hays offers steel and aluminum billet wheels with the aluminum wheel faced with a sintered bronze facing. This facing is first bonded to a thin steel disc which acts as a heat shield to protect the flywheel and to dissipate heat evenly at a controlled rate. The special steel rivets that hold the heat shield to the flywheel also aid in dissipating heat.

Schiefer produces flywheels in billet steel and in forged aluminum with the metal-sprayed copper and steel facing. This surface is then Blanchard-ground and shot-peened for stress relieving.

Weber has flywheels in forged aluminum, cast and billet steel. The aluminum wheel uses a steel facing riveted in place, then Blanchard-ground.

All the above-mentioned flywheels are balanced individually and may be used as is on stock engines. But with engine modifications, your pressure plate, disc, and flywheel should be balanced as a unit.

The B&M Clutch-Flite and Turbo-Flite automatic transmissions are "clutch" driven. Basically, the torque converter has been removed, and a special front plate, clutch release fork, and throwout bearing installed in its place. The automatic transmission is then coupled to the engine crankshaft with a standard or high performance flywheel, pressure plate, and disc combination.

This combination breeds the best of a stick transmission with an automatic. Missed shifts will be a thing of the past and there is no load on the automatic at the starting line—engine rpm can be brought up as high as needed without worrying about that converter stall speed.

Installation is very simple. If you use the transmission bellhousing the kit is an easy bolt-up job, with the main work being cutting a rectangular hole in the side of the housing for the release fork to operate. If you're going to use a combination safety shield/bellhousing, the transmission bellhousing is cut off just in front of the main case and a new adapter housing bolted on. Each type of kit comes complete with all hardware right down to a new input shaft for the clutch. They can be operated on the street as well as the drag strip.

Special bellhousings are necessary if you install a Long-type pressure plate on Chevy or Pontiac engines equipped with Borg & Beck or diaphragm units. The Long-type unit requires more area radially than the other types, so it's not possible to use the standard housing. When this is the case, it's best to switch to a scattershield bellhousing for safety as well as gaining the necessary room for the conversion.

Since the high-revving 1955 Chevy was introduced, flywheel and clutch explosions have been a problem, and will always be a threat to driver and spectator with rpm in the six, seven, and eight thousand or more bracket.

Any safety shield used should be the approved type—AHRA, NHRA or better. Naturally, safety shields are required at sanctioned drag events and they should be used on all hot street machinery too—explosions are not limited to the drag strip alone. Donovan and Lakewood Industries make excellent products which are hydroformed from solid, one-piece sheet stock. In addition to this type of shield most pro drivers are using an inner lining of heat-treated alloy steel or aluminum that fits snugly inside the bellhousing and is only about ⅛ inch thick. Liners are made by Lakewood Industries and Don Long Chassis. The liner gives that extra ounce of protection and strength to the bellhousing if a red hot clutch is loose inside. Another safety item that has rapidly become favored is the safety blanket. The safety blanket consists of fourteen layers of heavy nylon shaped to conform to the bellhousing. Several big heavy-duty nylon straps and buckles similar to seat belt material hold the blanket securely to the bellhousing. Tests have shown them to withstand clutch disintegration. Besides being made for competition bellhousings, they are available for automatic transmissions as well. They weigh only ten pounds and are worth every ounce in the safety they provide.

Gear Ratios

Lugging an engine, which means running it too slowly, results in extreme pressures being built up inside which will wear it out very quickly. Over-revving an engine or running it too fast will have pretty much the same effect.

Through gearing, the transmission keeps the engine operating at the best speed where it puts out the most torque and can work the easiest, providing that the driver knows when to change the gears to correspond with road conditions. The driver who doesn't will be much better off with an automatic transmission. It will be a lot easier on the engine and maybe a lot easier on the transmission, especially if the driver is the type who clashes gears a lot.

Many mechanics who take transmissions apart every day do not know how to figure ratios in gears. It is simply a matter of counting the teeth on the gears to find out what's going on.

Suppose an engine is turning a gear with 10 teeth and this is meshed with another gear with 20 teeth, then a shaft runs from the 20-tooth gear directly to the rear end and then to the wheels of the car. Divide the number of teeth on the driving gear into the driven gear, or 10 into 20. The answer, of course, is 2; 2-to-1 gear ratio in the transmission. This means that the engine will turn over two revolutions for every one turn of the transmission output shaft.

Suppose it is a 10-tooth to 40-tooth relationship. Then the engine would turn over four times for every one revolution of the output shaft on the transmission. Whenever two gears are meshed, the one with the smaller number of teeth turns faster. If you had your hands on a boulder and you could just barely move it, your hands would move the same distance that the boulder would move. But if you put a long 2X4 under the edge of the boulder, with another rock close to it to pry on (as a fulcrum point), and you got out about 6 or 8 feet, you could move the boulder with very little pressure on the 2X4. Your hand has to travel a much greater distance in doing this than it did when you moved the boulder directly. When we hook up the engine to the small gear in the transmission we are accomplishing the same thing. It gives the engine leverage to do work, but at the same time the engine has to travel quite a bit farther.

Suppose you had 15 teeth on the engine gear and 29 teeth on the gear that meshes with it. The same arithmetic still applies. Divide the 15 into the 29 and you get 1.93 as your gear ratio. In other words, for every one revolution of the transmission output shaft, the engine will turn 1.93 times.

There isn't any transmission that only goes through two gears, however. They all go through four, but don't let this throw you. You simply take each pair of gears in turn and figure out the ratio of the pair. Then multiply the ratios together to get the overall transmission ratio. Take as an example the most popular transmission ever made, the 3-speed Chevrolet. In low gear, it has two pairs of gears, meshed. The first pair has 19 and 27 teeth, the second pair 14 and 29. In each pair, divide the driving gear into the driven gear and get ratios of 1.42 and 2.07. Multiplying those two ratios together gives 2.939 or 2.94, which is the overall ratio of the Chevrolet transmission in low gear.

To get the overall ratio of the whole car, carry this a step further and multiply the transmission ratio times the rear end ratio of 3.36 which gives 9.88, which is the number of times the engine turns for each rear wheel revolution.

With the transmission in second gear the power flow is also going through four gears or two pairs, so the same division of teeth and multiplication of ratios would give you the overall ratio in second gear. If you have a 4-speed transmission, third gear would amount to the same kind of calculations, but then when you get into high, which could be third or fourth (depending on the number of speeds your transmission has), the power flow is not going through any of the gears, so there is no multiplication. Then you are running on the ratio that is in the rear end.

There are three major arrangements of gears in a manual transmission. They are planetary, sliding, and constant-mesh gears, all of which have been tried by different car makers throughout the history of the automobile.

The planetary gear arrangement in the Model T transmission was really primitive and not very dependable. If the transmission bands lasted one year the driver was very lucky, and it was possible to burn them out completely on one long steep hill.

Sliding gears are still used in manual transmissions. All this means is that a gear is splined onto a shaft and when the driver wants to mesh it with another gear he moves a lever that slides the gear along the splines until the position is correct.

The first sliding-gear transmissions were of the progressive type. There was no H-pattern as we know it today. All the driver had to do was to move the shift lever in one direction and he would go through all the forward speeds. He moved the shift lever in the other direction to get into reverse. Thus all shifts were made in a straight line. It sounds like a great idea, but when coming down to a stop he had to gear back through second and low to get a neutral. If he waited until he came to a full stop, then he had to jiggle the shift lever to mesh with second gear then wiggle it again to get into low and finally he'd make it into neutral. To get into high gear he had to go through low and second.

The progressive transmission was really nothing more than an adaptation of the old back gears on a lathe. It was out of date before World War I when most manufacturers had gone to a selective transmission. The selective transmission has shift rails and a lever which can be moved through a gate from one rail to the other to select any number of gear positions from the neutral position of the lever. Most selective transmissions use the H-pattern.

The selective transmission can be either a sliding-gear or constant-mesh type or a combination of the two. In a sliding-gear type the actual gears are moved back and forth to mesh with other gears. In a constant-mesh type the gears are in a fixed position and the connection between is made by dog clutches. These dog clutches usually have some type of synchronizing device which is supposed to prevent clashing of the teeth on the clutch. However, if a person is inept enough it is possible to make a lot of noise and do a lot of damage with any transmission.

The advantage of the constant-mesh type is that it is easier to shift and if a shift is missed, the resulting clash will not be as damaging on a dog clutch as it would be on the gears. All automotive transmissions made today are of the selective type. Even motorcycles use a selective gearset but their linkage is hooked up so that it is applied in a progressive manner thus giving straight-line shifting.

Circle-track racing cars, such as sprint cars and midgets, do not have any need for a clutch or transmission because their speeds are never outside the range in which the engine produces usable torque. Race car builders found out long ago that by eliminating the clutch and transmission a lot of excess weight was pared off and they could go faster.

They still had to have some way to disconnect the engine from the wheels so that the engine could be warmed up with the car standing still, and also some way to make stopping easier. The in-and-out box was just what they needed, and it has been used for many years in all kinds of race cars. It is not used in championship cars or at Indianapolis, however, because those cars are required to have a reverse gear for backing up in emergencies. They also have two or more speeds forward in their transmission, besides reverse.

In-and-out boxes have one lever coming out the top of the box between the driver's legs. When he wants to engage the engine with the wheels, he pushes the lever down; he pulls up to disengage. He engages the engine only when the car is standing still and the engine is dead. Disengagement can be done at any time, but if he wants to re-engage he has to come to a complete stop, shut the engine off, and then call for the push truck to start him again.

The problem with a full power shift is in keeping the engine from over-revving during the time that the shift lever is moving from one gear position to the other. If the engine increases in speed, chances of getting the synchros meshed are poor. You can never be sure that the engine won't speed up the minute you pop the clutch, but one way to minimize this overspeeding is to wait until it is wound out completely, almost peaked in the lower gear before you shift. The trouble is, it's not the best time to shift at the most opportune moment for maximum acceleration and make it fast enough so that you don't miss.

Any sloppiness in the linkage or excessive end play in the synchros will increase chances of a miss so the transmission has to be in top shape for speed shifting. If you do a lot of drag racing there is a modification you can make that will almost insure your full power shifts. A synchro ready to mesh with the teeth on a gear has to be turning at just about the same speed as the gear. If the speeds are different the teeth will start skipping over each other because there just isn't time to get them meshed. The answer to this is to use the same sized teeth but with wider spaces in between.

The wide spaces are not necessary in normal shifting because the synchronizer with its brass rings does a good job of matching the speed of the teeth so that they can mesh. In drag shifting, however, the brass rings break, wear out, and literally fall to pieces.

The modification was developed by Chrysler transmission engineers for use on their 4-speed box but it will work on any box—even an old fashioned 3-speed—with good results. The engineers figured that with wide spacing on the synchro teeth the brass rings wouldn't be needed at all, and they were right. What the modification amounts to is taking the brass rings and the springs and the little spacers that hold them in position completely out of the transmission, then grinding or machining every other tooth off the gear hub and the synchro sleeve. You end up with a lot of back lashes, and you have converted back to an old-fashioned clash box.

There's one thing you should do to help any transmission live a little longer but particularly with a modified one. Before you pop the clutch off the line, let it drag just enough to take up the slack in the gears. If you don't do this you may let the clutch in when the gears are at one end of the back lash.

Shifting is about the only area where modifications are needed in a modern transmission. You may hear of transmission men who drill holes in gears or bushings to provide more oil flow, but for the most part transmission gears last so long and work so well that these modifications are unnecessary.

Automatics

Despite its complexity, you can understand an automatic transmission. Modern automatic transmissions are composed of three main sections: a torque converter, a gear system, and a hydraulic control system.

A torque converter is really nothing more than a fancy fluid coupling, and a fluid coupling can best be described as a couple of propellers fighting each other inside a housing. If you had a propeller and moved your hands so that water was forced against the blades, the propeller would turn. You would have, actually, a fluid coupling between your hands and the propeller.

To make it a little more efficient you could use two propellers spaced fairly close together so that one prop would force water against the other and make it turn also. Enclose the two propellers in a housing, hook the car engine to one, the rear wheels to the other, fill the housing with a light oil, and you have a fluid coupling that will actually move the car.

The propeller that is driven by the engine forces oil against the other propeller and that causes the rear wheels of the car to turn. There is no actual mechanical connection between the engine and the rear wheels. You can put the brakes on, stop the car dead, and the engine still keeps turning its own propeller, but the one connected to the rear wheels is stopped. That is the advantage of a fluid coupling, whether it's hooked to an automatic transmission or to a standard transmission with the usual three or four speeds. When the car is stopped, the engine does not have to be disconnected by shifting the transmission to neutral.

The propeller that's connected to the engine may be called the driving member, the impeller, the pump, the driving torus or the driver. The propeller connected to the rear wheels is called the turbine, driven member, driven torus, or the runner.

If the fluid coupling were really efficient, it wouldn't allow you to stop the car with the engine still engaged or to start off in high gear. Slippage in the fluid coupling was its one big disadvantage. It resulted not only in poor acceleration but in poor gas mileage because the engine was doing a lot of work churning up that fluid and the car wasn't getting anywhere.

In the modern automatic, the impeller and the turbine do not look like propellers at all but they perform the same function. Instead of having two or three or four blades as a propeller does, the impeller and the turbine have many blades set very close together. The angle of the blades is carefully set so that the fluid coupling will operate with the greatest efficiency. The difficulty is that when the angle of the blades is set for maximum efficiency, the fluid— as it leaves the turbine—shoots back at the impeller at an angle that has a tendency to slow the impeller down. In other words the engine is trying to slow the engine.

Oil inside the fluid coupling is not just churning away as it would if we had an egg beater in a bowl. It is actually being directed by the blades on the impeller to strike the turbine with a maximum amount of push, and is constantly circulating in a definite, well-planned pattern.

After the engineers reached the limit of design abilities on the fluid coupling, they decided to put in some extra stationary blades so that the fluid leaving the turbine would not come back against the impeller with retarding force. The extra blades are mounted in a full circle within the fluid coupling and are called a stator. When a fluid coupling has the extra stator blades it is a torque converter.

By putting a stator into the fluid coupling engineers got rid of the retarding effect of the oil leaving the turbine and gained an unexpected bonus in that it ceased to be a plain fluid coupling and was now a torque multiplier. More torque actually came out of the torque converter than was put into it.

A manual transmission multiplies torque because it gives the engine leverage to work. It's the old story of fulcrums and levers. The torque converter accomplishes the same type of reduction only it does it through fluid mechanics and the angle of the stator blades, instead of through gear size.

This torque multiplication comes into play whenever the impeller is turning faster than the turbine. Back off the throttle so the engine is just pushing enough to keep the rear wheels going, then the impeller and turbine are turning at about the same speed. All of the fluid in the housing is turning at the same speed as the impeller and turbine but there is no flow through the blades at this time.

While the impeller and the turbine (and the fluid) are turning at the same speed, the stator blades are not turning so they are creating a drag that tends to slow everything down. To get around this problem the hub upon which the stator blades are mounted is a one-way roller clutch. When the stator blades are redirecting the flow of fluid back into the impeller, the roller clutch does not permit rotation of the stator. But when the turbine catches up with the impeller, then the fluid rotating inside the housing strikes the back side of the stator blades and the stator goes along for a free ride, with the roller clutch permitting it to turn in the same direction the impeller, turbine, and fluid are rotating.

Multiplication through a torque converter can run as high as 2.5-to-1 or a little bit more. The faster you rotate that impeller the harder the fluid is going to press against the turbine, and the faster it will come back through the stator and be redirected against the turbine again.

Because of the torque multiplication, the torque converter does not slip nearly as much as the old fluid coupling. But it does slip a little at all times, even at highway speeds. Whenever the slippage exceeds 10 percent the torque multiplication starts because the flow of oil through the turbine blades strikes the front side of the stator, the stator locks up on its roller clutch, and the oil is redirected into the impeller to help it along.

While slippage in a fluid coupling is a pain in the neck, slippage in a torque converter is desirable because it results in this torque multiplication and gives greater acceleration. Maximum torque multiplication comes at full stall when the car is stationary and the throttle is wide open.

Many modern torque converters have the stator blades set at a fixed angle. But some have a hydraulically controlled piston within the hub of the stator assembly which changes the angle or pitch of the blades depending upon the load and speed of the engine.

In all modern transmissions torque multiplication is used along with gear changes in the automatic transmission that multiply the torque even further. The gear changes are made by the hydraulic control system at the proper speed and load.

Planetary gears used in an automatic transmission are similar to the planetary gear sets used in the Model T and also in an overdrive. They are arranged differently, usually with two planetary gear sets mounted together so that more gear reduction combinations are possible.

A simple planetary gearset has a sun gear mounted on a shaft with three or more planet pinions encircling it and meshed with it. The planet pinions are rotated on pins, and these pins are firmly attached to a cage so that all of the planet pinions operate as a unit. Around the planet pinions is a large ring gear with internal teeth that mesh with the pinions.

The gears are in mesh at all times. There is no sliding of the gears or unmeshing in the planetary system. The trick to planetary gears is that they are arranged in the transmission to apply power to any one of the three members—the ring gear, the planet pinion carrier, or the sun gear. We can also take power output off any one of the members.

The third method of operating the planetary gearset is to immobilize any one of the members so that it is held firmly to the transmission case. Not all of these possibilities occur in any transmission but if they did we could get reduction in two ways, direct drive, reverse, neutral, and overdrive—all out of the planetary gearset without doing anything but changing the power input, the power output, or holding one member.

Drive to various members of the planetary gearset is obtained by clutches inside the transmission which are operated hydraulically. The holding of various members is done by brake bands which are also operated hydraulically.

To get direct drive in the planetary gearset, lock any two members together with a clutch or combination of clutches. Whenever any two members are locked together the ring gear, planetary gear carrier, and the sun gear will all rotate as a unit. There is no gear reduction and we have a 1-to-1 direct drive ratio.

If we drive the sun gear with the power from the engine and hold the ring gear stationary, the sun gear will force the planet pinions to walk around the ring gear. The output shaft is hooked to the planet pinion carrier which rotates considerably slower than the sun gear does. With that condition we get a big torque increase which would compare to the low gear in a standard transmission.

Suppose we want gear reduction but not quite so much. Then we apply engine power to the ring gear and hold the sun gear—with the output shaft still connected to the planet pinion cage. We still get the same walking action between the pinions and the ring gear but they are also walking around the stationary sun gear. Thus we get a gear reduction that would be about the same as second gear in a standard transmission.

To get reverse we drive the sun gear, hold the planet pinion carrier stationary, and connect the output shaft to the ring gear. The planet pinions can rotate on their pins only, which causes the ring gear to turn in a reverse direction but also gives some gear reduction.

Many different arrangements of planetary gears have been tried in an automatic transmission. Most of them have evolved into an arrangement whereby two planetary gearsets are used with a common sun gear. Thus, the ring gear and the pinions can apply power to the sun gear, which in turn transmits the power to the pinions and the ring gear of the other planetary gear set. With an arrangement of clutches and bands for holding or connecting the various members, it is possible to get the gear ratios we want for efficient operation of the transmission.

The clutch assembly is a series of plates with some plates joined to the hub and the others joined to the drum or cylinder; a multiple-disc clutch is similar to the type used on some race cars today. They were also used on passenger cars in the early days of the automobile industry.

In a multiple-disc clutch the plates are free to float back and forth because they are just held by grooves in the hub or the drum that accept tangs on the disc. When the clutch is disengaged the set of discs that is connected to the hub is spinning away while the other set connected to the drum is stationary. It could be the other way around too, with the hub stationary and the drum spinning.

With one set of clutch plates spinning and the other stationary, there's a bit of bouncing around and friction in the clutch when it is released. Transmission fluid lubricates the clutch so that this friction doesn't bother anything. A clutch is much more dependable than a band. Because of this extra dependability, some transmission designers have tried to do away with bands entirely, using clutches instead.

Built into the clutch cylinder is the clutch piston, which is right next to the plates and rotates with the whole assembly. In order to apply the clutch a valve admits hydraulic fluid under pressure to the clutch piston and it squeezes all of the clutch plates together. It does a pretty good job of squeezing, locking the plates up tight into one solid mass so that the hub is locked to the drum.

To release the clutch a valve releases the hydraulic pressure and a spring pushes the piston back. There's nothing holding the clutch plates together so they float apart and the hub starts moving independently of the drum. The release spring can be a flat washer or coil springs.

There has been quite a variation in the number of plates used in clutches through the years. One of the problems in reassembling an automatic transmission is in getting the right number of plates back in. Of course if too many are put in, the clutch will not release and if too few are put in, the clutch will not engage tightly enough to lock the hub and drum. To be sure of putting in the right number of clutch plates, the transmission man has to have a book for the particular year and make of transmission he is working on, or he has to be familiar with the transmission.

The big swing to automatic transmissions in high performance automobiles hasn't been a long romance, and only recently has the mechanical brain come into its own as a hot rodding wizard. The Power-glide, Turboglide, Dynaflow, and Cruise-O-Matic designs have been okay for granny and the grocery store hop, but hopeless for any kind of decent performance. Of all the early American automatics, only the General Motors HydraMatic has proven itself worthy of a quick quarter mile.

The HydraMatic has been around for so long, it is too often overlooked as just another mainstay of hot rodding. But in many respects, it is still without peer for specialty heavy-duty work. Created back in 1939 for the luxury Cadillacs, only a few of the dual-range units are acceptable for the hot rod treatment. These include those produced for the '53–'56 Oldsmobile, '55–'56 Pontiacs, '53–'55 Cadillacs, and '53–'55 Lincolns. HydraMatics produced outside of these years have changes that, although perfectly all right for street use, are incompatible with the torture of high horsepower and maximum traction.

Perhaps the greatest distinction of the HydraMatic design, at least to the layman, is the type of hydraulic or fluid coupling used between the gearbox and engine crankshaft. Any kind of fluid coupling is intended to eliminate the standard clutch by using oil to transmit torque. In a Hydro, this coupling is a high performance type, and all the gears shift in sequence. Of course, the difference in application determines exactly what kind of HydraMatic a person may use. For a high horsepower gasser, equipped with supercharger and all the goodies, a full competition unit is necessary. But for ordinary heavy-duty use, such as in a pickup truck or towing a trailer, something much milder on the shifts is advisable. To this end, Hydro's are available in many different stages.

During modified Hydro development, it was found the stock front pump would not deliver enough hydraulic pressure. It could muster between 75 and 90 pounds per square inch, but over 185 psi was required. When there is not enough pump pressure, the transmission will shift "softly," that is, the friction clutches will not engage quickly enough. When there is too much pressure, the unit will "bog," or rather, the second and third speeds will try to engage at the same time.

The clutch assemblies in a Hydro are vital, as they determine how much torque will be delivered to the rear end. B&M Automotive has found that standard discs can be used with engines having torque in the 175-to-200 horsepower range, but these same discs are like paper in a reworked transmission. To cure this, they use a high porosity, nonmetallic disc facing good for engines up to 400 horsepower, with a waffle pattern grooving across the face to increase oil flow and cooling tendencies. For the big bears, or engines over 400 horses, a semimetallic material is used.

Just how well a modified HydraMatic will work and live depends almost entirely on initial installation and maintenance. That goes for all modified automatics, for that matter. Of course, all this really starts even before the unit is purchased. The prospective buyer should always be absolutely clear about what he will use the Hydro for. For instance, a Hydro-Stick is available in four different versions, and there is little overlap in purpose.

The unblown Hydro-Stick is recommended for limited horsepower cars weighing 3500 pounds or less. It should be used primarily on the street. The unblown Competition unit is made for unlimited horsepower, nonsupercharged cars weighing up to 5000 pounds. The blown design is strictly for hard-nosed competition with engines of unlimited horsepower. It has no weight limitation. Racing is expected of both competition models. The fourth version is the Traveler, intended for very heavy-duty pickup camper use, where there is not a lot of horsepower or torque involved, but the total vehicle weight may easily exceed 5000 pounds.

After the buyer has decided what his Hydro will be used for, he must follow installation directions carefully or expect eventual trouble. If the directions are followed and normal maintenance procedures are adhered to, a beefed Hydro can log upwards of 100,000 miles without the slightest problem.

Because of the many different weight and horsepower variations given a beefed Hydro, the correct operating pressure must be set by the individual, and the right pressure is imperative to trouble-free operation. All pressure changes are made at the regular plug, which is located on the forward left side of the transmission. Symptoms requiring a change are: soft full throttle 2-3 shift (corrected by raising pressure one shim at a time, maximum of three shims, until engine bogs on 2-3 full throttle shift, then remove one shim. If more than three additional shims are required, get a longer pressure spring. Champion spark plug washers make excellent shims); bogging full throttle 2-3 shift (too much pressure, remove pressure regulator spring and cut off ½-inch length of coil at a time. Coil must be cut from the regulator plug end of spring).

A bogging full throttle 2-3 shift is when the engine falters or pauses momentarily. An extreme bog is when the transmission shifts from second to fourth and then instantly back to third. When the pressure regulator assembly is removed for a pressure change, or a slipping condition occurs for no apparent reason, check the two rubber seals on the regulator valve for cracks or damage.

Maintenance is really limited to keeping the linkage in proper alignment, all the external bolts tight, and good fluid in the box. Under extreme hard use, the oil can break down. When this happens, it will lose its distinctive odor, and clutch failure may follow shortly. A good beefed Hydro should last a long, long time, if it is given the courtesy it deserves.

Under the FoMoCo heading, there are only three automatic transmissions worthy of consideration by performance-conscious hot rodders. Of these, the C4 and C6 are absolutely top drawer, with the earlier three-speed Cruise-O-Matic functional as a street unit.

Extensive modication to the C4 and C6 has been the concern of the factory until recently, simply because such development takes time. At any rate, the factory has been able to produce some very effective units, although the purchase price for such an item is quite high. This will come down as the independent builders become involved. The big improvement is use of the C4 Econoline (Falcon) converter to give better stall speed characteristics. This unit, which is 10¼ inches in diameter, has a stock torque capacity of only 275 pounds and a stall torque ratio of 2.40:1. However, by increasing the construction material thickness to .187-inch wall and using higher carbon steel, performance is far better.

Until there is considerable in-use evaluation of the C6 and smaller C4 transmission design, particularly by hot rod sources, the ultimate potential will remain relatively unknown. Early tests show, however, this to be equivalent to both the TorqueFlite and TurboHydro as a high performance automatic.

Although American Motors has one of the hottest-selling sporty cars going in the Javelin, its automatic transmission is not up to top performance standards. Even the potential is not really there.

It is basically a Borg-Warner three-speed very similar to the earlier FoMoCo Ford-O-Matics. The problem lies in inadequate clutch capacity, which in turn restricts clutch life under heavy-duty conditions. The friction material involved is not adequate for an engine giving much over 300 foot-pounds torque, virtually ruling the unit out as a serious hot rodding item. It seems limited to street use.

It is rumored, however, that the AMC engineers have been keenly aware of this problem for some time, particularly since the company has decided to get on the specialty-car performance bandwagon.

The series 300 TurboHydraMatics produced by General Motors are really just a step up from the PowerGlide, but they are strong. Strong enough to take the punishment of a fuel funny car without extensive reworking. The problem is simply that such a two-speed requires an engine with bundles of horsepower to become effective. That kind of horsepower and torque just isn't available in the passenger car.

Still, the 300 Turbo would be a good replacement for the softer

PowerGlide in a number of instances, such as with a 1500- to 2500-pound street roadster. For ordinary street use where the overall package weighs around one ton, there is no need to modify the innards.

General Motors types were forced to sit back and endure the slings and arrows of outrageous fortune for several years while Chrysler Corporation automatics put everything but dual-range Hydro's on the trailer. During the early 1960s any big drag meet looked like a Dodge or Plymouth factory parking lot. Although GM officially announced its withdrawal from automotive competition, the potential for winning races was never removed from the cars. This must have been a strong supporting argument for development of a new super-strong three-speed automatic, the Series 400 Turbo HydraMatic.

After the demise of the dual range HydraMatic of the mid-1950s, GM was faced with an endless assortment of nondescript automatic transmission designs hardly better than nothing. They all work fine for retirement-community elders, but suffer miserably under strenuous conditions. The Turbo has cured all that.

The new series 400 automatic was introduced on the 1964 Buicks and Cadillacs, followed in succeeding years by all the other GM marques, until it is now standard equipment, or recommended option, on most of the performance image cars. The Turbo is about 60 pounds lighter than its popular predecessor, the dual-range Hydro, and about 15 pounds above the Torque-Flite. Surrounded by a die-cast aluminum housing is a three-element hydraulic torque converter and a compound planetary gear set, the latter operated via friction of three multiple-disc clutch units, two sprag clutches, and two friction bands.

Initially there were two separate Turbo converter designs, identified as either a fixed or variable pitch (VP) stator. In all cases, the converter includes a driving member (pump), driven member (turbine), and reaction member (stator). The stator design used in a particular unit previous to 1968 depended upon vehicle requirement. For this reason, a fixed pitch stator was common on the higher-priced cars while the lower lines got the VP.

In the VP design, the individual stator blades are hydraulically operated to assume either high or low angle, low angle being approximately 18 degrees to plane of rotation at blade tip. This is the position for maximum efficiency. At wide throttle settings, where good acceleration and overall performance are demanded, especially for small engines, the blades switch to a high angle of about 26 degrees. This high angle is also used when the engine is idling and transmission is in gear, to reduce tendency to creep.

With a fixed stator design the blades are stationary at the maximum efficiency angle of about 23 degrees. For better performance at increased throttle settings, a part-throttle downshift from third to second gears is involved. Because this fixed stator design has proven versatile on even the smaller cars, the variable stator idea has been dropped.

The Turbo's torque converter has the function common to all such modern three-speeds in that it is primarily a fluid coupling to smoothly transmit engine power through oil to the transmission gear train. During the procedure it multiplies engine torque. In the two stator designs, the fixed unit multiplies by 2:1 while the variable unit is higher at 2.5:1. Stall speed for the fixed stator assembly will be between 1200 and 1400 rpm, while the VP unit stalls at a higher speed around 1800 to 1900 rpm. For this reason, a big engine with gobs of power can effectively use a fixed stator, while a small engine must have a VP. This lets the little banger get up to its operating rpm for drag racing starts. To get maximum stall speed with minimum efficiency, a VP converter from a V6 Buick or ohv Pontiac six should be used, as their diameter is about ¾ inch smaller than the standard V8.

The turbine shaft, which is about 9¼ inches long, ends in a forward clutch assembly. This clutch is the means of connecting and disconnecting the gear train from the converter and consists of a clutch housing splined to the turbine shaft; steel clutch drive plates tanged around the o.d. to fit the clutch housing; composition-faced clutch-drive plates tanged inside to a clutch hub; clutch piston that hydraulically applies to lock the plates together, and clutch release springs to retract the piston and release the clutch when hydraulic pressure is released.

The mainshaft connects at the forward end to the clutch hub and at the back to the rear internal gear of the compound planetary gear train. During use, reaction forces tend to rotate the front gear of this set in the wrong direction, so it is held stationary by a reaction carrier bolted to the transmission case. A sprag assembly inside the reaction carrier lets the final drive turn clockwise, but not the reverse. Thus, the front planetary pinions drive the front internal gear and output shaft in reduction at a ratio of about 2.48:1, which combined with the maximum converter ratio of 2:1, gives an overall first gear starting ratio of approximately 5:1.

As car speed increases, less torque multiplication is necessary, so the intermediate sprag assembly and clutch are installed ahead of the sun gear unit, but connected to the latter by a hollow shaft. This intermediate clutch and sprag assembly is similar to those already described, but it produces a final drive in second gear of 1.48:1. The direct drive ratio of 1:1 is the function of the direct clutch assembly, locking all drive components together. Two external friction bands hold either the front carrier or direct clutch housing to give reverse, and deceleration for first and second gears. These bands are not used in the all-out competition Turbo's, thereby allowing the transmission to freewheel in first and second gears.

For severe competition, the kind administered by seven-second funny cars and cleaner than clean Gassers, only a few (but significant) modifications are required. The converter housing must be cut apart on a lathe, making the cut at the original factory weld.

At B&M Automotive, where most of the TurboHydro racing development has been staged, a new-model higher-capacity pump is installed (it's deeper and necessary because of higher internal pressure requirements). The turbine shells and pump are furnace brazed, which is imperative.

It has been found that the stator assemblies need not be changed, but the turbine shaft diameter should be turned down about ⅛ inch between the bearing surfaces. This creates a torsion area which reduces shaft breakage under severe loads. After the converter housing is heli-arc welded together again (this weld is the difference in good and bad performance later on), three extra drive lugs are welded on the housing face, then the converter is balanced to within .200 ounce-inch. A bronze bushing is installed in the new front pump as a safeguard against seizure of the turbine shaft.

Apart from the valve body hydraulic pressure routing, the major changes are restricted to the clutches. Oil is in the clutch assemblies all the time, as a lubrication and as a built-in slippage for a smooth shift. During a stock assembly shifting sequence, oil displaced from between the clutch discs leaves through two holes drilled in the outer housing. To speed up this flow, eight holes of ³⁄₁₆-inch diameter are drilled in the direct-drive clutch housing, and the hubs of both direct and forward clutch assemblies are likewise drilled, each with twelve holes of ³⁄₁₆-inch diameter.

To continue improved clutch lubrication, the bronze thrust washers are grooved in two places on either face from the i.d. to o.d. The stock washers have two small V-grooves on either face, but the new oil routes are filed 90 degrees to them, and about ½ inch wide.

B&M has designed special steel and friction material discs for both the high gear and intermediate clutches, doing away with warpage common to stock units under high loadings, and at the same time increasing the friction material's coefficient of friction somewhat. The valve body is modified if the unit is to be a full competition item featuring manual shifting, simply by blocking or removing all the valves but one (other than the control valve), which is the check for reverse. A special transfer plate is used for each specific transmission type, closing off all the necessary passages.

Because the stall speed of the series 400 TurboHydro is below 2000 rpm, use of this automatic behind a smaller Chevy engine (anything below the 396) without a ClutchFlite is almost impossible. However, with a little machine work, things can be made to work. All that's necessary is a Chevy PowerGlide converter to bolt ahead of the Turbo gears, in essence reducing the effectiveness of the converter at the bottom end.

Such a high stall unit is made up from any 11 ¾-inch diameter PowerGlide converter (the stock Turbo converter is 13 inches in diameter). The first order of business is chucking the converter in a lathe and cutting the case open at the weld bead. A special turbine hub must be machined from billet stock, or a ready-made hub is available from the speed shop. Such a ready-to-use hub is made from 4130 steel, with inside splines to match the turbo input (turbine) shaft. The stock hub cannot be bored and broached to the larger diameter, and different spline pattern cut because the hub snout o.d. is too small.

After the new hub is mated to the turbine housing, both the turbine and pump housings are furnace brazed, necessary because of the extreme pressures fed into the vanes during operation. This is one of the reasons Ford increased the thickness of the small C4 converter housings when used with the big engine/C6 transmissions.

All other machine work should be done after the furnace brazing, which compensates for any distortion caused by the high heat of brazing. The pump drive gear slot is milled ¹⁄₁₆ inch deeper to keep the converter from bottoming on the pump with resulting damage. At the other end of the pump drive snout, inside the housing, the thrust face is trued. The stock phenolic thrust washer is replaced by a Torrington needle bearing washer. The stator remains unmodified.

Much work is done to the front cover. The input shaft of the PowerGlide is supported by a bushing in this cover, but the Turbo shaft is supported in the transmission, and must run free up front. Therefore, the bushing must be removed and the hole bored out to 1⅞₆ inches for turbine shaft clearance. Three additional drive lugs should be welded to the housing, then trued. After this, the thrust face on the inside of the front cover is trued, and the converter is ready to be heli-arc welded back together.

With this smaller converter in place, the small displacement engines can be spun to the 3000 rpm range before the stall speed is reached.

The very first Chrysler Corporation TorqueFlite was introduced in some 1956 Imperials, but it was far cry from the current king of the drag strips. Designated the A-466, it featured a cast-iron base, weighed a young ton, and isn't exactly ideal for the go-fast crowd. It can be modified, however, following the basic rules applied to later versions.

Because the TorqueFlite only weighs 158 pounds with converter, and since it has been refined extensively by the factory, it has proven exceptionally reliable in drag racing use.

As with the other three-speed automatics, something must be done to the converter if hard racing is anticipated. A modified wedge engine 12-inch version will work with bigger engines, but must have the four driving lugs drilled and tapped for larger ⅜-inch SAE bolts. These lugs must also be heli-arced to the housing. Early converters must be furnace brazed, but late units come this way from the factory. The blades can be machined slightly to increase stall speed an additional 500 rpm without affecting the overall efficiency.

To raise the stall speed even further, getting it up to 2600 rpm or so, requires use of the hemi converter, which is little more than a modified 273 unit. This unit has a different inner race, a larger neck on the pump drive, and a different hub and splines in the turbine wheel. The hub support is larger, as is a double ring gear with spacer, all adding up to a price of nearly $200. Still, such a converter is vital to successful racing.

When using the small converter, the front pump must be machined .100-inch (from the housing face) for clearance. The rear face breather hole is machined .110-inch, then the breather baffle outer edge is radiused to clear the wide hemi retainer. A high performance pump rotor is required, which includes a slight chamfer on the driving tang edges to reduce stress concentrations. A bronze shaft bushing is set in the wide front retainer, and is an important replacement for the earlier narrow babbit bushings.

The turbine input shaft should be of the high performance type (made of Hytuff), identified by red dye on the splines. New clutches and plates have been developed by B&M, increasing the transmission life considerably. While the stock output shaft has proven strong enough for most applications, the very powerful cars have created need for something better, thus a Hytuff treatment is necessary for them.

Some problems have arisen with the TorqueFlite, primarily due to insufficient band strength and carrier failure. To counteract this, steel carriers have been developed along with double wrap bands. With both, explosions have been all but eliminated.

While the A-727 is the best TorqueFlite for the bigger engines, the A-904 should not go unnoticed for lighter-duty applications. Especially for the smaller engines and lower class drag racing competition. This automatic is generally supplied with the slant six and 273 engines, and is merely scaled down from the big 727.

The small TorqueFlite can be modified for either street or racing use, with the converter being the important area of modification. In either case, a manual shifting control is desirable. The backside of the stator is machined for more clearance and the fin angles on the oil pump are changed, giving a high stalling speed and better high-rpm efficiency.

The stock clutches may be retained, but the early clutches (part number 2205203) are better for competition. The oil flow to the clutch pack can be increased by opening the pump delivery orifice to .090 inch, at which time the hydraulic pressure should be raised five pounds via the valve body. A double wrap 1-2 shift apply band is essential to racing use, and an excellent investment for the street.

For racing, the valve body can be changed to a manual shift unit. This entails removing metal from the transfer plate (PN 2466886) in three places. The valve body separator plate (PN 2538049) fits either the 904 or 727 transmission, but it must be modified to fit the small transmission by elongating one of the mounting holes.

The valve body orifice must be drilled to .120 inch. Next assemble the throttle valve, spring kickdown valve, and detent plug; then install 1-2 shift valve governor plug and end plate. Insert a ¼-inch diameter rod, 2%₆ inches long, in the 1-2 shift valve bore and install shift valve end plate. The 1-2 shift valve, 2-3 shift valve, and governor plug and springs are left out. Install the standard manual valve lever and throttle shaft, and install standard shuttle valve cover plate. Note that the shuttle valve, springs, throttle plug, and E-clip are also omitted. Use the standard regulator valve train, converter valve train, springs, and spring retainer. Install the one large valve-body steel ball in the valve body, but omit the five small steel balls. The transmission is now ready for racing.

The Rear End

The idea of drag racing is to get from the starting line to the clocks in the shortest possible time. Top speed in the trap at the quarter's end doesn't mean a thing if the other car gets there first.

An engine will deliver a certain amount of power at a certain number of crankshaft revolutions per minute. Two gears in a drive-line must enable maximum advantage to be taken of this power. In most instances the engine must be allowed to run at maximum power output as much of the time as possible after the car leaves the starting line until it gets to the finish line.

If your engine is one of the big-inchers, your car needs less final gear in first speed than it would for a smaller engine that has less torque on the low end. But now another problem: the final gear ratio depends on both the gear ratio in the transmission and the rear axle ratio. This ratio must be such that the engine will just be passing through the rpm where it twists hardest on the drive-shaft when the car passes the end of the quarter. If the engine reaches this rpm before the car reaches the strip end, the rate of acceleration will drop off before the car reaches the finish line; if it reaches this point after the car passes the finish line, the car isn't accelerating hard enough at some point before it reaches the finish.

What rear axle gear ratio is best for the car? Something between 4.00 and 5.00 to 1 will probably do the job. This is a wide range, and the right number depends on a number of variables. What make and model car is involved, and what size engine is in it? Is the engine stock or has it been modified in some way. What is the engine's mechanical condition, what sort of tires are on the car's rear wheels, etc., etc.?

Any decision as to what rear axle gear ratio would be best for a specific car for drag racing is pure guesswork unless the en-thusiast making the decision has had experience with cars of that particular make and model. Figures for engine speed of maximum power output and the car's maximum speed at the end of the quarter can be estimated and applied to a gear ratio formula, but the answer is going to be just as uncertain as the estimate for engine and car performance. The only way to find the correct ratio is to install gears that either a formula or common sense indicate to be somewhere near correct, and try them. If the engine quits pulling before it reaches the lights, install a numerically higher ratio; if the engine is pulling well at the lights and continues to pull past them, install a numerically lower ratio.

Determining whether the most is being obtained from an engine by driving a car on a drag strip isn't easy unless the driver has had considerable drag racing experience. Perhaps the best thing to do is to depend on the strip's clocks. Try to drive the car in as consistent a manner as possible for each run and use the gear ratio that gives the best average elapsed time.

There are several formulas that involve car speed, engine speed, and gear ratios but only two are necessary: one to determine the rear axle ratio for certain engine speed-car combinations and one for final ratios when the transmission is in its different speeds. For engine speed-car speed combinations the formula is:

$$\frac{RPM \times W}{MPH \times 168} = R$$

RPM = engine crankshaft speed
MPH = car speed
R   = rear axle gear ratio
W   = tire size
168 = constant

Tire size is determined by measuring the distance from the center of one of the rear axle shafts to the road surface when the tires are inflated to their normal hot operating pressure and the car is loaded as it will be for racing.

Using the figures of 6000 for RPM, 100 for MPH, and 13 for W, the formula becomes:

$$\frac{6000 \times 13}{100 \times 168} = R$$

This reduces to:

$$\frac{78000}{16800} = 4.64$$

A 4.64 ratio is close to 4.56, which would be close enough to do the job.

For final gear ratios, the formula is Transmission Ratio × Rear Axle Ratio = Final Ratio. With a 2.20 low and 4.56 rear axle, 2.20 × 4.56 = 10.03 Final Ratio. With a 2.54 low and 4.56 rear axle, 2.54 × 4.56 = 11.58 Final Ratio, and so on.

6

The Chassis

The evolution of the automotive chassis has followed the pre-scribed pattern for the entire vehicle—improvement of a basic idea, with radical changes easing into the pattern only gradually. Since all aspects of automobile engineering are a constant learning experience, it is natural that the earliest chassis would be adapted from wagons, with improvements geared to engine and riding demands.

The early frames were simple "ladder" affairs. That is, two side rails connected by cross members. Things stayed this way for several years until the Budd company developed the all steel body. This helped the fame absorb some of the tremendous torsional forces, but the first real advancement in frame design came when Cord and Auburn introduced the X-member frame in the late 1920s. This X-member created a far stiffer frame at about the same weight.

The difference between the Model A '32 Fords and the '33 and later Fords is a prime example of this advance. The post-'33 Ford frames have a massive central X-member in the frame. Consequently these cars have an excellent reputation for frame rigidity.

Naturally, suspension and frame advances were matched by body construction improvements. Fisher Body led the way with their Turret Top all-steel body in 1934. This body did away with the cloth insert in the top and had steel stampings as a part of the body structure in the sides and floor. Unitized construction was introduced about this time also. The body and frame are really one piece, with the powertrain bolting directly to the combination structure. This is the kind of construction used by the prewar Studebaker and made so popular by Nash in the early '50s. Some engineers prefer unit construction, others lean strictly to separate bodies and frames.

If you're driving a late model Ford, the frame is of the Coke bottle configuration. It is of a rather narrow bottom-to-top cross section, boxed for maximum rigidity and strength. Cross members are virtually nonexistent, with a transmission carrier under the front floorboards and a thin hunk of tubing just behind the rear seat. The frame squirts out toward the outsides just behind the front wheels and then narrows, just ahead of the rear wheels. In the suspension department, the Ford uses semi-elliptic springs on outboard frame mounts at the rear and unequal-length coil-sprung A-arms at the front. The front has ball-joint-carried spindles.

This type of frame suspension combination is hardly adaptable to traditional hot rod building. It is best left unmodified (as are most of the new chassis).

The Chevrolet, Caddy, Buick frame varies quite a bit from Ford. With both GM and Ford, the change in body height forced drastic frame redesign. Ford sets the seat down inside the frame, while the General Motors approach has been to squeeze the mid section of the frame together, setting the seats down outside the center hump. This means that these cars have a rather heavy frame, with the suspension members attached to "add-ons." The front end uses ball and joint spindle carriers along with unequal length A-arms and coil springs. Coils are also used at the rear, with the rear end located by heavy stamped steel radius rods connecting to outriggers on the "wasp" frame.

MoPars use a combination unit body/frame. The area from the firewall forward is a bolt-on frame that holds the engine and front suspension. Chrysler products all use torsion bar front springing, which is a definite assist in the handling department. With this type of springing, the lower stamped steel A-arm serves as the locater for the front end of the torsion bar. The bar runs rearward alongside the framework and stops in an adjusting casting. A heavy bolt may be screwed in or out to adjust spring tension (and relative height of the front end). Rear springing of a Chrysler product is by conventional semi-elliptic springs.

Automobiles which utilize unit construction have no separate frames. The stresses and loads imposed by suspension and propulsion systems are distributed over the entire body-chassis structure by the placement of reinforcing members at the proper points. Even the body panels are "stressed" to carry their share of the loads. While it is difficult to envision the thin sheet metal used in body construction as being capable of containing a high horsepower engine and resisting the tremendous loads imposed by the suspension, steering, and power train, clever engineering has made this possible.

Unit construction derives its popularity from the fact that it is "tight." There is a notable absence of rattles or noise which may otherwise be produced by the bolt-on contact between body and frame. Unit construction is largely confined to stock automobiles and has little interest for the hot rodder who wishes to convert a stock car to a street or competition machine. However, a few race car builders have forsaken the familiar tubular frames for monocoque construction.

If any frame is to be described as being "conventional," it must be the familiar box section frame. These frames have side rails formed by channel sections, usually with a kickup at the rear to provide clearance for a conventional rear axle. The cross members have various sectional configurations and in most cases provide both cross bracing and separation bracing between the side rails.

At one time a certain amount of flexibility was considered desirable in a frame. This was supposed to contribute to road-holding qualities and passenger comfort. To some extent this was true. Flexing of the frame made up for some of the deficiencies in suspension systems, and the "give" in the frame aided in keeping the wheels on the road to contribute to handling qualities.

With the advent of independent front wheel suspensions, the need for a stiff frame became immediately apparent. The former solid-beam front axles tended to distribute the shock of road bumps more or less equally to the frame side rails through leaf springs. Independent front wheel suspensions were anchored to the front corners through coil springs and while this new concept in suspension gave the front wheels new-found ability to negotiate bumps, road-holding qualities and passenger comfort were largely nullified by excessive flexing of the frame.

To take full advantage of the benefits of independent front wheel suspension called for some extensive revisions in conventional frame design. Cross bracing was introduced into these new frames and channel sections were boxed to increase stiffness. Rigid front cross members were designed to form a solid base for the suspension system and to tie the side rails firmly together.

A tremendous amount of engineering knowhow has been incorporated into conventional frame design. The accepted structural shapes, including channel, I-beam box, and tubular sections, have been employed where their configuration will take maximum advantage of the metal from which they are formed with minimum weight. Lightening holes have been cut into members to reduce excess weight without sacrifice of strength. The end result has been frames with great rigidity which will withstand stresses imposed by rough roads, crash brake stops, and the surge of high horsepower engines.

Probably the most sophisticated frames are the tubular variety used in competition cars and dragsters. Tubular sections are extremely strong in relation to their weight and full advantage has been taken of this fact. In competition cars, small-diameter, paper-thin tubing is welded into a bridge structure that is a marvel of strength and lightness. The skillful placement of bracing makes these frames literally "bird cages." In fact one of the versions of the Maseratti competition sports cars was popularly known as the "bird cage."

The tubing used in the super-lightweight competition car frames is generally one of the chromium-molybdenum alloy steels which are popularly known as chrome-moly and characterized by extreme toughness. Very recently, competition-car builders have built frames of titanium alloy tubing which is 40 percent lighter than its equivalent in steel. One such frame in a track car, complete with its suspension components, weighed a mere 55 pounds. This is a dramatic contrast to a conventional frame which may weigh several hundred pounds.

To consider a titanium tubular space frame would be carrying things a little far afield for the average hot rodder who may wish to build a street or show rod from scratch. Two courses are open to this individual. One is to make necessary modifications to an old frame to update it to modern standards and the other is to purchase one of the frame kits presently available, and advertized in hot rod magazines.

Many rod builders, particularly those that are handy with the welding and cutting torch, prefer to modify their own frames by using stock frames as a base. Ladder-type frames made from mild steel are inexpensive and easily obtainable. Two types are suitable for use under a rod: those having absolutely straight side rails and those having a kick up at the front, at the rear, or both. Model "T" and Model "A" frames are good examples of the former and early Chevy or 1932 and later Ford frames are examples of the latter.

Before applying the torch to any frame, or even considering its use in stock form, the rod builder will be extremely wise to check its condition. It should be cleaned thoroughly and the areas around rivets inspected closely for cracks. The side rails should be carefully checked for straightness and the entire unit inspected for any twisted or bent members. Minor deviations in alignment may be corrected in the home shop and slight cracks may be welded. If any major deviations from alignment are detected, or if there is major damage, the only solutions are to entrust the repairs to a frame shop or seek a new frame.

If the builder is to be concerned with a frame that is to stay relatively unaltered, then he will be primarily concerned with small modifications. Such a situation would exist if the builder were to construct a slightly modified Model "A" roadster on a stock Model "A" frame. Assuming that this car could achieve a lower appearance by channeling the body, extensive changes in the frame would probably be unnecessary. Minor changes such as shock absorber mounts, new engine mounts, and miscellaneous braces are a relatively simple operation.

Most roadster builders will wish to incorporate some lowering into the frame and suspension system. This complicates the modifications but does not make them particularly difficult. If the car is a 1934 or older Ford, it will have the spring positioned above the axle. If the car is a 1935 or later Ford the spring is mounted ahead of the axle. If the later model front end is used with the earlier frame, the wheelbase will be shortened approximately five inches. This will work fine with a car without fenders but will require extensive body modifications if the wheels are to clear the fenders.

If the rod builder wishes to install a complete 1940 Ford front-end assembly in a pre-'35 frame in order to take advantage of the hydraulic brakes, it is not a difficult task. The operation consists of welding a ¼-inch plate, properly reinforced with gussets to the top of the front cross member. This plate is centered on the cross member and extends forward five to seven inches. After the welding operation, the plate may be drilled to accept the 1940 U-bolts which secure the spring. The normally high arch of the spring will clear the frame horns if it is in good condition and has not taken a permanent set. This is also a way of using a later model front end while keeping the wheelbase constant.

In cases where it is desired to make the frame very low, some modifications of the standard cross members must be made. Where '32 through '34 Fords are concerned a couple of inches of drop may be accomplished by the substitution of a Model "A" unit for the stock front cross member. If even more drop must be obtained in an "A" or later Ford, it is usually necessary to fabricate a new front cross member.

If the car being reworked has fenders, it will probably be necessary to retain the frame horns. This dictates the limits within which the frame may be dropped, and if more drop is desired, the usual method is to replace the cross member with a new one fabricated from channel-section steel. Here caution must be applied because most radiators are designed to fit the front cross member and any variation in the stock status of the frame must be considered with the radiator in mind. If no hood is to be used or more length in the engine compartment is needed, it is likely that the radiator can be mounted ahead of the front cross member.

If the rod is one of the fenderless variety, the frame horns will not be needed and considerable drop may be achieved by installing a hand-fabricated front cross member. Square or round tubing may be used and an old center section of driveshaft will serve very well. The stock cross member is removed and the front edge of the new member is positioned ¼ to ½ inch behind the rear edge of where the front transverse spring will finally be secured.

The frame horns are cut off and a new spring perch welded in place projecting ahead of the cross member. Before this is done, however, the whole situation should be sized up to determine just where the axle should be in relation to the frame, and the frame to the ground. Above all, it will be wise to check the clearance for the oil pan. Pan clearance of 5 inches is normal.

Spring perches may be built in a number of ways and at any height. The usual procedure is to weld a plate about 4 inches wide and 5 to 8 inches long to the top of the cross member and to reinforce it with substantial bracing. Locating holes for the spring centerbolt and U-bolts finishes the job. If the car is designed for an extreme rake at the front, giving the spring perch a slight upward tilt will facilitate front end alignment when the complete chassis is assembled.

The type of engine and transmission used in a rod will probably dictate the necessity for changes in the frame center cross member. For example, if it is planned to use a Ford '32 transmission in a Model "A" frame, the center cross member must be modified. This can be done by putting a '32 center cross member between the "A" rails. To accomplish this, the '32 cross member must be narrowed slightly and carefully fitted between the side rails before it is welded in place. Ford frames of 1933 vintage and later have an X-type cross member which makes the frame very rigid. The use of this member in other frames is both possible and practical.

If a tubular center cross member is fitted into the frame, it may be routed either above or below the transmission. In some cases it is routed above the transmission to provide a support for the brake and clutch pedals. The simplest method, however, is to route this center member below the transmission.

The rear cross member may be treated much the same as the front. If the floor at the rear of the body is not to be disturbed, then lowering must be accomplished in the spring mounts. One method of dropping a '32 frame is to replace the cross member with an

"A" cross member and spring. There are countless variations of the rear cross member which can be executed by the substitution of other stock parts or the fabrication of new members.

Modifications to the frame side rails includes "C-ing," "Z-ing," "double Z-ing," "stepping," and "boxing." Each of these techniques has evolved over the past years to serve a distinct purpose. C-ing, for example, is not a lowering technique but serves to restore the spring travel that was probably reduced when the suspension was modified to lower the car.

In C-ing, a small section of the frame side rails is removed where the rubber bumpers on the frame contact the rear axle or front suspension components when pushed to the limit of their travel by a bump. The car height is not changed but the increased spring travel distance can eliminate unpleasant and undesirable "bottoming."

If the C is to be performed at the front, a section about 2 inches deep and long enough to clear the upper A frame or other component of the front is cut out of the lower edge of the side rail. The frame may then be beefed up at this point with a reinforcing fish plate.

At the rear the C-ing procedure is similar. The cut in the frame is made semicircular in shape and about 2½ inches deep depending on the depth of the side rail and the amount of spring and axle travel desired or necessary. A piece of ¼-inch steel plate is cut to conform with the shape of the frame section and the C-cut and welded in place to provide reinforcement.

Because of the depth of the frame side rails only a limited amount of C-ing is possible without reducing the strength of the rails to the danger point. C-ing may not provide sufficient clearance for the rear axle and spring travel and in this case "stepping" is a possible solution. In stepping, a box section in the shape of an inverted U is fabricated from steel plate and welded in place over the rear axle area. After the step is welded to the frame the original frame between the legs of the step is cut away.

Z-ing, which is often called "kicking," is a lowering technique
that is usually applied to cars equipped with transverse springs.
It consists of altering the frameside rails so that they are kicked-up
at one or both ends so that the spring perches at the extremities
of the frame are located considerably higher than the central
portion of the frame upon which the body rests.

Z-ing or double Z-ing (when both ends of the frame are reworked) can be accomplished in a number of ways. If only a small
amount of kickup is desired it is entirely possible that diagonal
cuts can be made through the side rails and the short pieces
welded directly to the top of the center section. If the frame
already has a stock kick up at the rear, it is possible to cut
V-notches in the side rails and double them back upon themselves. In still other cases, it may be necessary to add a hand-
fabricated channel or box section to obtain the desired amount of
kickup.

Boxing frames is a relatively simple operation and may be a
highly important one if a heavy, high horsepower engine is used
in a rod. Some of the early model channel section frames lack
the rigidity necessary to stand the stresses imposed by big engines
and torrid competition. Boxing is accomplished by simply welding a light steel plate to the flanges of the channel sections to form
a box section. This will increase the weight of the frame but a
large part of the added weight can be eliminated if the added
metal is liberally punctured with lightening holes. A little common
sense will dictate the size and placement of these holes and if the
lightening job is done judiciously, there will be little sacrifice of
rigidity in the frame members.

Building a tubular space frame for an all-out dragster or other
type of competition car can represent a sizeable chore for the
amateur builder. Fortunately this chore can be circumvented by
purchasing one of the ready-made frames available for dragsters,
altered drag coupes, sprint cars and super-modified track cars.

In order to properly handle basic hot rod chassis building, the enthusiast should learn the techniques of handling a torch and arc welder.

Arc Welding

During the construction process of a rod, the necessity of arc welding one part to another inevitably crops up. Arc welding seems to be some sort of powerful secret weapon wielded by a mystic society of leather clad men found only in tiny, dimly lit buildings set aside for practice of this jealously guarded art.

As defined by the American Welding Society: A weld is made when the separate pieces of metal to be joined combine and form one piece as they are heated to a sufficiently high temperature to cause softening or melting. Pressure may be used to force the pieces together, or filler metal may be added to fill the joints. The melting point of the fill metal must be above 800° F or have approximately the same melting point as the base metal.

Metallic arc welding with the transformer welder is based on the fact that when one side of the welding circuit is attached to the work, which then is brought into contact with an electrode connected to the other side, an arc will be established. When the arc is properly controlled the metal from the electrode will pass through the arc and be deposited on the work. When the electrode is moved along the work at the correct speed, the metal will deposit a uniform layer called a bead. Sufficient temperature is generated by the arc to cause the electrode metal and the parent metal to fuse, resulting in a sound weld.

Electricity flows along an unbroken conductor path called a circuit. When this circuit is broken, the electric current (amperage) ceases to flow unless the electrical pressure (voltage) becomes sufficiently high to jump the gap. When the electricity jumps the gap a momentary "spark" is called an arc. The amount of current and the force of the voltage present determines the length, heat and intensity of the arc. The electric current used for welding may be direct current (DC) or alternating (AC).

Alternating current constantly changes its direction of flow. The alternating current commonly used in this country operates at 60 cycles . . . meaning it goes through a complete cycle of change in direction of flow, from positive to negative and back to positive, 60 times per second.

The exact welding current selected for a job depends upon the size of the pieces to be welded, size and type of electrode and the position of welding. Generally, a lower current will be sufficient for welding on a small part than would be necessary to weld on a large piece of the same thickness. Similarly with a given size of electrode, a lower current should be used on thin metals than on the heavier sections. The figures below give typical examples of how current selection is determined by rod size and welding position.

SELECTION OF ELECTRODES AND WELDER SETTINGS FOR ARC WELDING

	Diameter	$5/64$	$3/32$	$1/8$	$5/32$	$3/16$	$7/32$	$1/4$
	Flat	20–55	20–75	75–130	100–175	150–225	175–250	200–375
AMPS	Vertical	20–55	20–65	75–115	100–150	150–200	....	....
	Overhead	20–55	20–65	75–115	100–150	....	....	....

Striking the AC arc creates a very high temperature at the point of the arc. The arc core develops a temperature of about 8000° F. Under the intense heat developed, a small part of the work to be welded and the tip of the electrode are brought to a molten state. The molten parent metal of the piece to be welded is agitated by the arc flame. This agitation, or puddling action, is caused by the alternating effect of the current as it changes its direction. The alternating or pulsating characteristic of the arc insures that the valuable alloying elements in the electrode covering, the electrode core metal, and the parent metal are evenly distributed. In addition, the pulsating action of the arc tends to send to the surface of the molten pool the nonmetallic slag of low specific gravity. The result is a uniform dense weld which is stronger than the parent metal.

Before attempting to weld on an actual job there are several basic techniques to be mastered. The first step is striking the arc.

To start an arc is really a simple matter. If the electrode is slowly scratched over the metal until the sparks are flying and then gently lifted until the tip of the electrode is about ⅛ inch over the metal, you're under way. During this procedure you should move slowly with no fast motions until you become thoroughly familiar with striking an arc. This action is exactly like striking a match and certainly as easy. Most beginners try to strike the arc by a fast stabbing motion straight down on the metal. The result is usually that the electrode immediately sticks to the metal or withdraw so fast the arc is broken on the upswing. (We must note here that there is another accepted method of striking the arc. Known as the "tapping method," the electrode is brought straight down and immediately upon contact withdrawn to the proper arc length. This method is okay for pro's or for DC welders, but the scratching method is preferred for the beginner.)

If you purchase an AC welder suitable for home shop work (such as those made by Birdsell, Forney, Hobart, Lincoln, Marquette, etc.), you will probably receive a helmet with the welder. You may even get a dark helmet lens, too, but if you don't you can pick one up at the welding supply store. The number of the lens designates how much light it restricts, thus a number 9 passes more light than a 10, etc. You'll probably have to do some experimenting here.

Most arc welders use a ground clamp of some kind and an electrode holder. Most holders are reasonably lightweight and easy to grip. When placing the electrode into the holder, note that notches in the holder jaw allow various positions of the electrode, from 90 through 45 degrees to straight out. If it ever becomes absolutely necessary to have an angle other than one in the holder, then bend the electrode. The 45-degree position seems to be the best for learning. Always hold the holder in the same manner for uniform results, usually with the electrode release near the thumb.

To help quiet those shaking hands when you're first learning, we suggest the feeding procedure taught by Lincoln Electric Company. Place the holder in the right hand (or left, whatever the case may be) and place the closed left hand under the right. The left elbow is then rested on the work or pulled into the left side, whatever is more convenient. Now, guide the electrode with the right hand, use the left hand to feed the electrode into the work.

You should weld from left to right (for right-handed people) whenever possible, since this procedure seems to work best and you can see the work better. The electrode should be slightly tilted in the direction of travel but must be in a 90-degree angle as seen from the end.

Actual determination of the right arc length is rather difficult, as there is no ready means of measuring it, but we may define it as the distance from the tip of the electrode core wire to the base metal. Once you strike the arc, the correct length becomes highly important. This guide for mild steel will help: $\frac{1}{16}$ inch arc length for $\frac{1}{16}$- and $\frac{3}{32}$-inch electrodes, $\frac{1}{8}$ inch arc length for $\frac{1}{8}$- and $\frac{5}{32}$-inch electrodes. The method the author has found best is sound. A good, short arc has a distinctive crackling sound (like bacon frying). An incorrect long arc has a hollow "hissing" or "booing" sound. (A too short arc and you are stuck!) You'll soon learn to tell these sounds apart with practice.

When a short arc is used, the molten globule of metal from the end of the electrode is protected from the atmosphere by the arc flame. A long arc doesn't protect the globule which becomes oxidized en route to the base metal. With a long arc, penetration is less and the weld is spread out on top of the base metal. And, a long arc leaves all kinds of splatter which means much cleaning up afterward. Not to mention all those tiny little hot goodies that tend to find the most crowded places in one's tight-fitting coveralls.

Here is a place where the first one to the finish doesn't always win. The right speed will become apparent to you after a few passes over a piece of flat practice metal. If you're going too fast the bead you've just deposited will be wormy and uneven. It will appear rather flat and in all probability you'll have all sorts of splatter on the plate because the excessive speed is conducive to a long arc. On the other hand, if you are too slow, the final bead will have assumed mammoth proportions. This situation you'll quickly spot, and besides, you use too much rod this way. An excellent definition of the right welding speed is contained in the Lincoln Company's Student Guide: "The important thing to watch while welding is the puddle of molten metal right behind the arc. Do not watch the arc itself. It is the looks of the puddle and the ridge where the molten puddle solidifies that indicate correct welding speed. The ridge should be approximately ⅜ inch behind the electrode."

Usually the beginner tries to go too fast. Welding on thin plate will require welding faster while thick plate means welding slower to get good penetration. If you experience prolonged difficulty in making straight beads or maintaining the proper speed, you might suspect your vision, or perhaps your welding posture.

A good practice for striking the arc, proper arc length and speed may be done by running some beads on a flat place. Run the first bead parallel to the top edge, the second bead parallel to the first, etc. The ninth or tenth bead will look considerably better than the first and you have an easy way to check your progress.

The shortest distance between two points is a straight line, so as a beginner you need not attempt fancy or difficult patterns with your bead. Just go at a steady rate of speed in one direction only. We will mention the weaving method, but caution you to use it only after you are an accomplished welder.

Weaving is used if it sometimes becomes necessary to cover a wider area than normal with but one pass of the electrode. The electrode is moved from side to side in a set pattern. Be sure to use a uniform movement. Weaving is especially helpful when building up metal, but straight passes will achieve the same end. Incidentally, it is easiest to weld in a flat position.

There are numerous electrodes designed for use by arc welders. Since this story is confined to the AC welder, and more specifically the small shop/farm unit, we will consider only certain basic electrodes. Of the mild steel rods around, the most commonly used ones are designated 6013 and 6011 (Lincoln). The 6013 electrode is distinguished by a brown dot while the 6011 electrode has a blue dot marking. These dots are found on the bare end of the rod. Of the two, 6011 seems to be the better for general rodding use.

The 6013 (brown dot) electrode is almost universally used because of the beauty of the bead. But it does not handle dirty material well, it leaves a large amount of slag, and its penetration is less than 6011.

The 6011 (blue dot) has the characteristic of not leaving a large amount of slag, is easy to weld with because of this. It has strong, deep penetration, is excellent on dirty material, is excellent for overhead and vertical welding, and it costs less than other types. Actually, it is hard to make a bad weld job with 6011.

The electrode size most commonly used around the garage is ⅛ inch. The average setting for ⅛-inch rod and a limited input (shop type) welder (using blue dot rod) is 100 amps. Naturally, thinner material means less amperage, thicker material means more amperage. Variance in electrode size will also affect the amperage setting.

There are five basic types of welded joints common to hot rodding: butt welds, fillet welds, lap welds, edge welds, and corner welds. Virtually everything that is welded on a car will fall into these categories. Of the aforementioned five welds, the butt and the fillet welds are the two most common.

The most widely used weld is the butt type. It occurs when two pieces of material of the same thickness, or different thickness, are set together and welded. Generally speaking, a space one-half the thickness of the metal should be left between the two pieces. This space provides room for necessary weld penetration and possible parent metal expansion. If you don't leave space, be sure you have a big hammer and strong arm to straighten the metal when you're through. That is, if you have enough penetration to keep the metal together while you pound. When you're joining metal you would do well to place a small tack at each end of the intended weld area to keep the metal from "crawling." If the material you are welding is quite thick, you should bevel the joint on one or both sides. On butt welds, unless a weld penetrates close to 100 percent, the weld will be weaker than the material welded together.

The first thing about fillet welds is that no space is needed between the two metals being joined. A fillet weld is a bead of metal of triangular cross section positioned in the corner of two surfaces at right angles to each other. The fillet may be large or small depending on the requirements of the job and/or the size of the pieces being joined. In making the fillet, the weld deposit should be equally divided between the two metals being joined. It is important, especially for the beginner, that the electrode intersect the weld area at a 45-degree angle to the two pieces being welded, otherwise the metal will not distribute itself evenly. If the weld metal tends to be built up on the lower piece of metal, chances are the electrode is being pointed too much that way. The same goes for the vertical piece of metal. A fillet weld usually requires the beginner to go a bit slower than butt welding.

A lap weld is made by joining two pieces of metal with one piece lapped over the other. A fillet weld mates the edge of one piece and the face of the other. This type of joint normally requires two fillets so that the overlapping pieces are joined on both sides.

Edge welds and corner welds are not difficult to do and usually demand a power setting and procedure similar to butt welds. Penetration on the edge weld will be near the same as the corner weld, and the use of proper electrodes will mean a strong connection.

A weld in the vertical position may be done either in an up or down direction. Vertical up is used whenever a strong, dependable weld is desired. Vertical down is used primarily on sheet metal for fast, nonpenetrating welds.

The problem that arises when welding in the up direction is to put the molten metal where it is wanted, and make it stay there. If too much molten weld metal is deposited, gravity will pull it downward and make it drip. Usually in your pants cuff. Therefore, a certain technique should be followed. A fast freezing electrode (such as blue dot 6011) should be used and placed in the holder so that it sticks straight out. When welding, the electrode should be kept horizontal or pointing slightly upwards. Strike the arc and put some weld metal at the bottom of the pieces being welded. The arc is slowly moved from 3 to 4 inches upwards before too much molten metal is deposited where you started. This takes the heat away from the molten puddle, allowing it to solidify. If the arc isn't moved slowly away soon enough, you've got lots of molten metal trying to drip in your shoes. This upward motion of the arc is done by a very slight wrist motion, not by moving the arm in and out. Moving the arm makes vertical up welding complicated and hard to learn. If the upward motion of the arc is done correctly with a wrist motion, the arc will automatically become longer, thus depositing no metal. During this process, watch the molten metal. As soon as it solidifies, slowly bring the arc back and add a few more drops of metal. This entire process consists of slow, deliberate movements. There are other methods of vertical up welding, but this one seems best for learners.

There are various techniques for applying an overhead weld, but in the interest of simplicity for the nonprofessional welder the following method is recommended. Use blue dot rod in your holder as for vertical welding. Hold the electrode in an angle approximately 30 degrees off vertical as seen from both the end and the side. As you have already found out if you've ever done any overhead welding with an arc, the most important thing is to hold a very short arc. Long arcs result in a bad case of the "dribbles" with accompanying personal discomfort to the welder. If it is necessary, a slight back and forth motion with the electrode will help prevent dripping.

The horizontal weld is one that is quite common to rodding, especially when repairs "in the pits," etc., are being made. Only one type of joint truly falls in this category and that is the butt weld between two pieces of metal in a vertical plane. The horizontal weld is accomplished by moving in a straight line along the joint. A pattern is not recommended when making this kind of weld. Horizontal butt joints on sheet metal up to $\frac{1}{16}$ inch thick may be made from one side only. If the seam has numerous gaps, use a back-up strip. All metal over $\frac{3}{16}$ inch thick should be beveled and welded with several passes.

Gas Welding

A major tool for the home workshop therefore is the torch. You can get most everything you need for around $75–$100. The equipment includes welding blowpipe and tips, oxygen and acetylene regulators, hoses, friction lighter, goggles, and combination spanner wrench for the various fittings. In addition, you'll need a pair of pressurized cylinders of oxygen and acetylene; these cost an average of $80 for the pair, outright, but may be refilled for about $4 each. Some welding supply outfits will lease the cylinders for a flat rate which includes refilling.

Although there are some welding jobs on cars that should be handled with electric arc welding equipment a comparison with the versatility of the gas method makes this type of equipment an excellent choice in most cases. With an oxy-acetylene torch, welding, brazing, and cutting may be done with the same torch, merely by changing nozzles and certain valve controls. Welding is joining two metals together by heating them to the melting point, meanwhile adding more of the same metal (in the form of welding rod) to fill up any gaps caused by irregularities in their surface preventing full contact. Given full contact, the addition of rod may be omitted in true welding. This is the big difference between welding and brazing—brazing requires the rod used to join the two metals.

In order to successfully weld two metals together, they must have similar melting points—that is, when heated together they must reach the molten state almost simultaneously, otherwise one piece will get too hot and start to burn away from the torch before the other is hot enough to form a good bond between the two. In brazing, the melting point of the rod used is the consideration governing the heat of torch, so that it is possible to unite two metals of widely differing melting points through this method. In some cases, therefore, brazing is not only superior to welding, but actually the only way. Another nice feature concerning brazing is that a smaller amount of heat to unite the two metal pieces can be applied because of the use of the rod, thus decreasing the chances of causing warpage. This can avoid many hours of working out ripples and waves in body panels which have been buckled by excessive heat. In addition, the bead left by brazing is softer and easier to file smooth, since the metals used in brazing rod are softer than those in welding rod.

But the big thing to learn in gas welding is how to properly light the torch and regulate its flame. For practice, try joining together two pieces of steel in a simple butt joint, with the two straight edges of the pieces facing each other, not beveled or overlapping.

Light up your torch and then take it in your writing hand. Hold it naturally, not tightly as in a death grip. Now tilt the tip of the torch in the direction you're going to weld; if you're right-handed that will be toward the left. For left-handers the opposite will apply.

Apply the flame to the metal to be welded only after tuning it in. When the flame actually comes into contact with the metal, watch the surface closely. As the temperature goes up, you will find the metal surface will begin to glow. As it gets hotter, the surface will start to glisten, almost as if it were wet. This indicates it is about to melt. Watch closely now as the melting state is reached and a small puddle of molten metal is formed. Bring the welding rod in your other hand into play. Be careful not to just hold the rod in the flame and drip it over everything; this is a sign of a real novice and results in an unsafe weld. Instead, insert the tip of the rod right into the puddle where the flame is playing. You'll see the rod deposit a ball of metal into the puddle—now direct this ball by moving the torch through a small segment of an arc, using your elbow as a pivot point. As you move along the seam, add more rod as necessary to keep the bead going.

When you've mastered the straight-seam butt, try welding pieces together at angles. This gives the same effect as beveling edges on a butt weld and provides better penetration, especially when you work from "inside" the angle. When you achieve the kind of bead that is straight, consistent in width and radius, start concentrating on "penetration," because that's what makes the difference between a weld that will break and one that won't. When your welding looks consistent throughout the seam and penetration is uniform, you're ready to do some actual welding work on your car. But tackle little jobs first; if you move too quickly into major welding projects before you master the hang of it, you're headed for real trouble.

For instance, proper penetration depends more upon heat control than any other factor. Should the metal be too cool, penetration will be poor. If this is the case, try holding the torch a little closer. Too much heat, on the other hand, will cause "burning through." Hold the torch farther from the work. Only experimentation and practice can teach you everything you need to know in the art of torch welding.

After you have mastered the techniques of handling the torch and making the proper oxygen and acetylene adjustments on your controls for true welding, you are ready to learn welding with the use of flux, or the brazing method of welding two metals together.

Generally, a lower torch heat is required for the bonding of metal using the brazing method, reducing the possibility of warpage problems which are especially prevalent in such welding projects as hood panels, rear decks, and large flat areas of metal surfaces. In brazing, you don't actually melt the two pieces of metal to be joined; you merely get them hot and the bonding is accomplished by the brazing flux and the third metal, the brazing rod.

You use a smaller tip on your torch to keep the heat down where you want it. Brazing requires that the metal to be worked on be absolutely clean—not just clean in appearance, but chemically so. Unless this is done first, the brazing rod will not stick to the surface, but instead merely run off. Proper handling of the rod, flux, and control of relative temperatures is the knack of brazing—one that you can soon master with a little practice.

Heat the brazing rod and dip it into the flux. If the rod heating is the right temperature, you will pick up just the right amount of flux. Then, in order to effect proper bond, both the rod and work surface must be heated at the same time. Even, equal heating of both rod and surface insures easy flowing of rod in the opening between the two metals to be joined. After brazing the metal, you should have a bead built up between the two surfaces or in the hole area, if this is what you are doing.

Torch cutting of metal requires still another technique. Metal in thicknesses of ⅛ inch and greater are cut with the torch. All you have to do is to change to a cutting tip—the torch, or blowpipe, has a button beneath the handle which administers straight oxygen to the work on demand. With some outfits, a separate cutting attachment is usually required. It consists of a different blowpipe which incorporates an additional oxygen passage. Straight oxygen is administered by a regulator lever, or control, when required. Connection of the cutting attachment to your tanks and regulators is similar as with the ordinary welding blowpipe.

Before you begin, you should select the correct size cutting tip for the thicknesses of metal which this particular torch is capable of handling. Install this tip in place instead of your welding tip, light up the torch, and "tune in" the flame for cutting. This is done by setting the acetylene gauge at about 15 pounds pressure, and the oxygen control at approximately 35 pounds pressure. As you see, greater pressure is required for cutting with the torch than when you do torch welding or brazing. Actually, the cutting torch eats the metal away through oxidation. A steady stream of oxygen is on tap for doing the actual cutting, but first the metal must be heated to its kindling point by acetylene gas.

In performing the cut, you play the flame along the path you want the cut to follow. This is the preheating procedure. When the area to be cut glows bright red, the metal has reached its kindling temperature. You then press the oxygen control that administers the oxygen "needle." You're now beginning the cut, unless you've misjudged the temperature of the metal and it isn't hot enough yet.

If the pure oxygen added to the flame does the job at the start, move the torch along the path you want the cut to follow, keeping the preheating process going alternately and not traveling too fast to allow the metal to reach kindling temperature all the way along. Be sure to wear gloves while cutting as your hands will be close to the red hot metal at all times during the operation. When the metal is cool enough, check the edges of the cut. If beads have raised up along the edges, you have used more than enough preheat. A clean cut indicates preheat technique was correct.

7

Suspension Systems and Brakes

Suspension Systems

There is often some confusion as to what constitutes an automobile chassis and what makes up the suspension system. In hot rodding, the enthusiast considers the basic framework as chassis and all those pieces that support and control the front and rear end as suspension. Essentially, then, suspension means the springs, shock absorbers, and control members that connect wheels to frame.

Not much thought is given springs and hangers when a hot rod is being built, which is unfortunate, because nothing so affects the way a car rides and handles. A hot rodder can't be expected to approach springing as would an automotive engineer, but many problems must be understood to get maximum results from any building effort.

With a few rare exceptions where air or oil or other fluids are used as substitutes in a suspension system, springs may be divided into three categories: leaf springs, coil springs, and torsion

170

bars. Leaf springs consist of a stack of long, narrow, and relatively thin steel strips of spring steel which have unequal lengths. The individual "leaves" have no "arch" formed into them and the spring action is derived from the arch and the sliding contact between the leaves. The leaf spring reacts to a wide range of compression and rebound factors because of the different degrees of resiliency imparted to the spring by the various lengths and stiffness of its various leaves.

The mounting of leaf springs in a suspension system has taken many forms in the past. These mountings have been described as the quarter, semi, three-quarter, and full elliptic systems. The full elliptic and three-quarter elliptic springs have long disappeared as automotive components. The full elliptic consisted of two semi elliptics pivoted together at the ends of their longest leaves. The upper semi-elliptic section arched upward toward the frame where it was anchored and the lower section arched downward, where it was secured to the frame. The quarter elliptics are simply one half of a semi elliptic. Quarter elliptics are still used in a few suspension systems but not in conjunction with semi elliptics.

Leaf springs are mounted either transversely or longitudinally to the frame. In the case of a transverse mounting, a shackle is necessary at both ends where the spring is secured to the axle. As any leaf spring is compressed, its overall length is increased and this lateral movement of the spring is given freedom by the shackles. In a transverse system, the springs cannot hold the axles in the necessary perpendicular alignment to the frame and radius rods are necessary. Radius rods at the front run from the frame to the axle and are pivoted in such a manner as to permit up and down movement while canceling out any fore and aft movement of the axle. At the rear the function of the radius rods is similar, however, they also serve to transmit the driving force from the rear axle and wheels to the frame.

Semi-elliptic springs when used in a longitudinally mounted

suspension system have shackles at their rear anchor points. Front ends of the pairs of springs are secured to the frame and hold the axles in alignment. At the rear, this type of mounting also allows power to be transmitted from the rear axle to the frame through the front half of the rear springs.

Coil springs came into prominence in the automotive field with the advent of both front and rear independent wheel suspension systems. The methods used to incorporate coil springs into a suspension system are varied. However, the basic design elements are similar to those encountered in a transverse leaf spring system—keeping the wheels in alignment and transmitting power from the rear axle to the frame.

The torsion bar, which is really just a straight coil, is not a product of the atomic age. The ability of a piece of material to twist and return to original shape has been recognized for decades. (Even a wooden 2X4 will act as a torsion bar to some extent.) It wasn't until 1934, though, that this property of steel was utilized for automotive springing. In that year, Citroën of France pioneered the torsion bar in a production car. The next major development was by Dr. Porsche, when he adopted torsion suspension to his awesome Auto Union racers of the late 1930s. Mercedes and BMW also introduced torsion bars prior to World War II, and the majority of modern European-built automobiles use this type of springing in some form. The system remained relatively obscure in the United States until the mid-1950s. The ill-fated Packard incorporated a self-leveling, full torsion bar system just before the marque fell. The big change came in 1957 when Chrysler announced torsion springing for the front ends of their complete car line. Naturally, the company had to embark on quite a public education campaign, as distrust of that "skinny little steel rod" was widespread. The success of the system is now well established.

American racing cars have used torsion bars for many years,

but not until the Indianapolis 500 Kurtis roadsters did the system gain widespread popularity. Weight reduction and increased wheel control soon led to their use on practically every form of American race car, from midget to Bonneville streamliner. Even karts have used the arrangement.

In hot rodding, always try to use a "scrounged" torsion system in a situation similar to the original. That means a bar originally used on a 2000-pound car with near 50-50 weight distribution should only be used on another vehicle with approximate values. As an example, the bars from a Dodge Dart GT—1700 pounds on the front end—would be a good starting point on a '50 Ford or '37 Chevy. They would not be so good on a lightweight aluminum-engined fiberglass street roadster.

Size and operation of a torsion bar is always important. Usually, the torsion system used on a passenger car has long bars, while a race car will have a shorter overall length. This is the result of space and stress limitations. The longer the bar of a given diameter, the easier it will twist with a given length operating lever. In application, it works like this.

If a bar is 20 inches long and one inch in diameter, the longer the operating lever the easier it is to twist the bar. However, the energy within the bar itself remains the same no matter how long the operating lever. A major problem in making the system fit a car is the available room for the operating lever and the available travel at the end of such a lever.

Actual practice usually calls for a lever from 10 to 15 inches long, so how much springiness you have (spring rate) will probably be determined by bar length and diameter. This is a basic assumption, since a highly sophisticated suspension will normally require less spring rate than a more conventional counterpart.

For example, a street roadster weighs in at just under 1500 pounds street ready. On this car, the original front torsion bars are 36 inches long, have a ⅞-inch diameter, and use an 8-inch-long lever. At the back, they are 42 inches long, but of the same diameter and lever length. Early testing revealed the overall handling excellent but the ride was too harsh. Subsequent tests proved that bars cut down to ¾-inch diameter maintained the handling qualities, but passenger comfort was increased considerably. Care must be taken in decreasing the diameter of a torsion bar, since the strength of the bar will also be decreased. It will take less force to permanently twist the bar to a new shape.

For a typical Chevrolet 283-powered '32 Ford, weight ranges about 2200 pounds equally distributed. Chrysler Corporation bars would have to be turned down in diameter (a risky business, since they are shotpeened and preset), but Morris Minor bars would work very well. So would Jowett, Mercedes Benz, Datsun, and Jaguar, to mention a few foreign cars using acceptable torsion bars.

The Volkswagen/Porsche suspensions, both front and rear, can be adapted to virtually any car with similar total weights. Cars slightly heavier can utilize the VW bus suspension. Use of the VW components, however, should be restricted by weight—don't exceed the original weight (modification of the components for a lighter car is okay). In some cases, slight additional weight has been successfully compensated for by adding overload coil spring/shocks.

Usually, the torsion bar itself is a snap compared to the headaches of mounting. This shouldn't really be the problem it is made into, but if the original mountings cannot be duplicated some ingenious ideas are in order. For instance, the Morris Minor bars are adaptable to most all forms of lighter homemade cars. What was originally the rear-end adjustment lever often becomes the primary operating lever. The main part of the bar is a smaller diameter than either end, requiring some kind of split bushing support.

A solid axle, such as on the front of pre-'49 Fords and the rear of most vehicles, is the most difficult to hook up. On an independent front suspension, such as the Chrysler, the front torsion bar is located on the inside pivot point for the lower control arm. If your car uses independent suspension anywhere, the bars can be designed to work in much the same way.

On a beam front axle, it's all a matter of dissimilar arcs. If the spring from an early Ford is removed, the axle is free to move up and down and sideways, but not fore and aft. The long radius rods from the axle to the frame maintain wheel alignment. If the radius rods are 30 inches long, and a parallel connecting arm is only 10 inches long, the arcs swung by the axle ends of each rod are not nearly the same. If the axle is so located, up and down movement will be drastically limited.

The same holds true if operating levers run across the chassis parallel with the axle. If the ends are connected directly to the axle, the arcs normally made by the lever ends would bind the axle. The answer is shackles, since the long radius arms take care of any fore/aft movement. If the torsion bars run across the chassis and the operating arms either lead or trail to the axle, small shackles and a good track bar must be used. If the bars are run parallel to the side frame rails, shackles and shocks mounted at a slight angle will not suffice.

At the rear end the same thing applies, with complexity depending on application. Closed drive rear ends require shackle connections, as do most applications where some kind of long torque rod is used. Shackles are absolutely necessary if the operating arms run parallel to the axle housing. On installations where the bars run cross chassis, the operating arm end may be bolted directly to the axle housing with no shackle, provided a parallel housing locator arm is used. If the operating lever extends forward and connects to the top of the housing, the locator (torque rod) arm should connect a like distance below the housing and may run forward or aft to a frame mount. In this way, the rear end is free to move up and down with no bind. Heavier cars (over 1800 pounds) using levers of less than ⅝-inch thickness will also need track bars. Actually the anti-sway track bar device is recommended for all occasions.

There should be some kind of provision for bar adjustment after the car is on the road. On Chrysler products equipped with torsion bars, this adjustment is via a bolt and lever. If the front of the car begins to sag, the bolt is turned against a static plate, moving the short adjustment arm and putting more tension on the bar. Bars made for racing use a similar adjustment device. Others clamp solidly at the rear and use a splined bar/lever mating at the front. By removing the lever and moving the desired number of splines, bar tension is increased or decreased.

The bars must be clean and free of all nicks or scratches. Imperfections in the metal can lead to a fatigue crack, so carefully smooth off all burrs with a file. It is common race car practice to wrap the bars with plastic tape, giving a form of protection against kicked-up rocks. If the car is subjected to severe use, such as track or strip racing, all parts of the system should receive periodic magnaflux inspection.

Springs have a marked effect on roadholding, to say the least, largely due to their relative "stiffness." This is precisely why the first-time hot rod builder may create a bone-crushing monster rather than a silk-smooth jewel. Spring rates should be as soft as possible without reaching their bump stops or excessively decreasing roll resistance. The basic aim of springs is to keep the wheels on the ground as much as possible (extremely important to racing cars), while allowing each wheel to rise on surface bumps with the least amount of bump effect transferred to the car. In theory, spring systems can only be perfect on a smooth road.

If a car hits a two-inch bump, the springs will compress by two inches at time of impact. Immediately following this jar, the springs will recover, or bounce back, from the compression. If the car does not have shocks, this recovery will far exceed the compression distance of two inches. With shocks, the recovery is not so pronounced, but it still is greater than two inches. The springs, therefore, actually magnify road irregularities.

However, if the car did not have any springs at all, the reaction of the car would be instantaneous when a bump is hit. The spine bone would immediately receive an acceleration of several G's, making a wild bronc ride seem tame by comparison. The spring, then, acts as a cushion; along with the tires and upholstery padding.

If a car of specific weight hits a bump at the same speed and angle time after time, the spring reaction should always be identical. If there were no dampening effect, or shock absorbers, the springs would oscillate at the same general rate. That is, the springs would want to continue to compress and recover for quite some distance after the bump had been hit. Controlling this oscillation is the biggest problem of engineers and, to some extent, hot rodders. It is desirable to have "soft" springs, which means a low frequency or low rate. The spring rate is the load in pounds required to give a deflection of one inch.

An initial deflection of more than six inches is not normally possible. With this amount of deflection there would have to be at least six inches between the spring stops, or the limit of up/down spring travel. Such a great distance is not available in hot rods. A travel of around five inches is more common. But with the six-inch deflection, our two-inch bump would have an acceleration factor of about one-third gravity (with a spring rate of 77). The passenger would hardly feel the bump with this figure. A softer spring would create too spongy a situation for good handling. A stiffer spring would aggravate the bump effect. Working out a compromise is the hot rodder's dilemma.

Keep in mind also that dips in the road will have a direct effect on the springs. For instance, if the spring is compressed three inches due to the car weight, and maximum down travel is only four inches, then four inches is all you have to work with. Suppose you go sailing down the road and hit a quick dip. If the dip is sharp enough and deep enough, it is possible for the wheel to sail off the lip and hit with a thud on the far side. Hardly conducive to good riding. This is an oversimplification, but enough to start one thinking.

In general applications, the hot rodder works with all three basic automotive springs: leaf, coil, and torsion. The leaf spring is by far the most common, because it is the simplest. It is conceivable that within twenty years, however, both the coil and torsion bar will have replaced it. Such a trend is already well under way in hot rodding, with coils fast replacing the transverse Ford type leaf.

A leaf spring as applied to a hot rod needs considerable modification for maximum performance. For instance, the typical rod chassis of 2X4-inch tubing will retain an early Ford front and rear spring. Assuming the car has a Chevy V8 engine and fiberglass T body, weight will be about evenly divided between front and rear wheels and total nearly 2000 pounds.

This is roughly how the Model A stacked up, too. But the difference is in vehicle performance. The A-bone chugged along at 50 mph over dirt roads, with handling and ride purely coincidental to transportation. It would seem that forty years after the Model A, such considerations would rate more importance. A road racing car does not have to ride harshly to go fast or handle well. For example, consider the small rear-engined car versus the old Indianapolis roadster. You thrashed the roadster around the brickyard, you drive the new cars. Quite a difference.

If the stock Model A springs are utilized with the hypothetical rod, then the best possible springing is not being achieved. Some modification is necessary. The small leaves are the very backbone of a leaf spring, and contribute much to the stiffness. The effective radius of action of a leaf spring, in locating the axle, is three quarters of the half length of the spring. As the spring leaves are stacked, increasing the travel at the spring end will compound the resistance (or "spring"). One spring leaf (such as on the Chevy II) will travel over quite a distance. Two leaves together, one shorter than the other, will start the travel softly but gradually get stiffer, etc.

To soften the Model A springs, remove some of the spring leaves (there is no hard and fast rule that tells just how many). As a general rule, a rod with 1000 to 1300 pounds on the front end, and with a typical Ford-type suspension, can have the 1928–1934 spring so modified. Remove the third, fifth, and top leaves. This will soften the ride considerably. The 1935–1948 springs may lose their third and fifth leaves only, since the spring length is longer.

At the rear, there is more work. With the high-arch Model A spring, remove leaves 2, 4, and 6. With the flatter springs, remove leaves 3 and 5.

Friction between leaves is a great thief of handling and ride in leaf springs, and this is bound to be present in older springs. Special rubber tip glides are available, but since these hardly look sanitary on a nonfendered rod, builders usually discard them. The next best thing is lubrication.

The spring should be completely disassembled and each leaf cleaned of all rust. If small depressions are worn in a leaf (where the leave tip above has rested), the depressions should be feathered out with a grinder. If the depressions are more than $\frac{1}{16}$ inch deep, replace the leaf. After each leaf is cleaned, the spring may be reassembled with good grease between each leaf. To keep the grease in place, strips of screen wire between the leaves will work, then wrap the spring with plastic tape. Often the difference between a stiff and limber spring is merely rust buildup and binding.

As a general rule in rod building, use the longest, flattest transverse (cross chassis) spring possible. This is often difficult at the front end because of spring mountings, but if a special tubular axle is used, provision can be made to incorporate the long 1935–1948 springs.

The coil spring is ideal for hot rod use, particularly at the rear, but causes no end to problems if improperly located. Ideally, the coil should be mounted as near the wheel as possible, so that the spring works to a greater degree with each inch of wheel movement. However, some rodders have mounted the coils well inboard on the dead axles, thereby reducing this spring movement and effectively reducing both ride and handling characteristics.

The type of coil spring utilized usually depends on availability. Nothing wrong with this, although there are spring manufacturers in the larger cities who can wind a coil to exact specifications. With a hot rod, there are normally limiting factors of available space, load requirements, and appearance. The latter usually receives the most importance. It has been found through experience that Corvair front springs work well at the rear of a typical 2000-pound hot rod. With lightweight engines, such as the Chevy and small Ford, these same coils work well at the front also. With heavier engines, the rear Corvair coils are better. In selecting coils, find a spring that will work within the space limitations and which was designed for a car with similar weight characteristics.

Coil/shocks, or the spring system utilizing a coil spring wrapped around a shock absorber, are fast finding favor because of their simplicity. However, except for Monroe, few American-made units are acceptable for hot rod use. The best bet with this design is to create your own combination by using overload designs and having special springs wound. This is mostly a trial and error situation, unfortunately; but the individual springs only run around nine dollars each, so the cost isn't prohibitive.

How the springs are mounted is very important to both handling and ride. The length and angle of the shackles should be near stock length, or about 3 inches long. The angle should also be nearly normal, roughly 45 degrees, angling outward from spring eye to perch.

Axles and A-Arms

In the search for front end systems applicable to hot rod design and construction, only two designs are finding widespread use; the solid axle and the trailing link systems. There are two types of solid axle. The Elliot axle is the standard beam unit used in many older cars and some present-day heavy-duty vehicles. It is a beam or solid axle having each end opened to form a squared-off C. The steering knuckles fit into the C and are positioned by kingpins. The type of solid axle most familiar to rodders is the Reverse Elliot. This features steering knuckles with yokes that fit the axle ends. The pre-'49 Ford axles were Reverse Elliot types. There are no appreciable differences in values or performances between the two types.

The most common axle found in hot rodding is the solid-beam type. The term solid-beam is used here to differentiate between tubular and beam units. The original-equipment axles found on early Fords are beam, except for a very few tubular units produced for V8-60 equipped cars in the late '30s. The very simplicity of the Ford chassis has made it a rodding favorite for years. Simplicity also accounts for the widespread use of Ford solid axle front ends. They are inexpensive, easy to modify, and parts are readily available.

Since most special straight tube and lightweight tube axles are manufactured solely for competition use, the street axle chosen will be of some standard automotive make. If the car in question happens to be a 1934 or older Ford, then an axle having the spring mounted directly above will probably be necessary. If this is the case, there are several approaches to use. If the car is to be restored, the original front end will probably be sufficient. If it is a rod with an accompanying heavier engine and hydraulic brakes, several changes are in order. If the car is a Model "A," but a very slight drop is desired along with a huskier axle, use a 1932–1934 Ford unit. If the car is any Ford up to the year 1935 and a major front end drop is desirable, special dropped axles are available from speed shops. A dropped axle has had that portion of the axle between the ends and the spring perch bolts reshaped to allow the spindles to ride higher than normal. Drops of 2½ and 3½ inches are common.

Dropped axles are also available for 1935 through 1948 Ford products. These axles feature spring perch bolts located a bit farther toward the ends of the axle than the pre-'35 units. This means that a more severe bend (or S shape) must be put in the axle ends to attain a drop common with the earlier axles. The tighter bend usually means that some portion of the spindle steering arm will hit the axle. The only solution here is to heat and reshape the steering arms on both spindles until they do not have such a lazy bend toward the rear. By heating and bending them in nearly flush against the backing plate, they will clear the axle. Be sure and align the arms properly after they are modified, or you may run into some steering problems. It is not advisable to cut and weld any portion of the front end. That is for real professionals who know their business.

If you want hydraulic brakes on early Fords, the same procedure applies whether you use a dropped axle or not. Ford did not put hydraulics on their cars until 1939. Everything up until that time had mechanical brakes—that is, the means of placing the brake shoe into contact with the drum was by mechanical linkage from the brake pedal to the brake shoe.

If you have a Ford front end that you want to use (one with mechanical brakes) and you want to install hydraulics but don't know what year the front end is, follow this pattern. If the spring is ahead of the axle, it is for a Ford '35 through '38. If you use this type of unit, the backing plates and drums from a '39 through '48 Ford should fit directly on the spindles. If the spring is above the axle, then you will probably have to purchase a special hydraulic brake installation kit from a speed emporium. Fitting hydraulics on the Model "A" axle (where you want to retain the Model "A" spindles) will mean the use of spacer rings between the new backing plates and the place where their counterparts formerly mounted. That is, the large center locating hole in hydraulic backing plates is larger than those in mechanical units, thus the spacers. The backing plate mounting holes won't align, so a little enlarging with a rat-tail file is in order. To use the later hydraulic-type brake drums, a small sleeve must be slipped on the spindle bolt to locate the wheel hub's inner bearing.

The easiest and possibly best way to get hydraulic brakes on the older Fords is to use the entire spindle setup from post-'39 Fords. Incidentally, it has been noted that many rodders have been mounting the spindle thrust bearing incorrectly. This is a round bearing that fits between the bottom of the spindle and the axle. The kingpin locates it. This is there so that steering isn't such a bind in troublesome spots. But some rodders, especially on dropped axle installations, have moved this bearing to a position between the top of the axle and the top spindle yoke. Here, it does nothing more than take up space, although it does give a bit more drop to the front end.

If '39 or later spindles have been used up front, there is no steering arm on the left front wheel to connect to the drag link. You can make such a unit simply, but for a very minor cost you can purchase one from the speed shop.

If you want to split and remount the radius rods (wishbone) on the front end, it is quite simple to do. Cut the solid C-shaped connection from the wishbone at the rear and swing the ends out to the frame. Weld the rod fittings into the ends, making both rods of equal length. Determine the height of the previous frame mounting from the ground, and construct new plates of sheet steel to either bolt or weld to the frame. These plates should be at least ¼ inch thick. They are located on the frame at the ends of the radius rods. Holes for the tapered tie rod ends are then drilled in the plates, the holes being the same height from the ground as the original mounting. Tie rod ends are then screwed in the radius rods and bolted to the new frame mounting plates. In some instances, holes may be drilled directly into the frame, no plate being needed. Remember that the caster of the front end is affected by the location of the ends of the radius rods. Close to the ground is lots of caster, higher up is less, etc.

Many of the dropped axles have the outer ends, or dropped section, filled and smoothed. That is, the ends look flat quite, unlike an "I" beam. Dropped tubular axles are rather common. Usually these are items from the aforementioned Ford V8-60 cars or trucks that have had the ends heated and dropped as with "I" beam axles. Because of construction problems, these axles are dropped less than the beams. In some rare cases, rodders have built special tubular axles with drops that look like the original. Mostly, however, handmade tube axles are either straight or incorporate a straight angle at the ends for the drop, rather than a tight S shape. Such axles are most prominent on drag cars.

If you have a tubular or beam axle and wish to mount it ahead of the spring, follow this procedure. Get the complete wishbone setup from a 1935 or later Ford. These front ends mount the spring ahead of the axle, the spring perches being incorporated into the front ends of the wishbone. Saw the wishbone off just behind the place where it bolts to the axle (about 3 inches). Turn the two stubs around, switch sides and bolt them to your axle. The spring perches, or we might call them hangers, are now behind the axle. Fill and smooth the cut-off ends, which now stick out front.

If you're looking for a really kookie tube front axle, you might consider a used one from a Chrysler product of the very late 1930s. These axles have semi-elliptic springs and a good drop at the ends. They also have a flat forward bend in the middle that is of little consequence on a rod other than in appearance. Ream the ends of this axle for the Ford spindles and kingpins if you want to, or use the hydraulic brakes and hubs from later Chrysler products. Get some spring perch bolts from a '34 or older Ford, and locate and weld them onto the axle. That's it. An unusual axle, especially for a show/street rod, and they are really easy to find.

Shock Absorbers

Selection of shock absorbers for hot rods is a pick and try proposition, since no company makes such specific units. They could not, and be successful, since every hot rod is different. The builder must content himself with selecting a shock that will do the job, and then mount it correctly.

There are three basic types of shock absorbers used in hot rodding: the pure friction unit, which has an arm compressed against a piece of leather, used primarily for drag vehicles; the Houdaille, which is a lever and piston arrangement common to 1948 and older Fords; and the direct acting piston shock, or tubular "airplane" design common on all modern cars.

Most hot rodders prefer the tubular shock, since it can be mounted in a minimum space and is inexpensive. This type of shock must have the lower end mounted as near the wheel as possible to get maximum travel on the shock piston. It should be mounted vertically for best shock control, but it is usually mounted to angle inward at the top, which gives away control.

When selecting any shock absorber, use a unit from a car of similar weight (overall, as well as distribution front and rear) as that of the intended hot rod. Since most metal-bodied rods weigh between 2000 and 2800 pounds, something from a Corvair, Falcon,

Datsun, etc., would be applicable. Fiberglass bodied cars are lighter, so shocks from a Volkswagen, Saburu, or similar light-weight cars would be good swaps.

Brakes

The advent of the early motor cars necessitated positive means of bringing them to a halt after their earth-shattering, 12-mph charges.

Those early braking systems were extremely rudimentary. Most featured a kind of external contracting design that employed bands made of cast iron, wire rope, hemp, leather, elm or cotton belting to produce the needed friction. Means of transmitting the driver's command began as a simple lever which slowly evolved into a rather complex series of rods, shafts, cams, and pivot points that required constant adjustment to ensure even the lowest level of braking performance. As time went on, the problem of stopping the ever faster and heavier automobiles eventually led to the demise of external contracting brakes and a switch to the more powerful internal expanding shoe-to-drum designs.

Further refinements incorporated the use of new linings made of woven asbestos impregnated with bits of metal, and a gradual switch to a four-wheel braking system brought on by various racing experiences.

The Roaring Twenties saw the first U.S.-built passenger car equipped with hydraulic brakes—an honor falling to the mighty Dusenberg. Most brakes during this period still depended upon mechanical linkage to synchronize and transmit the urge from the driver to the brake. Because women had arrived on the motoring scene, something had to be done to help them yank on the brakes. Because they couldn't muster the necessary pull or push those old brakes needed, there began a drift toward a sort of self-energized type of drum brake.

By the '30s, the era of the mechanical brake was drawing to a close, as the industry swung toward hydraulics. The years of World War II brought about many automotive innovations, with a revolution in the technology of brakes and linings just a matter of course. Big, heavy trucks, high-speed aircraft and lumbering armor—operating in some of the most forsaken spots under incredibly poor conditions—demanded and got brakes that could and would perform well anywhere in the world.

After the war the ever-increasing trend to lower and lower automotive silhouettes put the drum brake and its designers to even more of a test. The need for better and more consistent stopping power led to a new type of external contracting brake— the disc.

The use of drum brakes on any hot rod is literally restricted to what will fit what. Always match the front and rear brake systems. That is, never use brakes with small area (such as Corvair) at one end, and brakes with large area at the other. This unequal distribution of braking potential will create a monster, totally unreliable for any kind of high performance stopping. If a late model Oldsmobile rear end is used in a Model T, then the front brakes should have a brake lining area equivalent to a late model Oldsmobile also. The alternative is to reduce the Oldsmobile rear linings in size until they are compatible with the front. But that is defeating the purpose of getting superior brakes.

As a rule, it is possible to install larger and better brakes on most vehicles by using newer parts from the same type of car (Chevy for Chevy, Ford for Ford, etc.). In this way, 1954 Pontiac brakes will fit 1939 Chevy trucks, and so on. It is absolutely essential that hot rod brakes be far superior to those originally produced with the chassis. The addition of high horsepower engines quadruples demands on brakes.

Disc brakes are not new. They have been on the scene since the turn of the century (1902 to be exact), but with the braking technologies of the early 1900s they were not practical. Disc brakes then were merely another far-out idea.

Not until thirty-six years later did a couple of Britishers, working on a brake skeleton in the closet, begin to fashion a practical way of stopping high-speed military aircraft—their solution, the disc brake. Further experiments during the war proved their ultimate practicality on trucks and tanks. After the war, with its use in automobile racing, the disc brake came of age.

Detroit dropped the ball, unfortunately. Their early efforts ran into problems of money and prejudice, and while their interest waned, the Europeans (mostly British) began incorporating Girling and Dunlop disc brakes in many of their sports cars.

It wasn't until the early '60s that U.S. auto makers showed renewed interest in disc brakes. Seemingly out of the blue, the cost-conscious, conservative managers of Motor City found (after extensive testing) that disc were for real. A revolution took place that equaled the switch from mechanical brakes to hydraulics some thirty years ago.

Drum brakes, by nature, are losers in a modern combination of big-front-end sheet metal and fat, low-profile tires on solid mag-style wheels. Somewhere, buried in all that iron, are four brake drums starving for heat-absorbing air.

Aside from their inherent simplicity, ability to resist heat-induced fade, light weight and ease of maintenance, disc brakes offer a near-perfect solution to consistent braking action, under less-than-ideal weather or design conditions. Why? Because they are non-self-energized brakes.

The disc is a wheel-shaped steel plate (some with a set of turbine-like vanes sandwiched in the center to induce a greater cooling effect). This disc, or rotor, is attached to the turning wheel. Taking the place of a backing plate is a rotor splash shield to keep dirt, grease, and other foreign material away from the braking surface of the disc. Doing the actual work is a vise-like, hydraulically operated device called a caliper which is usually mounted to the spindle by a bracket. Applying the actual pressure to a biscuit-like pad or puck (bonded or riveted to a thin steel plate) are a set of pistons, housed within the confines of the caliper. How many pistons drive the pads (pucks, shoes, etc.) toward the rotor depends upon its intended use, but most modern passenger applications are being currently equipped with C-clamp style, full-floating, single-piston calipers. Racing versions, on the other hand, can feature any number of multipistoned calipers attached to various points on the rotor.

A disc brake has the same effect as a two-trailing-shoe brake. That means that disc brakes depend upon hydraulic pressure (and lots of it) plus great big pistons rather than any self-energizing to create the needed friction. Drum brake self-energizers use a rebounding principle to self-increase brake producing pressure. The discs—by being non-self-energizing, and coming on all at once—tend to give a much more progressive braking action. That is, the harder you press on the brake pedal, the greater the braking effort at the point of pad-to-rotor contact. Disc braking is a boon in foul braking conditions. They resist erratic braking and fade, and are a relatively trouble-free means of stopping. But, it takes a lot of line pressure against massive pistons to get the desired non-self-energized effect—the primary reason you'll use full-power boosting equipment in your hot rod.

There are a number of special disc brake kits available for all American cars through speed shops and performance equipment mail order houses. In addition, it is possible to adapt foreign and American stock car disc brakes by careful selection of drum bearings and homemade caliper brackets. The latter is perhaps the most economical method for budget conscious rodders, since stock items from a wrecked car usually cost less than $50 for the complete front end package.

8

Wheels and Tires

Wheels

In the scheme of archeology, wheels are a rather recent invention, having been introduced to society some five thousand years ago in the Middle East. At first, movement of large objects was facilitated by rolling them along on large logs. An effective method, but tedious. Someone then cut a roller from the center of a log and located it in a platform notch—the first vehicle was invented. Interestingly, these very crude wooden rollers were in widespread use for two thousand years before the wheel was refined by the Egyptians. And for the next three thousand years, the basic Egyptian spoke wheel remained little changed. Not until invention of the automobile did the wheel receive more than passing interest from the engineers.

With the self-propelled automobile and the pneumatic rubber tire came some very stringent requirements in wheel design. These requirements grow in importance as vehicle size and speed increased. The contemporary wheel of today may look like its

1920 disc counterpart, but it is totally different in manufacture, strength, safety, and endurance.

Almost everyone calls the wheel and its component parts by the wrong names. For the sake of clarity, the rim is what supports the tire. The dish-like part that fits inside the rim diameter and bolts to the brake drum is called the disc. The area of the disc that contacts the drum or hub is known as the mounting face. The distance between the mounting face and the outboard rim edge is the offset.

As might be expected, tire and wheel development proceeded together after someone discovered that rubber and air could cushion horse-drawn wagons. Bicycles got high pressure tires. Early motorists carried spare tires around for their clincher-type wheel rims. In the good old days, changing a flat tire was a major undertaking. Wheel development kept pace with the automobile, finding demountable, clincher-type rims for wooden spoked wheels by 1904, followed in one year by a universal rim. In 1913 the wire wheel was standard equipment, with the demountable rims by 1915. Disc wheels were introduced by the Mudd-Michelin Company in 1919, but didn't gain widespread use until the early 1930s.

This disc wheel is essentially the design still in use. Because of production methods, the rolled steel rim with separate pressed hub gradually put the wire and wood spoke wheel out of business in mass production. Wire wheels have remained on sports cars, but they are being replaced by the lighter alloy disc units now so common. The majority of wheels are now manufactured by auto companies and independents like Kelsey-Hayes, Motor Wheel Corporation, and the Budd Company.

Although the basic idea of the wheel has not changed drastically, the approach has, due principally to better tire design and automobile styling. If you want a low car, you need smaller wheels. But smaller wheels mean wider rims, and wider rims mean decreased brake cooling and subsequent inefficiency, ad infinitum.

The 14-inch wheel has been settled on, at least for the time being, as the best for heavier cars, and the 13-inchers are restricted to the smaller "compacts." But because of brake problems, sometimes alleviated by wider drums, better material, etc., most manufacturers offer 15-inch wheels as part of a heavy-duty package. These heavy-duty, or police, wheel options are generally recommended for trailer towing, hard driving, etc., and add very little to the initial purchase price of a new car. Such a wheel is normally fitted with a wider rim, and is often made of a heavier gage metal. For an extra-special stock-type wheel in this category, larger wheel and rim companies can build a unit on order, with chrome plating often available.

Of interest to the average hot rodder is the question of wheel interchangeability (what'll fit what?) and the special custom wheels now made for almost anything that moves. Unlike many other facets of automotive engineering, wheels are not necessarily interchangeable just because the bolt pattern is the same. Wheel design depends upon body styling, suspension engineering, and brakes. Consequently, there are several unapparent differences between wheels, even between those used on a particular make of car. Although the Chrysler Imperial wheel of the early '50s has a 5-hole, 5½-inch bolt circle diameter, and will bolt to a pre-'48 Ford hub, the mounting face and lug bolt seating angle are different. The Corvair wheel, which is wider, will bolt to the Falcon 4-bolt hub, but will shroud the brake drum more, making marginal brakes even less acceptable. And so the battle goes.

Of real concern is the matter of offset, or the distance from the mounting face to the outside rim. Most wheel people agree that a minor offset, up to ⅛ inch, isn't too great, but that trouble can easily develop with greater offset. If the offset is more than ⅛ inch, an extra strain is placed on the load-carrying components of the car. The rear axles and housings are designed to place a wheel center X number of inches from the middle of the car. If the wheel center is moved a couple of inches outboard, just that much more leverage is available to damage the housing, bearings, axles, etc. Rear end housings, prone to break near the center section anyway, are really liable to fail with deeply offset wheels.

At the front end the situation is even more critical. An automobile front end has been geometrically engineered to keep high load factors within the confines of design. That is, a Corvair spindle will carry the outside bearing load of the lightweight front end. But put a Corvair front end under an early rod with a heavy Oldsmobile engine and larger spindles are desirable. By using deep offset wheels on a spindle, the effect is the same as adding more weight to the front end.

When selecting a wheel to interchange, keep in mind that the offset shouldn't be much greater than the offset for the wheel it is replacing. Of course, reversing a wheel is different. The backside of most wheels features a gentle taper from the drop-center area to the rim edge, which is why reversing is so common on chrome units. The offset may hardly be changed by reversing. Further, when swapping wheels the bolt hole diameter must be nearly the same and the bolt hole taper should match up with the lug nuts used. It is often advisable to buy a set of lug nuts that fit both the hub bolts *and* the wheel taper, or machine the available nuts.

The center hole register diameter must be similar, since a good fit will further reduce strain on the lug bolt area. Naturally, always check carefully for wheel and tire clearance near the tie rod ends, fender panels, and brake drums. This clearance problem is especially critical if you're going from a large wheel diameter to a smaller one, such as 15 to 14 inches, and so on. Also keep in mind the kind of tires you'll be using, for some of the new oval cross-section tires will interfere with fender inner panels. As a general guide to interchangeability of wheels, it is wise to use a wheel originally built for a car of similar or heavier weight, never lighter. The wider the rim, the better the car's handling will be, but only if the wheel offset is minor, particularly at the front.

You can even use wire wheels on your rod if you've a mind to, with true knockoff hubs. There are a number of wire wheels made for certain American cars (Cadillac, Chrysler, Buick, Thunderbird), all with lug bolt attachment, but by some careful scrounging among the foreign cars in the local wrecking yard you can get some excellent swaps too. Wire wheels are generally classified as dual or triple laced, the designation referring to the number of wire spoke rows that go from hub to rim. As a general guideline, a compact such as the Corvair or Falcon can use the dual laced wheel from sports cars of comparable weight such as Austin-Healey, Triumph, etc. Heavier cars should have the triple laced spokes normally associated with the bigger, high performance sports machines, or the heavy duty American wires.

The Triumph TR splined hub assembly will bolt right onto the current American 4-bolt compact car hubs (with the exception of Dart and Valiant, which will require redrilling the spline hub flange), and wire wheels for this particular hub spline range from 13- through 16-in sizes. Heavier cars with the 5-bolt lug pattern can use either Austin-Healey or larger sports car splined hubs. One note of caution: always make sure the spokes are tight, as they easily loosen after prolonged use.

The biggest single concern of the modern rodder, especially if he has a post-1948 car, is getting "just-right" wheels. The Mag-type special wheel is the current rage among the late-rod set, while the early-rod gang is going back to chromies with bullet (baby moon) hub caps or painted wheels with beauty rims. Whatever kind of special wheel is used for a street-driven car depends entirely on the desire of the owner, but there are a number of special maintenance tips for such wheels.

Few can afford the luxury of real magnesium alloy wheels on the street. But if you have a set of these primarily racing units, keep in mind that they must be kept clean at all times, and perfectly free of nicks and scratches. If you have real mags you'll probably be tinkering around with them every weekend. A small rock will fly up and nick the cast alloy rim slightly. If the sharp edges of a nick or scratch are not sanded round and smoothed out, a stress concentration may set in and fatigue cracks can quickly follow. Such a failure normally happens before the owner has any idea that trouble is brewing. For this reason racing organizations require test certificates on mag alloy wheels every year.

An aluminum wheel doesn't have this great maintenance requirement, but it's still wise to keep them free from stress concentrations. Further, a tremendous number of wheels have been put on the market using all grades of aluminum alloy, both inferior and good, so always keep a close watch for minute cracks around the bolt circle and/or spoke areas. Not just on the outside, but inside next to the drum, too.

The question of what kind of "mag" to buy—full casting or alloy center/steel rim, welded construction or riveted, etc.—is again a matter of preference. Naturally, it's always wise to go with a proven design. Don't buy a set just because they're inexpensive; your life may depend on the few dollars you saved. As to construction techniques, the welded alloy center/steel rim wheel has a possible advantage in that there are no holes in the rim, making it good for tubeless tire use. On the other hand, riveted construction has been perfected to overcome this problem, too. A full casting alloy wheel, more in the category of a racing unit and therefore lighter, is more susceptible to rim damage if you hit a curb.

Although a full casting wheel does require more care during use, it can provide some excellent dividends. For a typical car, a mag wheel will save 10 pounds per corner, or 40 pounds overall. This is unsprung weight, where any weight saving immediately shows up in better vehicle ride and handling. Further, an alloy wheel, particularly magnesium, will allow much better brake cooling (that's why it has replaced spoked wheels on European road racers), which is an advantage when you are towing a trailer, climbing mountains, etc.

Somewhere in between the alloy center/steel rim and the chrome stock wheel comes the all-steel "mag." Here the stock steel rim is centered by a steel stamping made to resemble a cast wheel, with the entire unit chromed. Usually heavier than a stock wheel, this design is sometimes superior in appearance, one of the reasons for its popularity with custom show participants.

All special wheels must undergo continuing inspection for flaws, which should be included in the normal cleaning schedule. A chrome wheel must always be kept clean and heavily waxed if rust is to be circumvented. Should a spot of rust crop up, clean it off with any of the special cleansers available at the parts house, and then touch up the pitted surface with clear fingernail polish or a clear plastic spray. Never use a stiff brush or steel wool on any special wheel, chrome or alloy, as the surface may be ruined beyond repair. Aluminum wheels (discounting the chrome-plated aluminum items) will not need polishing as often as magnesium, but should also receive generous waxing often (both inboard and outside). The mag wheel is difficult to keep shiny, but as it becomes discolored an enamel paint rubbing compound used prior to the mag polishing compound will ease the chore. You can wax a mag, but nothing really does much good.

No matter what kind of wheel is on your machine, it must be treated with respect. You can't go around banging into curbs and expect wheels to live a decent life. Taken care of and inspected periodically, wheels will usually outlast the car.

For the beginning rodder a full set of alloy or chromed wheels is often too expensive. In that case, the rodder must use his ingenuity. The answer is a reversed wheel, which may or may not be offset, painted nicely and equipped with a baby moon hubcap.

The first step is to see if the wheel can be reversed or not. If the wheel itself does not have a deep recess on the inside, reversing may not gain any distance. Some of the early Ford and Chevy wheels are like this, and are therefore useless for the purpose. At the same time, if the vehicle fender is going to interfere, it's better to leave well enough alone. In most cases, though, a reverse is possible.

Sharpen up that old cold chisel and chip off all the rivets holding the rim and hub together. Make sure the wheel is lying flat on the cement so the rim isn't bent, because you'll have to swing a heavy hammer to bust the rivets loose. After the rivets are decapped, knock out the remaining pieces with a punch. Mark the hub and rim for reference, then carefully hammer the hub out. This usually takes patience, since the rim drop-center is normally bent slightly into the hub during original assembly.

After the hub is removed, turn it around and, using a reference mark to put the piece back together as they were originally, hammer the hub back into place. Initial alignment is accomplished by putting the rivet holes back together, lined up by the punch.

Now mount the wheel on a drum. If you want to make up some kind of an alignment jug from an old axle or front hub, go ahead, but just using the car hub is faster. Use a tri-square as the reference for alignment by setting it against the outside edge of the rim and marking the ground. By rotating the wheel (all the time keeping the square on the ground mark), you find high and low spots (in and out) on the rim. Tap the rim for final alignment. When the wheel is aligned, the original rivet holes will be very close also.

If you don't have access to an arc welder, you'll have to have someone tack weld the wheel in three or four places around the diameter, running the tack bead into the original rivet holes. Check alignment as the welding is being done. Keep going around the wheel until all the rivet holes are welded shut; some wheels have eight holes, others twelve, etc. If at any time during the tacking process the wheel shows up out of alignment, break the welds and start again.

After the rivet holes are welded shut, the wheel will stay in position while the hub is welded to the rim on the back side. Finally, the rivet holes are ground smooth and rewelded if necessary to ensure against pinhole leaks (not important if a tube is used). If the valve stem is to be repositioned, locate it the same distance from the rim as originally, then drill a hole and file the edges smooth. Weld the original hole closed. Some prefer the smooth look of the rim, therefore the valve stem is always left on the inside.

After the welding is done, chip away the slag, lay into the rim with some sandpaper, coarse steel wool, or paint remover. Clean it good, spray with quality spray-can paint, and you're ready for the tire. If you can't spring for a set of baby moon caps just yet, dig around at the local junkyard. The most inexpensive cars in a line are usually delivered with very simple hub caps, caps that might be exactly what you need.

Wheel Adapters

Hot rodders who have been around for several years are especially appreciative of the wheel adapters now sold by all speed equipment shops and mail-order outlets. Until recently any kind of wheel swap usually meant changing the hub bolt pattern; now it is a matter of installing inexpensive adapters.

The new wheel adapters, which will fit any American wheel (modern patterns, of course) to any U.S. car, are made in both aluminum and steel. The steel adapters are from ¾ to 1 inch thick, machined from castings of 1015 low carbon steel, and weigh approximately five pounds each. Of specific interest in the steel line up is the 6-bolt unit for Chevrolet pickups.

Aluminum adapters are lighter, about half the weight of steel, and arc machined from virgin 356 T6 heat-treated alloy. All aluminum adapters are $^{15}\!/_{16}$ inch thick, including the special spacers which are for problem installations (use of wide rim wheels, wide oval tires, disc brakes, etc., where clearance is the problem).

Thickness of an adapter is important, since any movement of the wheel centerline from the designed point will have a direct, and usually adverse, effect on handling and wheel-bearing wear. It is wise to keep in mind that combining an adapter with offset wheels may aggravate the situation (but also remember that a reversed wheel is not necessarily offset). Most American cars, particularly the larger, heavier versions, have a margin of safety engineered into the suspension. For this reason, bearing wear and failure is at a minimum. But on lighter-weight cars this margin is also less; while foreign cars are usually on the edge to begin with. A Volkswagen is the most significant example. When the wheel centerline is moved outboard an excessive amount, meaning more than two inches, bearing wear goes up at an alarming rate.

The weight of an adapter is important, since it is applied directly as unsprung weight. Therefore, if handling and ride are important, the lighter aluminum adapter is better than steel. Working as a heat sink, the aluminum adapter will also transfer heat energy to the airstream faster than steel.

The most popular adapters are early Ford drum pattern (5½-inch diameter, 5 holes) to late Ford and Chevy wheels. Of interest here is the fact that Chrysler and Buick wire wheels can be utilized without changing the drum bolt pattern. Adapters for all the four-lug bolt machines, such as Corvair, Falcon, etc., are available, and will bolt to many foreign hubs. With this in view, it would be possible to utilize the Girling disc brake assembly from a Triumph TR3 on a Ford spindle, then adapt to the Ford wheels, etc.

Although left-hand thread nuts are available from the adapter manufacturer, it is just as easy to grind the tapered lip from the standard lug nuts, which makes them thin enough to work with the adapter plate. Also note that in most cases the adapter holes don't line up perfectly with the lug bolt, because the bolts bend out of shape slightly during use. Light tapping with the hammer is dictated here. In case a bolt is bent too far out of alignment, run a lug nut on and tap it with the hammer to straighten.

As to the possibility of making your own adapters, go ahead; there is nothing involved a good machinist can't do. However, first consider the cost involved. You can buy the raw stock, aluminum or steel, and good forged lug bolts are as near as the local new car agency.

Of vital importance to any adapter is the center hole, which should be just large enough to fit the locating register on the hub. On the inside face of the hole, a chamfer will be needed to ensure a perfect fit of adapter and hub.

It is not wise to use the hole pattern from a brake drum as the only lug bolt hole guide, since these holes are purposely over-size. Instead, working from the adapter center, scribe a diameter exactly that of the wheel bolt pattern. If this is five inches and there are five bolts, then the center point of each lug bolt hole will be exactly 72 degrees apart along this circle.

If an adapter is not to be used, the original lug bolt pattern may be changed. This is definitely a machine shop operation, because precision is imperative to wheel radius. When changing a hub pattern, patience is the most important ingredient.

Tires

Not so many years ago, the possibility of getting a good tire for a fast roadster or coupe was uncomfortably slim. Even as late as the mid-1950s, few top quality premium designs were coming from the factories, simply because average passenger car performance didn't warrant them. A hot rod owner had to be content with getting the best tire possible, and making do, which meant tire failures at the dry lakes or Bonneville were to be expected. Indianapolis tires were used whenever available, but these were restricted in use and unsuitable for highway driving. A typical rod would use large tires at the rear, preferably 7.00x16, and the smallest that could be found on the front, 5.50x16 or so. The big tires helped traction and the small ones made steering easier (those early steering gearboxes can seldom be called keen). Besides, this made the machine look like an oval track racer.

The scene has changed radically during the last few years, with factories going all-out to produce maximum performance tires for Detroit cars. Whereas the big rear, small front tire combination used to be the vogue on everything, the modern rod is likely to feature a set of identical "Daytona" type weenies. Hot rodders can now have good tire design along with the maximum in safety.

Let's take a look at the overall tire situation, forgetting for a moment the special tires now in vogue, and see what has been happening in the world of rubber. First of all, there is a new organization that exists for the benefit of tire makers, appropriately titled the Rubber Manufacturers Association (RMA). A major part of RMA's yearly activity is taken up in testing tires, and their certified tire directory for any year will list tire makers with products tested an approved.

Interestingly, specific safety requirements for new passenger car tires only became effective on January 1, 1965 (industry wide), but already the test requirements have risen up to 50 percent. This means the current RMA standards are more stringent than any existing federal or state standard. Here's what the RMA does (through the Automotive Testing Division of Electrical Testing Laboratories in New York) in a typical certification.

First a group of tires are selected at random from a maker's line. They are put on a special test wheel and run under a constant test load and inflation for speeds accelerating to the equivalent of 100 mph. Of course, they can be run at higher speeds, but this is the currently accepted maximum for passenger cars. The tire is then run on a test wheel for 34 hours (1700 miles) under different overload conditions (at 65 mph) as a part of the durability testing. Strength is tested by inserting a ¾-inch steel plunger into the tire at five places to check carcass strength, with the energy values dependent upon tire size. The tire size also has specific minimums, of concern primarily to the manufacturer, but the bead test is of value to all ultimate tire users. Here, the force required to unseat a tire bead from the rim wheel is measured, with a minimum 2500 pounds pressure applied to the sidewall. This particular test simulates the load stresses encountered in sharp turns or cornering at high speeds on the highway. All this is in addition to the $25 million spent annually by the tire industry in product testing and the $100 million that has been laid out for lab and road testing facilities.

This kind of money can feasibly be spent on testing, in view of the staggering $500 million unloaded by consumers every year for tires sold under more than 2 hundred brand names. With this kind of market potential, it is to be expected that tire variety and quality will run from superb to poor, with the sales price in direct relationship to quality.

For the average car, including the custom and street rod, use nothing inferior to the original equipment tire. It stands to reason, also, that any modification to the car will have direct bearing upon tire requirements. For instance, a 1956 Chevrolet sporting a big, supercharged Chrysler hemi engine will need better tires on the front than the original equipment type.

As delivered by the factory no new car gets the absolute top tire. Instead, they are fitted with a second quality line proven entirely adequate. For the modern new car, this means a 2-ply rayon cord design, designated as a 100 Line Tire. The number is merely used as a reference point, with the best tires rated at 150 percent.

The 4-ply rayon and 2-ply Nylon cord tires come along at 115 percent, and lesser quality skins pull 90 percent, 80 percent, etc.

Naturally, you'll want to get the best possible deal on any tire you buy, and because there is such a margin of profit in tire sales, it's far wiser to shop around for a good quality tire at a discount than settle for cheapies. Some cheap tires are of such poor quality that a good retread on a premium carcass is better.

Some special cheater slick recaps are put on racing tire casings, but the majority are passenger car retreads. Because of the severe heat problems a racing tire encounters, it is engineered quite differently than its highway cousin. Cord angle, wall design, cord spacing, etc., are all different to reduce heat buildup. At the same time, since months and months of longevity are not involved, race tire rubber compound can be tailored to a specific race track and even to wet or dry pavement. Furthermore, a race tire does not scuff too many sidewalk curbs, so there is virtually no sidewall protective gum. This last factor is a significant reason that true racing tires should not be used on a street machine.

A recap is just a piece of rubber glued on an old tire casing, but great differences in quality are possible. What might be plenty good enough for a farm wagon is zero-zero for a modern passenger car, especially a high performance street job. In the first place, there isn't a great deal of difference in the basic procedure of creating a new tire or a recap. In both instances, the final tread rubber, or gum, is laid over the cord by hand and heat does the melting and bonding.

But where recaps have gotten a sometimes sour reputation is in this molding process, and from unsatisfactory tire casings to start with. When a tire is to be recapped, the casing must be absolutely free of any defects! All too many one-horse recappers will use inferior casings, working on a percentage or failure theory. That is, it's cheaper to replace a few comebacks than to insist on prime casings at the outset.

A recap seldom sheds the new rubber because of ineffective

rubber bonding, but rather because of cord separation or similar casing failure. If a casing is porous and tire air can seep through the cord area, it will settle between the cord and rubber, where it will expand when heated, forcing the original rubber away from the casing. If a recap goes on properly, and on a good casing to begin with, it will serve as well as a new tire. To help win the recap war, use tubes, thereby preventing air from seeping through casings.

The creation of a special recap is much like ordinary recapping, with certain refinements. After the casing has been carefully inspected, it is just as carefully "matched" with another tire. This matching is of particular importance to the racing fraternity. There can be as much as a one-inch variance in the diameter of two identically labeled tires.

Only four-ply Nylon "textile" blanks (fancy for worn-out passenger tires) are used. Rayon is rejected because of a tendency to break down, as the old cotton cords did. The buffing process is critical to making a good drag slick or Indy tire. A tire due for the slick recap will be buffed, leaving a flattened surface. This helps to keep the tire edges built up and the final result is a flat racing tire with a cap from 5.5 to 8 inches. This same kind of flattened preshaping is used for the Indy style tire, where the tread must be wide.

After the buffing, the tires are placed on another rack and sprayed with a super heavy-duty cement. As the glue is becoming tacky, the tire is moved to still another machine and the special recap rubber applied by a cold chemical adhesion process. This is just to keep the recap rubber in place until the tire is put in the "oven."

An inflatable bladder (tube) and inner rim are added to the tire; then it is put into the special mold. The outer mold matrix has the eventual tire tread pattern on the inside surface, and when the tire is in place, the mold is forcing inward while the inflatable tube is pushing outward.

In the mold, the tire is heated to 300 degrees with 160 pounds of air in the tube, for exactly one hour and ten minutes. During this time the recap rubber completely bonds to the casing, and the tread shape and design is permanently set. Also during this time the rubber cures.

The chemical makeup of the recap rubber is as important as the method of production. Drag racing is a sticky business, whereas the average street tire must be a combination of tire variables. The highway tire must wear well, have good traction on either wet or dry pavement, have good design to control heat, and be reasonably priced. The race tire must win races, all else be hanged! There isn't a rubber engineer in the world who can get maximum results from the drawing board without some trial and error testing. Such research and development is further complicated by the numerous changes in race car design during the year. Every time a significant power increase occurs, or a new chassis is developed, the tires must change again too. It's a mechanical merry-go-round.

The kinds of tires to use on the street are a personal matter, but each type of tire was designed for a specific purpose and should be used for such. A slick may give excellent traction on clean, dry pavement. But just find a slightly damp surface and zingo! Spin city. The purpose of treads in tires is to give a place for the water (or sand) on pavement to be squeezed. Admittedly, tread isn't the perfect answer, but it works.

For the fella who digs at the drags occasionally, it is wise to remember that a recap cannot be used like a special racing tire slick. The recap is still using the passenger car casing, and it cannot be run with six or ten or fifteen pounds of air pressure. Instead, it must be run nearer normal pressures. Toward this end, the rubber has been compounded differently than the special racing slick, also. When racing is scheduled, fill the rear tires with 40 pounds of air, then stand on the loud pedal enough to lay a batch of rubber about five feet long. Study this pattern. If the pattern is darker in the middle than on the edges, reduce pressure five pounds and try again. If the middle is lighter than the sides, raise the pressure. The idea is to get a consistent amount of rubber across the tread width. You can't do much about lengthening the footprint, or the amount of tire in actual contact with the pavement, when using recaps. To do this you must go to around ten pounds pressure, a place where recaps won't hack it.

Tires, whether for racing or tractors, are basically of the same construction, the difference being primarily in construction technique, compounds, and quality control. In all cases, a bead is a part of the design, and serves to hold the tire in place on the wheel. This bead is made by covering a steel cable with strong rubber, with ply cords looping from one bead to the other.

The earlier cotton ply cords have been replaced by rayon, fiberglass, and Nylon, but the cotton strength specifications are still used. Therefore, a 4-ply rating may only include 2 plies of the modern cord if this is as strong as 4 plies of cotton. Nylon is stronger than rayon (and more expensive) and common in race tires, but it flat-spots when a car sits for any length of time, resulting in a bumpy ride until the tire assumes its natural shape after a few miles of driving. Also, just because a tire has a 2-ply construction doesn't mean it is half as good as a 4-ply. The cords may be larger or better, another reason for some 2-ply tires to carry a 4-ply rating.

The cord angle has much to do with tire design and performance. A low cord angle (the angle at which different cords intersect) gives a good ride and long life because the cords do not build up as much heat during deflection as a high angle design. A good example of this is the Radial tire, which the cord is almost perpendicular to the bead.

If only two radial tires are to be used on a car they should never, never be used on the front.

Radial tires not only look different, they are different. Their "stickiness" is only in very small part due to the rubber compounding and much more to the internal construction or lay-up of the cords. The usual tire has cords or fabric laid diagonally from bead to bead at an angle of around 30 to 40 degrees to the centerline of the tire. These cords are laid up in layers of two, four, six or more plies, each ply running opposite the next. The result is a firm, strong, bonded fabric that holds the tire in shape. The radial, on the other hand, has its basic cords running from bead to bead at 90 degrees to the centerline of the tire in two plies, each ply running parallel to the other. If this were all there were, it would be a pretty weak construction, but it isn't all. Surrounding these radial plies is a belt of metal mesh or of from four to six plies of cord running at about 16 degrees to the centerline. This belt is extremely stiff and does the job of holding the tire together laterally. It does something else, too. It provides a very stiff base for the tread that prevents squirm or distortion and, with the flexible sidewalls, holds the tread firmly flat on the road surface. The lack of squirm cuts the scrub factor considerably, which accounts for the long-wearing claims for radials. However, some manufacturers take advantage of this to use a softer, stickier compound and the bold, open, so-called aggressive tread. The result is sticky indeed, especially in the wet, where the open tread allows drainage and the softer compounding gives traction that simply isn't found in the harder crossply tire. It also makes for faster wear.

All is not roses, though. Eventually, even the flexibility of the radial sidewall has to come to an end. When this happens with a crossply, the tread picks up in an arc, reducing the bite gradually. When it happens with a radial, the stiff tread comes up more like a board lifted at one edge and the bite is gone very suddenly indeed. True, it happens later than with the crossply but when it does happen it happens with vigor. The fabric belted radials, being more flexible, are gentler about it, tending to give some warning. The steel belted tires tend to produce a condition like instant ice when the slip angles and cornering forces get high.

It is for this reason that radials should not be used on the front with crossplies on the rear. At high slip angles the crossplies tend to surpass radials in cornering force and the result of such a mixture can be instant understeer, severe understeer at speed, just when you don't want it.

In terms of roll, cornering, skid recovery, and breakaway the radial will show roughly 5 percent better traction in the dry and up to 20 percent better in the wet. They have other things going for them, too. Thanks to the stiff tread, they have a quicker response because the tread goes in the direction of wheel travel rather than squirming and then finally catching up with it, though this is to some extent offset by a time lag caused by the flexible sidewall. In fact, unless you have them mounted on rims at least as wide, or wider than, the tread width, you will have to get used to feeling as though you are riding on tires that are slightly underinflated. This effect can be combatted to a certain extent by running the pressure up to the maximum recommended (33 to 36 psi) at some sacrifice in ride.

A close cousin to the radial is the belted-bias tire. Originally developed in Germany, it was called a Halbgurtel or "half-belt" which is actually a misnomer since it has a full belt—"half radial" would be a better term. The basic construction is the same as a crossply but with a fabric belt or two layers of cords set at about 25 degrees to the centerline of the tire. In its original form it never really took hold although it can be laid up on conventional machinery, unlike the true radial. Armstrong in this country latched onto the idea but with a difference. Working with Owens-Corning, they developed a form of bondable Fiberglas and used that for the belt with a polyester cord for the base layup. The result is a tire with most of the qualities of the radial—stiff tread and flexible walls—that can be produced on existing machinery.

Both radials and bias-belts are first-line high performance tires and do not come cheaply; they run from about $45 up to as high as $100 a tire (Uniroyal Masters). In the larger sizes the radial will probably run just a shade more than the bias-belt but it is hardly noticeable. However, the greater cost is pretty well made up for by longer wear, although since they will put up with more nonsense this wear factor can be nullified by more exuberant driving.

In any tire, tread is specifically the gum molded to the carcass, or the rubber that touches the road (and wears out). It is responsible for traction, and is at best a compromise. Soft rubber gives good traction but wears fast, hard rubber wears well and is slick as grease at times. The tread pattern determines how the tire will react on different surfaces, with small cuts best for dry pavement and large cuts for wet weather. The tread compounds also vary according to use, with synthetics added to natural rubber as a prevention of deterioration caused by oil, ozone, and smog.

Of the hundred-plus brand names listed for American tires, fewer than two dozen do the actual producing. It is easy to see, then, that some judicious shopping can save you money, particularly if you don't happen to care about the significance of a brand name. As an example, the Firestone 500 7.75x14 blackwall sells for nearly $40 on an average, but the Montgomery Ward HST tire is the same thing, and costs under $25.

As a guide to what kind of discount is possible, keep these figures in mind next time you go shopping. The retailer has a margin of 36 percent on first line (OEM) tires, 45 percent on premium, and 30 percent on second line. The bargain basement third line has no real percentage breakdown. As an average, a 25 percent discount is plausible, if you're a good shopper. "Seconds" are structurally good tires, usually with some kind of flaw in the appearance, and can be good buys provided you take them with a guarantee that they will be true within 3 to 4 percent of inflated diameter and/or they are dynamically balancable. If the roundness has not been kept within limits, the tire will wear (tread chunk) quickly.

Naturally, the high performance racing tires are the best for top road handling, but they can also be incorrect for your car. For example, a tire built for sports car racing in the rain will have superb traction, but will wear out almost immediately. And a tire made to be used on a dry track won't have much wet surface traction—you can spin out in a mud puddle the size of a dime. Further, the honest racing tire isn't built to last months and months in everyday use, so the rubber will check and crack early. Because heat is retained by heavy sidewall rubber coatings, the racing tire is very thin here and highly susceptible to curb damage.

The best high performance tire to buy is the one sold as a sports or sports car type. A true Indy or Daytona tire may look super wild, but shouldn't be expected to give overall highway use. At the same time, slicks should never be run on the street. They make the car look like the drag racing variety, but it's a dumb thing thing to do. In the first place, if it's a very good slick, the soft rubber will wear abnormally fast. Second, it has no design provisions for cornering, and third, it's miserable on a damp surface.

Besides, slicks make the ride harder. Cheater slicks are better, in that they at least have a couple of tread grooves, but nothing is better than a tire designed for the street.

In general, when buying a tire for good handling, get the wider tread and a carcass designed for a wide rim. If you're going on long, hard trips, buy an additional ply rating design, and for high speed, naturally get the racing or high performance type tire.

Whatever you do, keep good tires on that rod. The cost is small compared to the possible consequences of tire failure.

9

Fiberglass Hot Rods

It is probable that fiberglass saved traditional hot rodding from extinction. There were just so many ancient Model T's and Model A's that could be saved from the scrap through the years. With the resurgence of interest in these cars as full restoration material, the hot rodder has been hard put to find something "really old" to transform. Perfect fiberglass replicas, lighter in weight and stronger, have been as much a revolution in the automotive sport as fiberglass hulls have been to boating. Now anyone can have a vintage 1923 Model T roadster body, or a "genuine" Austin Bantam, or even a 1934 Willys coupe. The selection is as varied as it is unique.

Plastic cars were introduced to the automotive sport during the early 1950s, although fiberglass had been experimented with for many years previous. Henry Ford made the front pages by banging away at glass fenders on pre-World War II cars, but the product remained an oddity. These earlier plastics required highly specialized manufacturing processes. This was all changed with the availability and introduction of low-cost fiber and polyester resins.

Fiberglass can be likened to concrete, a material well suited to molding but not exceptionally strong in itself. However, with the addition of steel reinforcements, concrete becomes the basis for fantastic architectural schemes. So with fiberglass.

By itself, resin is easily formed but has little strength. This is the job of glass fiber reinforcements which are available as interwoven blankets or as matted blankets (the latter formed by pressing individual filaments together with a weak binder). There is no use working with fiberglass unless you understand what it is.

Synthetic resins come in a number of forms, including phenolics, acrylics, epoxies, ureas, and polyesters. The entire enthusiast industry has chosen polyesters because they are easy to use and control—and are inexpensive as well. While the material for an aluminum car body may cost upwards of $500, the same body can be formed from fiberglass for less than one-fifth that figure.

Resins of polyester are a heavy liquid, weighing about nine pounds per gallon and ranging in viscosity between water thin and molasses thick (between 75 and 70,000 cps). Enthusiasts use a cps of about 700, since this is the easiest to work with and easily saturates both fiberglass matte and cloth.

It is the possibility of resin curing itself, or hardening, that makes it so desirable as a binder with fiberglass filaments as the core strength material. Resin hardens if a catalyst is added and the material is heated to 200° F for approximately two hours. However, if heat is not added, the combination of resin and catalyst will, several days later, begin to cause internal heat and subsequent hardening. This chemical heat, called exothermic, will turn the liquid into a solid, a characteristic that hobbyists use in plastic crafts.

Exothermic heat cures the resin just as the external heat will, but at a much slower rate—far too slow for the hot rodder. Since a big heating oven is not available, and long natural curing time is unsatisfactory, an accelerator can be added. This accelerator serves to "kick" the catalyst in a much shorter time, causing the exo-thermic heat to intensify. Thus the builder can vary the time resin will "kick" simply by the catalyst/accelerator combination he uses. However, the resin will harden much faster in a large mass (due to the exothermic heat involved) than when spread thin. That's why resin must be mixed in relatively small batches to avoid un-necessary waste.

The most common formula for resin, catalyst, and accelerator calls for about 1 percent catalyst and 1 percent accelerator by weight per 100 percent resin. This will hold true throughout numerous mixing sequences if good materials are used each time.

Room temperature has an effect on curing time, with the time speeding up on a hot day and slowing down on a cold day. If a bucket of pure resin is mixed with catalyst and accelerator at the 2 percent basis, it will start to set in about forty minutes and cure completely in two hours at 70° F ambient temperature. Using this as a base, the enthusiast can vary his formula to suit his own par-ticular conditions.

It may be difficult to select materials without prior experience, but the best guide is always to go for quality. There are resins for all kinds of different uses, some that do not cure at room tem-peratures, others that are inhibited by air and never surface cure. Tell the supplier what you have in mind and he will give you the correct materials.

Just as quality resin of the correct type for automobile bodies is necessary for any type of fiberglass work—whether molding an entire body or making a small patch—quality glass fibers for the reinforcement are necessary. A number of different reinforcements might be used, such as rayon, nylon, linen, cotton, etc.—but none have proven as suitable as glass.

Glass fibers are made by applying heat and pressure to glass which is in marble form, producing long filaments (called fibers or rovings) that can be bunched in various ways much in the manner of ordinary sewing thread. To make handling easier, a binding is sometimes included at this stage.

Two types of fiberglass are used in body manufacture and repair: woven cloth and matte. Woven cloth is practically the same as any other woven material, but the texture of the weave, which means the amount of glass contained in a particular square inch of cloth, has a direct bearing on cloth strength. For building a car, cloth from .010 to .015 inch thick and with a moderately open weave is recommended. This gives the strength of glass plus the texture for good resin penetration. Because fiberglass materials cost in proportion to amount, some manufacturers of specialty bodies try to control cost by using less material. This can only result in an inferior product, something many buyers learn the hard way. Always check the reputation of the builder first, and if possible inspect one of his products. You may be able to build up the strength of an inferior product, but this will raise the cost at least 50 percent.

Matte is designed to give thickness to a laminate, and consequent strength, at a reasonable price. It is not as strong as cloth, but is ideal for use as a thickness agent in conjunction with resin and cloth, reducing the cost over several layers of cloth. The glass fibers are laid so they run in one direction. A sheet is then laid against another with fibers running 90 degrees opposite; thus a kind of laminated plywood effect is obtained, insuring very good strength.

DuPont has long been producing a special treatment for fiberglass, but most companies have treatments that achieve the same results. DuPont calls their process the 114 treatment, but it really consists of two steps—treatment 112 and treatment 114. In the former, the cloth is run through towers where it is subjected to blasts of heat to drive off oils necessary during weaving. The cleaned cloth is then given treatment 114, which is a light chroming of the surface. With any treatment, the objective is a glass product easier to laminate, again giving extra strength.

Check with any body shop and chances are you'll find only one or two metal men thoroughly familiar with fiberglass repairs. It is a profitable repair business, but because of the products involved, it is not integrated into the overall metal repair trade as it should be. Each shop will have one or two specialists. Part of this problem stems from the fact that fiberglass can irritate the skin. This can be circumvented by using a protective cream on the hands, or rubber gloves. Wear long-sleeved shirts, button your collar, and use a respirator if necessary. Fiberglass dust kicked up by a disc grinder may irritate the nostrils.

Resin mixtures should be used in well-ventilated areas, since toxic fumes are involved. These same resins will tend to accumulate on tools, shoes, clothing, practically everything—so the resin should be cleaned while it is still soft. Lacquer thinner is an excellent cleaning agent.

There are three general kinds of fiberglass parts: matched metal molds, spray lay-ups, and hand lay-ups. In the first, chopped fiber and polyester resin are mixed, catalyst added, and the combination placed in a male/female mold. Heat and pressure are applied. The finished piece is ready in a few minutes, which means that the metal mold procedure is a fast and inexpensive way to produce fiberglass parts in quantity. However, the strength of the part may not be great.

With spray lay-up, chopped glass roving is blown into a female mold along with catalyzed resin. The mixture is then rolled by hand and allowed to cure at ambient temperatures. This type of lay-up is popular with smaller dune buggy manufacturers, although the builder must control the percentage of glass and resin to get correct strength. Hand lay-up is the general method of the low-volume producer, or the one-off rodder. This includes laying glass mat, cloth or roving—or a combination of these—in the female mold and saturating the pieces with resin. The entire surface must be carefully rolled, to ensure the proper mixture and balance throughout and the removal of air bubbles. Pieces formed this way are usually very strong and thick, but the process is more costly than the others.

Repair of any of these fiberglass parts will follow the same general scheme (even a metal panel that is heavily rusted may be repaired much the same way). To repair large or small holes, first remove the damaged material and bevel the edges to about 20 degrees. Grind off the paint and gel coat to reach the raw fiberglass. This should be done on both sides for maximum strength.

Special fiberglass repair kits are available for this type of work, and may be used on either steel or fiberglass. In the case of steel, however, an epoxy resin must be used rather than polyester, as the latter will not adhere well to metal. The epoxy kit can be used for both metal and glass.

Cut two pieces of mat so they will extend past the hole edges about two inches. Mix the resin and catalyst (hardener) per the container directions, then spread the resin through the fiberglass. A handy non-stick work area is made by a polyethylene sheet (suit bags from the cleaners work well). Coat both inner and outer surfaces of the hole with resin mixture; then when this mix is tacky, apply the saturated mat to both the inner and outer surfaces. Press the two patches together, working out any air bubbles, which should leave a saucer-like depression where the hole was.

Allow the repair to cure, and since this is a chemical action, as soon as the surface is hard, it is hard clear through. The curing can be speeded up by raising the temperature, easy enough to do by placing heat lamps about 18 inches from the work. After the spot is cured, grind the surface smooth and fill the remaining low spot(s) with plastic filler from the kit. If additional coats of resin are necessary, sand lightly between coats.

Closing a large hole is slightly different, in that larger, stronger patches are required. Place a piece of cloth on the polyethylene bag, cut larger than the hole, and saturate it with resin. Then place two pieces of mat on the cloth, both pieces cut larger than the hole and both thoroughly saturated with resin. Stick this thick patch to the underside of the hole after resin applied to the parent material is tacky, and remove air bubbles by pressing with the poly bag. The mat side is placed toward the body. Make a similar patch and apply it to the hole outside, then finish as before.

Fiberglass mat and resin can be used very well to reinforce areas subject to excessive stress, and for tying in parts of fiberglass to wood, etc. Pure fiberglass is best for this work, as it hardens when spread over the damaged surface. It is ideal when a mounting bracket is being replaced on a fiberglass piece.

To tie in a wooden piece, or a mounting bracket, coat the glass surface with the pure resin, push the tie-in piece into place, and apply more resin. Mat or cloth may be included if desired.

Repairing splits and cracks is very common with fiberglass bodies subjected to stress. Kits are ideal for this purpose also. Remove the loose material and grind a broad "V" down the fissure. Clean the inside of the split also. Cut a piece of mat and apply to inner surface with the resin mix. Use two pieces of mat if there is excessive stress in the area. Cover the mat with a piece of saturated cloth pressed firmly in place. Here the repair is much the same as with holes. The fiberglass structure is now reinforced and the crack may be filled with plastic filler. Sometimes small impact cracks may be repaired directly with pure resin and a filler, but the addition of a mat/cloth reinforcement is added insurance.

Unlike metal, a fiberglass body does not crumple when damaged —with a blow to one part being transferred throughout the panel. Instead, the fiberglass will resist considerable force and then crack or shatter. It is possible to rebuild a shattered area from the various pieces, much like a jigsaw puzzle. Unican's canned fiberglass is ideal for this type of repair.

Working from the back side, remove all the dirt and broken pieces from the structure edge. Find a piece that mates to the main structure and clamp into place. Smear a coating of canned fiberglass on both pieces. Repeat this process with each of the pieces until all are glued into a rough, basically reconstructed piece.

At this point, check for rigidity, as more canned fiberglass may be required on the backside. All the raw edges will be exposed to the outside. With a rough disc, grind the whole outer surface to shape, removing all the high points and corners. This leaves a thin shell of the basic shape desired.

A complete rebuild is now possible by cutting one-foot pieces of fiberglass mat and laying them onto this thin shell form. Saturate the mat and roll it into place. As the edges of mat will taper out when rolled, shingle the area for consistent thickness.

When an entire panel must be replaced, it is possible to purchase the panels from specialty supply houses or direct from the manufacturer. Corvettes and Avantis are the most common production fiberglass cars, but more and more, high performance metal-bodies cars are including fiberglass front panels, deck lids, etc. When a panel is being repaired, it is trimmed to fit the car body and attached with mat and cloth—as mentioned in hole or crack repair.

But it may be more economical to make up your own mold and repair the missing piece. Making a small mold is easy, and can be done by either backing the missing area with formed wire and cardboard (as a base for repair mat and cloth, a kind of rough male inner mold), or taking a female mold off a similar panel.

Consider the example of a damaged Corvette rear fender. On a similar fender mark off with masking tape an area slightly larger than the damaged area. Mask the surrounding area with paper, so spilled glass and resin will not damage it. Using Johnson paste floor wax, liberally smear the unmasked section of the fender, leaving a wet coat of wax over the surface. In some instances it is possible to lay a piece of Saran Wrap over the area as a mold base. This won't work with reverse curves, but the wrap will adhere to most other compound curves.

Thin layers of mat should be used. This mat is cut into small pieces ranging from 2x4 inches to 4x6 inches.

Saturate the small pieces of mat with resin and lay on the waxed surface, with the smallest pieces used around the edges. Lay on pieces in an overlapping shingle manner until the entire surface has been covered. The small pieces will conform to the curves better than a single large piece. To force the mat into crevices and indentations, use a small paint brush wetted in resin. Push the material into place with the bristle ends; do not brush back and forth. After the whole surface has been covered with one layer, allow the mold to harden at least one hour.

After the mold has thoroughly cured, gently work the piece away from the original fender, remove the wax and polish the fender. The mold will be slightly larger than the original damaged fender and will align with it. Glass the mold in place and then finish as with all other repairs, using mat to build up the area to the original fender thickness. This is slightly more complicated than making a backing of wire and/or cardboard, but it works much better in areas of many compound curves.

If a special fiberglass body is desired, it can be made up from a mold. This procedure is rather expensive, but is especially useful if more than one body is to be made.

There must be some kind of basis for the mold, and this becomes the mock-up. In the case of hot rodding, original metal bodies are usually used. The metal is carefully straightened to perfect condition, as with an old Model T body, and most of the hard work is already done. However, if a special design is called for, the mock-up must be built from scratch. It is possible to utilize a basic body as the mock-up foundation, changing the contours with various materials.

For a new design, a wooden frame mock-up is made (as with aluminum) and covered with wire. The wire is fixed between the plywood bulkheads, about one inch below the proposed surface and is used to keep plaster in place and thin. After the mock-up substructure is assembled, it should be sprayed with some kind of varnish or shellac to prevent the wood from extracting water from the plaster.

Short-time casting plaster is the most common material used (plaster of Paris). A thin solution is mixed, and small mats of "shredded hemp," "shredded rope," or "long fiber" are dipped into the solution and applied about ¼ inch thick over the wire mesh. This mixture is allowed to dry.

A thick plaster mix is applied over this plaster-hemp base to within about ⅛ inch of the finished surface. Apply this plaster to the entire model. Brush on a thin coat of orange shellac to prevent the bottom layer of plaster from drawing water from the final coats. A thin, flexible metal blade, called a spline, is used to apply the final plaster coats. This blade is about one inch wide by two or three feet long, and is used to ensure flowing contours. A thin mixture of plaster is applied to the mold and smoothed by running the spline guide across the templates. It is easiest to work with two sections (three templates) at a time.

After this first coat of thin plaster has been applied, but not dried, a second coat is applied and a shorter spline is used. The amateur can usually work only about three square feet at a time. The plaster is allowed to dry and is then smoothed with graters, sander, or file. An excellent grater can be made by wrapping expanded metal around a 2x4 inch piece of wood.

After the plaster is really dry, which takes about two weeks, it can be sanded. Spray or brush on thick coats of lacquer primer (this lacquer is important) and sand the mock-up as on any ordinary car. Paint the mock-up with a good gloss lacquer, and fill small imperfections with putty and filler as with a metal or fiberglass body. Be careful when sanding a high spot, as any breakthrough in the plaster must be carefully feather-edged and repainted.

A parting agent must be applied to the mock-up if a female mold is made (and this is highly recommended, since use of the mock-up for a male mold will produce a rough outer body finish). Several parting agents are available, with lacquer-type cellulose acetate solution the most common. To one gallon of acetone add a half pound of cellulose acetate molding compound. Polyvinyl alcohol, which can be dissolved in hot water, makes a fine parting agent. Whatever type of parting agent is used, the mock-up must be coated with a good wax—a thick coat—and then be highly polished.

The female mold is made by spraying on a coat of polyester resin, followed by a second coat. This rather thick coat of pure resin is necessary if imperfections in the female mold are to be sanded out. Next add a layer of cloth to the entire mock-up, thoroughly saturated with resin. Work out all trapped air with a roller. Allow this layer of cloth to cure, then apply two or more layers of mat, followed by another layer of cloth.

The mold may need to separate, depending upon the "draw" of the mock-up. Most sports car-type bodies split cross-wise in the cockpit area, Model T's split down the middle, etc. Pieces of plywood may be constructed into a framework and laminated to the mold as further support, also forming a bench to hold the inverted mold. Making the actual body is then a matter of glass lamination, using a good parting agent and wax in the mold. The body is made from resin and layers of cloth/mat applied over a gel coat.

Fiberglass is a perfect agent for the amateur and professional alike, as it allows inexpensive experiments with exotic body designs. It is not a difficult medium, and is definitely recommended for anyone wanting to make his own "special" car from scratch.

10

Custom Painting

Painting, whether a diesel truck or a Morris Minor, is something anyone can do as long as the basic steps are thoroughly understood and faithfully applied. Most painters learn their trade the hard way, by long apprenticeship at the feet of experts, but in the custom paint field, most of the big names are self-taught. That is, they began as teenagers, by puttering first with their own cars and then on friends' vehicles. Perhaps this slightly different approach accounts for the leadership these famous painters enjoy. They prefer to try different things, to experiment with unusual techniques and colors in an effort to express their individuality.

But becoming an individual doesn't happen overnight. Instead, the basic 1-2-3 aspect of ordinary painting must be successfully learned and applied. However, it is only a short step from the basics to the advanced, and the serious enthusiast can become a top custom painter within a year. Since the number of really good custom painters can be counted on ten fingers, it's obvious the country needs more of them.

After all bodywork is completed, every piece of chome trim is removed from the body. There are a few pieces that can't be taken off, for one reason or another, but the majority are removable. This initial extra work will save more extra work in the end. Taping the trim properly is a time-consuming project, and although it only takes about one-quarter the time of complete removal, there are other problems to consider. In the first place, if you miscue with the masking tape, you can botch an otherwise good paint job (this will be explained later). Second, if you take the trim off, the entire body gets paint protection, under trim and all. Third, the area around the trim is a perfect place for wax and other types of film to build up, and if you're not very thorough with your preparation, this kind of film will ruin the paint. And finally, it's just a lot easier to prepare, paint, and finish a car that's minus trim. Incidentally, if the trim is held in place by stationary clips (the clips bolt to the body panel and the trim piece snaps away), don't go to great effort removing the clip. Paint right over it!

In addition to the trim, take out the grille (so the cavity can be painted); remove the bumpers; remove the rubber bumpers from the hood, deck lid, and doors; and last, peel the rubber windlacing seal away from the doors and deck lid. Be careful, for you'll want to reuse this seal, either the standard or universal type. If you really want to be meticulous, remove the door upholstery panels and kick panels. These are difficult to tape off and the little extra effort is well worth it.

It isn't important whether you feather-edge the repaired areas, or sand the unblemished paint first. Because water sanding is the fastest, cleanest, and easiest method of sanding, you'll probably do the overall sanding first. This way, if the job stretches out over several days (nothing wrong with this), the slight surface rusting that's bound to cover the repaired areas will be taken off in the feather-edging step just before primer is applied.

Obviously, it's wise to pick a place that drains well for your sanding location. The residue from sanding actually acts as a mild stain, which discolors driveway concrete if left standing.

If possible, use a hose for water supply, with a bare trickle available at all times. If this is impractical, a bucket of water and a good sponge will suffice. Thoroughly wet the surface before you start, and if possible, do the sanding in the shade, if for no other reason than comfort. Another hint: figure on getting wet; you will before you're through.

The top is as good a place to start as any. Work down to the hood and deck lid before attacking the side panels. Hold the hose in one hand, keeping the end from making new scratches, and sand with the other. Direct the flow of water on the work area as needed, which means a fine film of water at all times. You won't get too much water as far as sanding is concerned, but the more water you use, the wetter you become. When you're getting just enough water, the paper will glide without grabbing, but will have enough drag to tell you it's cutting.

If a bucket and sponge are used, you'll have to squeeze the sponge regularly to keep the water flowing, which means you'll use up the water supply rapidly. You can hold some of the moisture longer by adding a cake of Lava soap to the materials. Work up a good lather and spread it over the sanding area.

The sanding pattern is extremely important and can have a drastic effect upon the finished job. Always go in one direction as much as possible, preferably lengthwise with the panel (much like the grain in wood), and never, never sand in circles. On many panels, such as the top near the windshield, the lengthwise direction will not get around the windows well, so the direction must be changed, but the pattern here will be a straight, crisscross effect.

The sandpaper may be held either by hand or with a semiflexible sanding block. A block is very good for large panels, but the hand conforms better to curves. If a sanding block is used, tear strips from the sheet just wide enough for the block. Use 220-, 280-, or

320-grit paper for pre-primer sanding. If hand-held, the paper is torn differently. A 9 x 11-inch sheet is turned on its side, folded together, and torn down the center. Each piece is then triple-folded, leaving one face toward the paint, one toward the hand, and one folded between the two.

When sanding by hand, keep the entire hand in contact with the surface, not just the finger tips or side of the palm. However, for specific areas, these two pressure points may be used.

After the entire area has been sanded, let it dry and then check to make sure every inch has been covered. Any missed streaks or corners must be touched up.

With the biggest part of the surface sanded, attention can be directed toward repaired areas, scratches and chips. Getting these places feather-edged properly is vital to a well-finished product! This cannot be overstressed.

After the initial fast cut, switch to 220-grit sandpaper and the block plus water, and repeat. The idea is to feather the break between paint and metal over a wide area. There will be at least two layers of paint showing, the color coat and the primer/surfacer. However, on older cars the number can be as high as eight or nine layers. The wider the band of each paint layer showing, the better the feather-edging job! A one-inch band means a much better job than a ¼-inch band. Finally, sand the feather-edged area in the direction of the overall panel sanding job.

Scratches are easy to remove if they are only one paint coat thick. Just a little more localized pressure on the paper will do the job, but the "trough" should be feathered as much as possible. Small rock chips along the car's front and around the wheel openings are harder to remove, and because of their sheer number, it is best to use a block or electric/air jitterbug. Incidentally, you can rent one of these handy gadgets for three dollars a day. When the rock chips are really numerous and deep, resort to an initial attack with 100-grit paper, then follow up with the finer grits before priming. The entire color coat area is usually removed, but the effort is necessary.

Chips on the rest of the car, such as around exposed hinges or door openings or what have you, are really the hardest of all to feather-edge—mainly because their size means the feather-edging will leave a sort of smooth crater. Although the paint may be thin, the crater will really show up (even if properly feather-edged) in the finished job if you're not careful. The best route to follow when fixing up chipped places is to make the feather-edge area several times bigger than the size of the chipped area. If there were several coats of paint on the car, the crater might best be filled with a thin coat of putty after the primer is applied. The important point is, make a chip crater as smooth as possible, flowing gradually into the surrounding paint.

Be careful when sanding next to chrome, aluminum, or glass, as the paper will cut these surfaces quickly. Next to chrome, slide the index finger (or little finger) off the paper and use it as a guide. The same goes for the other materials, too. With a block, just be careful.

The edges of all opening panels should be block-sanded to bare metal. This won't be hard, as the paint here is usually minimal at best. This procedure will do away with a large percentage of edge chips, and will keep the new paint's thickness at a minimum, which cuts down on the chances of future chips.

Doorjambs and door edges should be washed clean of all accumulated dirt and grease, then thoroughly sanded with both paper and 00 steel wool. The steel wool gets down in all the little irregularities the paper can't reach, ensuring that the final paint will bond securely.

Fenders should be loosened and the fender welt removed; then carefuly sand the mating edges, especially chipped places. This is one location where shoddy preparation will quickly show up. New fender welt (which only costs twenty cents per foot) may be added after the color is on. Don't try to mask it off!

Finally, turn to the repaired areas again. If a spot has been worked, sand the bare area well with 220-grit or finer paper, until all the rough file or grinder scratches are no longer noticeable to the touch. Don't use rough paper, and don't lay on the pressure. Be careful—lead and fiberglass will scratch before the surrounding metal will.

Should a fiberglass area have what appear to be blisters, further repair is in order. This sometimes happens, so just peel out the air-bubble blister with a knife blade and patch it with more glass or resin.

Special attention must be paid to a repaired area before primer/surfacer is applied. If lead was used, wash the entire area thoroughly with properly diluted MetalPrep, which removes acid and grease. Wash away the MetalPrep residue with water. With both fiberglass- and lead-repaired areas, clean thoroughly with grease and wax remover (even though they've been well sanded), then spot with a good coat of primer.

At this stage of the game, you'll want a compressor handy, which can be rented along with the paint gun, for about ten dollars a day. You'll only need it for a day (actually much less). The compressor should be able to maintain a steady eighty pounds of pressure, which is more than enough for painting.

Build up tank pressure, drain the tank of any oil (the renter will show you how), then blow all the dirt and sanding residue from the car. Be especially careful to clean all the little pieces of stuff that get in cracks around windows, windshield, hood, hinges, etc. Use a lint-free rag or tack cloth as you go along to clean the surface as well as all chrome and glass areas.

When the car is clean, tape off the trim, glass, and interior. Since the primer/surfacer will be either lacquer or acrylic, you don't have to sweat over spray sticking to everything. Therefore, you can cover the engine and the seats with an old piece of anything handy. Tape a width of newspaper around the engine compartment opening. Tape off the door upholstery panels and glass molding if they haven't been removed. Keep all this paper as flat as possible, so debris can't fall in the folds and blow out later, even if this is just the prime coat.

If you plan to become deeply involved in automotive painting, you will need to know the equipment in some detail. The paint spray gun is a device that uses air pressure to atomize sprayable material. For automotive refinishing, two types of paint guns are common, one having the gun (mixer) and the paint container (cup) integral, the other having the container separated from the gun by an extra hose. These types are further divided into bleeder and nonbleeder, external and internal mix, and pressure-, gravity- or suction-feed guns.

The bleeder-type gun is more common in the very inexpensive lines, and is designed without an air valve. The air passes through the gun at all times, which keeps the air pressure from building up in the hose. There are no air pressure control devices involved, so the gun is used with small low-pressure compressors. More suitable to automotive painting is the nonbleeder design which has an air valve to shut off the air as the trigger is released. Such a gun can control both the air and paint flow by trigger manipulation.

The internal-mixing spray gun mixes the air and paint inside the cap, but this design also is not well suited to automotive work. Better is the external-mix gun which mixes and atomizes the air and paint just outside the cap. A suction-feed gun uses the force of a stream of compressed air to cause a vacuum, which causes the paint to push out of the container. If the fluid tip is flush with the air cap, chances are the gun is of the pressure-feed type (commonly used on automotive assembly lines), where the paint is forced to the gun by air pressure in the container attached to the spray gun.

The air cap is located at the extreme tip of the paint gun, with a knurled face so it can be gripped and removed by hand. Such a cap may have one to four orifices for air which is directed into the paint stream to atomize the mixture. As a rule, the average shop gun will have two orifices, but the more orifices available the better. Heavy materials will atomize better with multiple-orifice caps.

A small, removable nozzle is held into the gun body by the air cap. This is the fluid tip which meters and controls the direction of paint into the air streams. The fluid tip is a seat for the fluid needle, the unit which controls the flow of material from the cup. These tips are available in a wide range of nozzle sizes. The larger the nozzle size, the larger the amount of paint that can be sprayed. The needle and the fluid tip come in matched pairs, ranging up to .086 inch (this size designation is stamped on both tip and needle), but for average use, something in the .036- to .045 inch range is best.

A suction-feed gun tends to apply an uneven spray on anything but vertical surfaces, because paint in a tipped container will flow over the vent in the cup cover. A partial solution is to unplug the vent periodically and keep it toward the rear of the cup. The same air flow that atomizes and sprays the paint creates a siphon. If very large areas are being painted, where the fluid adjustment is wide open for maximum pattern, the automization pressure can get as high as 35 to 40 pounds, which means the pressure required to operate the siphon is greater than that required to atomize the paint. The pressure-feed gun eliminates most of the disadvantages of the suction-feed gun, but it requires more skill since it applies a greater volume of paint faster.

It is absolutely imperative to keep all spray painting equipment as clean as possible, so you must clean the gun after each and every use. If the gun is not cleaned, the paint will dry in those difficult-to-clean nozzles. When cleaning the suction-feed gun, loosen the cup and hold the gun handle over it with the siphon tube inside the container. Unscrew the air cap several turns, then cover the cap with a rag and pull the trigger. Air pressure will be diverted through the fluid passages and will force any paint in the gun back into the cup.

Empty the cup and clean it thoroughly with thinner, then pour a small amount of thinner into the cup. Spray this solvent through the gun to flush the fluid passages. It is handy to keep a small can of solvent ready for gun cleaning. Either wipe the gun housing with a soaked rag or use a bristle brush, the latter being preferable.

The air cup should be removed and cleaned by soaking it in clean thinner. Dry the cap with compressed air. If the small holes are plugged, soak the cap longer, then open the holes with a toothpick or broomstraw. Do not use a metal object as this may enlarge the holes.

Never soak the entire spray gun in solvent, as this allows sludge and dirt to collect in the air passages or removes lubricants necessary for smooth gun operation. These lubricant points are at the fluid needle packing, air valve packing, and the trigger bearing screw. The fluid needle can be coated lightly with a petroleum jelly. Never use a caustic alkaline solution to clean a spray gun, as these solutions will corrode the aluminum and diecast parts. It takes only minutes to clean a gun shortly after use, but cleaning can require hours if the gun has been left unclean for a period of time.

Air compressors are normally grouped as either single- or two-stage. The single-stage unit has a single cylinder and will give pressure to around 100 psi. A two-stage unit has twin cylinders of unequal size with an intercooler between the cylinders and will pump well over 100 psi. In the two-stage design, air is compressed first in the large cylinder, then it is recompressed further by the small cylinder before being fed to the high pressure storage tank.

The size of compressor needed will depend entirely upon what the job calls for. A normal shop compressor is very large, since so many things in the shop are driven by air. The home craftsman can usually do very well with a good single-stage compressor that will hold at least 60 psi while the paint gun is being operated (80 to 100 psi would be better). There are a number of smaller, portable air compressors available through various sales outlets, but the compressor should not be purchased on the basis of price. Plan on spending well over $100 for a good portable unit unless you can find a good used compressor. Incidentally, a paint gun requires on the average 8.5 cubic feet of air per minute.

Seldom available, as an integral part of the new compressor, is a regulator (transformer), which is used to maintain a close check on the air supply to paint guns. The regulator also prevents oil, water, and dirt from entering the air lines. The regulator has numerous filter elements to trap foreign materials, and a drain cock in the sump to release oil and moisture. Gauges on the regulator show exactly how much pressure is available and how much is being used.

If the compressor is being installed permanently, steel pipe can be used to bring the air to convenient outlets. Usually, however, the home enthusiast will use the portable compressor equipped with hoses. It is vital that the correct size hose be used, since resistance to the flow of air increases rapidly as hose diameter decreases. There are two types of hose available, air and paint. Air hose is normally red, and paint hose is black or brown. Hose size is normally 5/16 inch inside diameter for suction-feed guns. Air pressure drop caused by friction in the line can be severe if the hose or pipe is long or the inside diameter is small.

When the entire car is taped, and the spray gun is ready to fire, mix up the primer/surfacer. Neither lacquer nor acrylic will go over enamel in color-coat form. This can be done only over a factory-baked enamel job, where the paint is dry clear through. Baked enamel is likely to blister when covered with the hotter paints. This applies only to the color coats, and not to the primer, which will cover the surface with no adverse effects.

No matter what kind of paint will finally be used—enamel, lacquer, or acrylic—use a multipurpose primer with the appropriate thinner. Mix according to the directions on the can, which is usually about two parts thinner to one part primer, then stir thoroughly. For primer, a good all-around spray gun head will do, something like a Number 30 on the DeVilbiss and Number 362 on the Binks. Adjust the gun so that the spray fan is about 8 inches wide, 12 inches from the gun head. If the fan is too wide, there will be a thin spot in the middle, or if it's two narrow the pattern will appear as a tight band. The fan adjustment is the top knob above the handle. The second knob is for material adjustment.

Make practice passes on a piece of cardboard, with the compressor set at 60 pounds constant. If you use the DeVilbiss, keep the gun 8 to 12 inches away from the surface; with the Binks, 10 to 12 inches. Notice that when the paint gun trigger is first depressed there is a moment when only air comes out, quickly followed by the paint. Practice making a smooth pass, keeping the gun a constant distance from the surface until the pass (which will average about two feet per swing) is completed. Start the pass on one side, swing horizontally to the other limit, raise or lower the gun nearly a fan width and go back. Keep the gun nearly a fan width and go back. Keep the gun nearly a fan width and go back again. The gun should be kept parallel to the surface, so that one end of the fan isn't closer than the other.

As soon as you feel confident with the paint gun (don't worry too much, because primer dries relatively quickly and it is easy to fix up a botched area), start with the doors, hood, and deck lid openings. Spray the primer on evenly, in smooth strokes. When these are done, allow them to dry for 10 to 15 minutes, then close the openings and start on the big outside metal.

Start spraying on the top, which is the hardest to reach, and follow these handy hints. Throw the air hose over one shoulder and hold it away from the car with the extra hand; wrap a piece of rag around the gun/cup connection point to keep paint from dribbling out when painting with the gun in a nozzle-down position (such as top, hood, deck lid).

If the paint is going on correctly, it will appear smooth and wet for just a bit after application. If it looks grainy (as is full of sand), the paint is too thick or you're holding the gun too far away from the surface. If the paint runs (you won't need anybody to show you what this panic is!), it is too thin or you are holding the gun too close to the surface. If the patch alternates dry-wet-dry, or wet-runny-wet, your pass is not constant. And don't stay in one place too long. It's just 1-2-3, 1-2-3, etc.

Primer is the basic foundation of a fine paint job, so don't skimp. It takes about one gallon of unthinned primer/surfacer for the average car, so keep going around the car until you're sure you've got it well covered. Cost is $10 per gallon for the primer, $3 per gallon for thinner.

Plan your time so that when you are through spraying you have at least two hours of sunlight left, and try to spray when the temperature is at least 60° or above. If you are spraying in winter or inside when it's raining, use special thinner (the paint store will decide for you).

Finally, if the car has slight waves in the panels that might be taken out by block sanding, a good trick is to spray a final coat of a different-colored primer. For instance, if the major primer color was light gray, finish with dark gray, or vice versa. Then, later on when you block sand, the thin top coat will come off, but the other color will still show in low spots. For panels that are particularly wavy, alternate several coats of primer color, which will show both light and low spots when dry.

After the primer has dried for twenty or thirty minutes, the tape can be removed. (Bleeder sealer, applied over paints such as red and maroon which bled through color coats, is put on over the primer later.) Although it is possible to go right ahead and sand the car (dry) and follow with the color coats of paint, it is best to allow the primer to cure for several days, or even weeks. The primer will dry and shrink, so allow about four weeks' time for a good job. In the meantime, you can drive the car.

The best painter in the world finds it difficult to put out a fine finished product if the initial work hasn't been done right or well enough. However, vital as the preparatory work is, painting is still a three-phase operation—preparation, application, maintenance.

Next, use the wax and grease remover solution again, completely washing the car, even in the tiniest cracks. This is vital, for any foreign substance will invariably ruin an otherwise perfect paint job. For instance, just the marks left by your fingers will leave dark splotches under the final color. When washing the car with the cleaning solution, always use clean, lint-free rags (don't use shop towels as they often are cleaned with low-grade solvents that contain contaminants detrimental to good paint adhesion). It's wise to use a special cleanser always, but in a pinch you can use lacquer thinner, applied with a very wet rag and immediately wiped off with a dry rag. Don't wait even a minute if you use thinner, as it is "hot" and will quickly soften the primer surface and may cause other damage below.

It's best to tape after the final surface sanding is completed and when all the little nicks and crannies have been blown free of water or sanding dust. Absolute cleanliness is a prerequisite to good paint jobs, so it's worth taking a few extra minutes rather than waste many hours of hard labor.

The car is now ready for the final color, and this is precisely where most amateur painters get the jitters. One step must follow the other in rapid succession. Having the procedures well established in your mind will ensure fine results.

What you do from now on depends a lot upon the paint you're using—the type, not the brand. Lacquer is the easiest to spray for the novice (several customizers don't even know how to use enamel properly!), followed by acrylic, then enamel. Lacquer and acrylic dry much faster, compensating for many errors in application—or at least for a few.

Basically, paint is a mixture of pigments (coloring matter, which can be mixed with many other elements and compounds, from bronze to gold, to silver powder, etc.).

The thinner, which is a vital partner to paint, is in fact the real paint base and makes drying possible. Obviously, the thinner also lowers the paint's viscosity so that the solution can be sprayed through a paint gun.

Enamel paint, although the hardest to actually apply, requires the least amount of overall effort, and is an excellent choice where maximum toughness is required. It gets glossiness (shine) from a varnish used by the manufacturer. Varnish is made of a solution of resins mixed with alcohol, turpentine, or amyl acetate. You must use enamel thinner with enamel paint. Although acrylic has received a big boost as a standard finish by several auto makers, at least one major company still uses baked enamel. A baked-enamel job is superior to an air-dry job (due to its durability), but unless you have a bake oven available, you're stuck with air-dry. For years, hot rodders have considered lacquer the only way to get a superb paint job, but such is not at all the case. It depends generally upon the painter. For the average person unable to afford a good lacquer expert, and not wanting to take the extra preparation pains necessary for lacquer, enamel is an obvious answer. It covers scratches well, and can be used almost anywhere.

Lacquer paints are made from cellulose, resins, and a thing called lac, which is a sticky substance deposited by insects on trees in southeastern Asia. But in this form, lacquer is very brittle, so auto lacquers have one or more plasticizers added for elasticity. Unlike enamel, which takes as much as four to six months to really harden, lacquer cures shortly after metal contact.

Acrylic is like lacquer, in that it dries right away, but it is plastic-based (lacquer is cotton-based) and undergoes a chemical change as the paint dries and unites with oxygen. Acrylic must be sprayed differently, since it will not dry to maximum gloss if put on in one heavy coat.

As in priming, before starting to spray color, it is wise to completely clean the spraying equipment, especially if it has come from the local rental emporium.

If enamel is to be used, thin it with two parts thinner to one part paint, pouring the paint into the cup through a strainer which traps bits of foreign matter. Tighten the pot until secure, as paint might otherwise drip from the connection (invariably right out in the middle of a flat panel). If you cannot keep such drips from occurring, wrap a shop rag tightly around the area as a trap.

Before ever blowing color at the waiting car, test the gun pattern. Start by opening the gun up by turning the spreader adjustment (top thumb screw above the handle) all the way out, and backing off the fluid screw (right beneath the spreader adjustment) until the first thread shows. Adjust the air-pressure regulator to give a constant 40-lb. pressure for lacquer and acrylics, of 60-lb. for enamel. Hold the gun 6 or 8 inches from the test surface, parallel to such surface, and give the trigger one full pull, then release.

The resulting pattern of paint should be uniform throughout, with fine atomization and no distortion. If something is wrong with the pattern, it will make the painting process exceptionally difficult for a nonprofessional.

The color coat is sprayed exactly like the primer/surfacer. However, some extra preparation might be needed if lacquer or acrylic is being applied over enamel. Just as a precaution, if the old paint is enamel, spray on a coat of DuPont Number 22 sealer, which will keep the enamel from raising due to the hotter lacquer thinner. If you're not sure, you can always spray a test patch first, but a sealer is the best bet.

All the previous work will come to naught if the final color coat spraying is done haphazardly. Before actually spraying any paint, practice the proper spraying swing. At all times, the nozzle should be from 8 to 12 inches from the surface (individuals vary in technique, that's why the distance is only approximate). Picture yourself standing facing the side door of a car. You want to paint each individual panel, or panel group, with a full stroke, thereby reducing the number of overlaps to a minimum. With gun held at the left edge of a panel and the nozzle distance correct, twist the wrist so the gun is actually pointed lengthwise to the car. As the trigger is pulled, twist the wrist back toward the car, which makes the initial application of each stroke blend in. As the gun comes to point directly at the surface, begin the stroke across the panel—not too slow, and not too fast, just so. If you go too fast, the stroke will look misty, if too slow the paint will pile up and run. At the end of each stroke (which will usually be at the end of the panel) twist the wrist, and nozzle, away from the car in the opposite direction.

The entire spraying operation, too often overlooked by professionals when explaining paint, is a sort of rhythm, like dancing. Just remember, 1-2-3, 1-2-3, twist-stroke-twist, etc. The length of the panel will dictate the length of the intermediate count. It's very easy, and lots of fun once you catch on.

Because you're spraying a panel at a time, you must get in the habit of spraying consistently. Don't put paint on one area heavily and go light on another. As you start a panel, you might begin each stroke slightly in from one edge, and stop slightly short of the other. Then, as the next panel is painted, the overspray from both strokes will combine to give the right amount of coverage. This will take time to learn.

The single biggest problem the amateur faces is stroke inconsistency. The paint must overlap everywhere, otherwise it will appear streaked when it dries. It might be advisable for the neophyte to make horizontal strokes on the panel first, followed by vertical strokes (the gun laid on its side to keep the fan pattern right), and finished by crisscross strokes. The idea is to get the same amount of paint everywhere.

If lacquer is being used, you can paint merrily on your way. However, acrylic must be allowed to "flash,"—that is, surface harden—before the next coat is applied. Following the enamel procedure works well with acrylic. Enamel, being a very slow dryer, cannot be applied all at once. The first time around the car, apply a very light, or tack coat. This will become sticky in a few minutes and helps make subsequent spraying easier by increasing adhesion. The second coat of enamel is sprayed normally, but the amateur should never try to get all the paint (two gallons required for the average car) on in one pass.

Starting with the top, spray each stroke evenly. If you load up a particular area, which is easy to do, expect a run. But don't panic, just keep right on with the job, but ease off on the amount of paint. When the first cover coat is finished, dip a tiny brush in the enamel thinner and remove as much of the sag (run) as possible. The idea is to soak up the excess, not spread it around. After the excess is removed, gingerly fog a little paint over the area. If you do the job well, the little boo-boo won't be apparent (good painters can completely eradicate runs). On the next coat, go easy in this area, just lightly fogging over the top of it.

Usually, an enamel job requires three passes—the tack coat, first color, and second color. After the last coat, wait a couple of minutes, check for sags and repair them, then leave the car to dry overnight. In fact, since enamel should be painted indoors, leave the car if possible for a couple of days before detailing.

A note about enamel and moisture. Moisture and paint just don't mix, so if you wash the floor to keep the dust down, let it dry before painting. This also might be a good time to discuss temperature and paint. Temperature shouldn't be under 60° or over 100° F when you paint a car, otherwise special steps are required. Remember, this is the temperature of the metal. If you're painting lacquer or acrylic out in the backyard, that hot sun can make the body sizzle.

Special additives are available to control the drying time, such as DuPont 3656 (rather than normal 366/g) for acrylic, which will slow drying down if the temperature is too hot. If painting when it's wet or cold, the color can "blush"—that is, moisture is trapped in the paint, so a slower acting thinner or special retarder might be needed. The local paint salesman will guide you here. At all times, follow the mixture directions of the manufacturer explicitly.

A note about the spraying environment. It is possible to rent the facilities of a paint shop over the weekend, thereby gaining the equipment and paint booth. However, the only real requirement is that enamel should be painted in a dust-free atmosphere. A fly walking across the surface before becoming trapped is also a mess. Again, don't mind an overspray on everything. Enamel overspray will stay, while lacquer and acrylic will dust off or wash away. Lacquer and acrylic can be sprayed quite well outdoors.

Although an enamel job can be done all in one spraying, lacquer and acrylic require more elapsed time for the best results. If you have the time, spray the latter in several good coats, then allow to dry for a couple of days. Water-sand with 600-grit sandpaper then spray with several more coats. Whereas enamel doesn't require any special after-spray attention, lacquer and acrylic must be sanded with 600-grit paper before final rubbing out.

It is always advisable to consider stock paints and colors for a street-driven car. The reason is obvious—maintenance. It's very difficult to repair chips and hurt spots in a specially prepared color. The new cars, especially the higher priced models, have a tremendous range of glamour colors available that are very close to the special "candies" and "flakes." For instance Corvette's

Nassau Blue is a very good near-translucent and is comparable to light candy blue.

Although actually putting paint on a car is the hardest part of any refinishing operation, keeping the color like new is perhaps the most frustrating. The value of a good paint job seldom shows itself if the final finishing isn't well done.

In case you have ended up with some sags (runs), which is easy to do if you've used enamel, very lightly water-sand the run ridges after the paint has set at least two weeks, then lightly fog the area with new paint.

An enamel paint job doesn't require color sanding. In fact, since enamel never really dries underneath, sanding it will often cut away the vital layer of surface sheen and you'll never get a shiny result. In all cases with enamel, let the car stand in the paint booth as long as possible before removing the tape, paper, etc. If possible, leave the car for two nights before starting the detail work.

Although an enamel paint job will feel dry to the touch, even after a month or so, the paint underneath the hard surface is still soft. In actuality, the paint doesn't feel hard, but rather like plastic. Whatever foreign object you leave on the surface of a new enamel paint job (discounting baked enamel, which is ideal) is likely to cause a pattern or outline in the paint.

Enamel only a couple of months old is also very susceptible to water spotting. When you wash a new enamel paint job, use only clear, cool water and the softest of rags. Then carefully dry the entire surface with a very soft chamois. Do not leave even a speck of water, as it will spot the paint.

If for some reason you desire to rub out an enamel paint job, do so only after the paint is three months old. A professional will do the rubbing sooner, but it's best to take the extra few weeks as a precaution. You can use a machine polisher if you've gotten in a little recent practice, but if you're not sure of yourself, do it the hard way. By hand. When rubbing out enamel, use very fine enamel compound, and go very, very lightly. Often, tiny particles of dust will imbed in the thin outer layer of an enamel job, and although repeated washings will remove many of them, a light rub-out is necessary for maximum smoothness. Enamel should never be rubbed out too often. A good guide is after three months, then once a year thereafter. Don't wax a new enamel paint job until the paint has had a good chance to dry. Wait roughly three to five months.

Lacquers and acrylics normally require a color sanding for maximum effect. This sanding may come either during the actual painting process, or after, or both. The number of coats involved in a lacquer paint job is not necessarily indicative of the quality of the work. The more paint on a surface, the greater the possibility of early paint failure.

While painting the car, color sanding may be worth while. No matter how carefully the body work has been done, not all of the tiny little ripples or dings can be found during the original sanding. Many painters spray on a light lacquer or acrylic color coat just to find these imperfections. With color on the car, they show up readily, and can be eliminated with a thin touch of putty. Color sanding follows after three or four coats of color have been applied; color block sanding will further smooth out the overall surface and remove any imperfections.

The final color sanding cuts away the surface imperfections of these fast-dry paints, irregularities that appear because the paint dries quickly and does not flow together like enamel. Color sanding is possible because the paint is thoroughly dry from its outer to inner surface. Such sanding is always done with 600-grit wet-or-dry paper, chased with generous amounts of water. Some professionals use white gas or similar products, but the amateur had best stick with water. Make sure the surface of the paper is clean at all times, as a grain of dirt or built-up paint will deeply scratch the surface. Color sanding has been described as a sort of blending process.

When the surface has dried after color sanding, it is dull but very smooth. Next is the polishing procedure, and like everything else connected with painting, it requires a light touch. You can rent a good polisher for a couple of bucks, and the compound is not expensive.

Hand rubbing a car may sound exotic, but it's a perfect waste of time. You'll eventually end up with a hand-rubbed finish anyway, so start with the machine polisher. If possible, practice on another car before you attack your new paint job, just to get the feel of the polisher.

It is vital that you use the proper compound for polishing. Because hand rubbing is not nearly as efficient, the compound for it is very coarse. Machine compound is much thinner, but if you don't have it available, mix ordinary hand compound (which looks like thick, gooey clay) with water until you have a thin, watery paste. It's better to have machine compound too thin than too thick.

Most polishes are merely a thin form of rubbing compound, and perform the function of a light abrasive. If you were to use polish over and over for a long enough period, you would have no paint left. If you use a thick hand-rubbing compound with a mechanical polisher, it is very easy to cut right through the paint to the bare metal, so go slowly until you get the knack of it.

After you have machine-polished the entire car, working each panel until the paint becomes shiny, you can use a hand compound to get around all the little places—door handles, grille moldings, fender corners, etc. This will take almost as long as the machine polishing, and you will then know why initial hand-rubbing is so futile. Finally, wipe the car with clean, soft rags and hand-rub any areas that aren't sparkling. If you've followed all the necessary steps to this point, the car will glisten like a jewel.

If you really want to come up with a super job, repeat the rubbing procedure, using a finer compound (subsequent uses of polish accomplishes a similar end). Sometimes (although most custom painters don't go this far) you can finish it off with ordinary kitchen corn starch, which is a very fine, powdery abrasive.

Following the rubbing, wash the paint with clear, cool water to remove any small grains of abrasive. As with enamel, never leave water standing on lacquer or acrylic finishes, or they will spot. This becomes especially critical if the car is washed in the hot sun. In fact, all work on a new finish is best done in the shade.

When it comes to waxing, you're on your own. Carnuba wax is always recommended, but generally the better the wax, the harder it is to apply. With lacquer and acrylic, get a top quality wax on the car as soon as possible, and keep the car waxed from then on.

Lacquer and acrylic tend to scratch easily (the former is worst), breaking along the line of impact much like the jagged edges of a zipper. A heavy coating of wax will help keep this problem to a minimum.

No matter how careful you are with a paint job (and it can become ridiculous), paint is bound to get little chips, nicks, and the like during normal service. Even carefully handled show cars get their share of paint problems.

The solution is not to throw a tantrum, but to repair the chipped area immediately. The edges of doors, deck lid, and hood are most susceptible to chips, while the front end and lower sides generally receive a dose of rock nicks. In either case, touch up the chips or nicks with a matching color, or a tone very close to matching. Use a small brush or frayed paper match stem, and dab on the paint in successive layers until it has built up to nearly the original thickness. Then, very carefully color sand and/or rub the area, blending the edges smooth. Very large scratches can be repaired this way, surprisingly enough, and even the most amateur job will come out looking good. Incidentally, you can fix up chrome scratches with plain old fingernail polish, which will keep the exposed surfaces from rusting.

In the event that you have applied a special custom color including lots of clear lacquer or acrylic, this clear will often fail after one or two years (acrylic lasts much longer). The resulting "check" cracks can sometimes be color sanded out and it's always worth a try.

Special custom colors should not be expected to last forever, although many will. The more clear required for the paint job, the less durable—generally speaking—it becomes. Also, the more metallic used, the more susceptible the paint is to fading. If you protect the paint with lots of wax, keep it clean, and repair all scratches, you can expect a good paint job to last for years.

Special Paint

Unlike custom body work, which is expensive and not in great demand as a full-time profession, custom painting enjoys widespread popularity, primarily because it is well within the reach of most enthusiasts. We are in an era of the specialized car, and a special car must look different from the norm.

There are a number of special paint shops across the nation. They turn out fine body and fender work, but concentrate on producing outstanding paint jobs. Interestingly enough, this special painting may not be so special after all, but merely a better-than-average application. Dean Jeffries is famous as a custom painter, yet his Hollywood shop does a land-office business in basic paint jobs on Aston Martins, Bentleys, and Rolls-Royces. Dean stresses quality above all else, which has made him exceptionally successful. Naturally this same kind of attention to detail is followed elsewhere at most famous custom shops. People like Joe Bailon, who invented candy apple; Gene Winfield; Watson; Junior; the A Brothers; Anderson—all are sticklers for minute detail. The custom appearance of their paint is a matter of technique rather than some great dark secret

Perhaps this philosophical approach is best explained by Joe Anderson, a successful Southern California painter who has pioneered the use of enamels in custom paints. "I can't paint all the cars in the world, so why try. There are no real secrets in painting anyway, since any professional who has an interest in special paints can quickly duplicate anything new." Apparently the Anderson philosophy has been working, as he spends several hours a day on the telephone, helping beginners and professionals alike get the best possible results with his custom-mixed paints.

The key to any good custom paint job is not so much the color selected, or the type of paint, but the detailing. A straight maroon paint job on any car might cost $125 at a typical body shop, yet the custom painter charges three or four times that much because he is so meticulous. And the difference in the two jobs is immediately apparent.

Preparation is the basic foundation on which any custom paint job rests. The metal must be ready and as free of flaws as possible. No tiny dents, no waves, no scratches.

A custom paint job really means that everything humanly possible has been done to make the finished product perfect. This means that everything is painted, including the firewall, beneath the hood and deck lid—everything! There is something very distinctive about a thorough paint job, something that sets it apart from even those high-quality factory finishes.

Nothing should be overlooked during preparation for a custom paint job. This cannot be overemphasized. Remove the chrome trim and the rubber around the doors, hood, and deck lid. Remove any identification plates on the doorsills (these can be replaced with metal screws or blind rivets). If the firewall is to be painted, along with the inner fender panels, remove such things as horns, voltage regulators, etc., from the panels but leave all the wiring connected. Cover the engine with a nonporous material (plastic, oil cloth) and tape off bulky items that should not be painted (windshield motor, brake cylinder, etc.).

All inner surfaces can then be sanded, although the rough panels won't be as smooth as the exterior panels without resorting to metal work or filling. They will look fine, however, if they are sanded well with 320-grit sandpaper (wet) and the rough places are cleaned with 00 steel wool. Then thoroughly wash all inner surfaces with a high-quality grease and wax remover.

The difference in preparing the outside panels for custom paint is again in detail. It is absolutely vital there be no nicks, dings, or ripples to spoil the looks of the finished job. As a beginning, sand the entire car with a rubber block and 320-grit wet sandpaper. Keep the paper wet all the time for faster cutting. In areas where there are high and low spots, sand to metal in the high spots, by using the original paint as low-area filler. The more paint you load on a panel, the greater the chance of premature failure; using the original paint as a filler will guard against this.

The reason for using water when sanding is simple; it cuts down on the amount of clogging, eliminates dust, and leaves a smoother finish. Solvents should not be used at all, particularly gasoline. Besides being dangerous, gas has the added disadvantage of leaving an oily film on the surface.

The amount of work involved in this initial preparation stage will directly determine how the finished product will look. For example, look at a repainted Corvette. Unless the body has been very carefully block-sanded, with the waves filed smooth, the new paint will accentuate the ripples normally found in production fiberglass cars. Fiberglass-bodied cars also tend to have many small cracks in their high stress areas, cracks that must be repaired. If not, they will only grow larger and ruin an otherwise good paint job.

When there is a very high spot that cannot be taken down with a light amount of filing, the spot must be worked with hammer and dolly. Unless the panel has been damaged, such spots are not likely to occur. The small rubber sanding blocks available through auto paint stores are fine for preliminary sanding; longer blocks are a distinct advantage if the car has a number of low-crown panels. This includes most late model cars. Such blocks can be made from a piece of good hardwood, about ½ inch thick, 4 inches wide, and from 8 to 14 inches long. These long blocks will show up curves and long ripples not found by the shorter rubber block, something very helpful if the finish color is to be black or very dark, as dark colors tend to accent ripples.

When the surface is ready for a primer/surfacer, it should be thoroughly washed as outlined previously. Masking and taping are also the same. Remember too that a primer, which is designed to go over bare metal, is not a scratch filler.

The type of primer/surfacer to use depends upon the type of original paint being covered. As a guide, always use automotive synthetic enamel primer/surfacer (this is not the same as a primer only, but is a combination product), particularly if you're not sure what the original paint was. The synthetic primer/surfacer fills minor scratches and will not have a chemical reaction with the base paint. At the same time it forms an excellent undercoat that will grip the metal and the original paint as well as the new paint. A further advantage comes if you are using a glazing compound. Glaze cannot be spread over enamel in any quantity, as it will cause the paint to raise. However, it will work over the synthetic primer/surfacer.

When applying glaze to bring up some of the low spots, it should be put on in thin coats one on top of the other and allowed to dry thoroughly between each application. Glaze is not a substitute for plastic or lead fillers, and will crack if it becomes too thick.

Finally, synthetic primer/surfacer can be used as a nonsanding sealer over a lacquer, which means it does not need to be sanded before the finish color paint is added. Such a sealer is not unusual; there are several special sealers available, but any quality primer/surfacer is so versatile that it reduces the need for keeping a large inventory of priming materials. Unlike lacquer primer, however, the synthetic does not flash (surface dry) within a matter of minutes. Synthetic does dry relatively fast, however, to the touch, but must be left for some time before sanding. Generally speaking, the longer the better, as it will have a chance to thoroughly shrink before any paint is added.

When the primer/surfacer is ready for sanding, it is often given another flash-coat of primer, which is lighter or darker in color. This will dry rapidly and can be sanded right away. The advantage is that when the primer/surfacer is block sanded, the different color will show up any high or low spots that may have been missed the first time around. And there are usually many. This final sanding will require very smooth sandpaper; enamel should have 320-grit wet, while lacquer should have 400- or 600-grit wet.

Spraying special custom paint is basically the same as spraying any paint, although the particular technique may vary slightly between cobwebbing, Metalflake, candy, and so on. Experts are emphatic on one point, however: have everything ready to go! Once the spraying is started, there isn't time to be looking around for a missing can of toner or some more thinner.

Painting translucent (candy) colors is not hard, but is rather like a series of building-block steps. The underbase is the secret, as it is highly reflective and actually shows through the covering transparent toner. The four common underbases for lacquer are ordinary gold, copper, silver, and pearl metallics. Each color works in combination with the toners to give a specific effect. For example: Copper underbases tend to darken the final color, and have a warm tone, or richness. Gold helps create a vivid brilliance under any color, although still warm, yet retains a definite sparkle.

Silver tones down the color, but gives a sort of deep chromed look beneath the color.

The toners and blenders are available from any automotive paint supply store. A clear blender is imperative. When mixing the underbase, don't use too much powder, or the underbase will tend to separate . . . and don't prepare the underbase mixture until ready to spray as it will jell if left out in the air even for a short period of time.

Shoot the underbase in a normal manner, under low pressure (35 to 40 lbs.), and thin the paint with equal amounts of quality, slow drying lacquer thinner. Try not to get a dark or light spot while covering the car completely. You can effectively spot such an area, so if those spotted panels appear, just shoot the car again. After the underbase has dried for a half hour or so, spray on a coat of sealer to keep the underbase from bleeding. Figure on using about one gallon of underbase for an average American car.

Eleven of the thirteen most popular candy colors can be applied over the above underbases. The two exceptions are Pagan Gold and Mother of Pearl. Pearl must be applied over a white or silver base, and Pagan Gold over the gold underbase. The formulas for mixing color coats are included in this chapter.

The final tone is determined by the toner used, and the number of paint coats applied. While the paint is still wet you can get an approximate idea of what the final color will be.

Spraying the color coats is not difficult, but increase the pressure to about 50 to 65 pounds for lacquer and acrylic. The color should be sprayed within one or two hours after the underbase sealer, and should be thinned 1:1 or 1½:1 with quality thinner. Fog the color on slightly dry, then cover with clear, so it will flow together. Avoid irregular strokes. An intermediate color sanding with 600-grit wet sandpaper after eight hours' drying time is then followed by a couple of surface flow coats, which are mixed 2:1 or 3:1 with a quality slow-dry thinner. Wait a couple of weeks if possible before final color sanding and rubbing out, as this gives the paint more time to dry and shrink.

The number of paint coats applied will not necessarily indicate how good the job is; indeed some custom painters apply the same amount of paint with half the number of coats. This is something personal and depends upon a particular painter's technique. On average, a candy color paint job will have around thirty-five coats of paint when finished, Metalflake perhaps twice as many. Still, the less paint applied, the better it will last.

For the enthusiast who must drive his pride-and-joy and cannot treat it as heirloom china, custom enamel is the answer. Enamel has long been considered the best of all general-purpose paints, and it is even better suited to automobiles since the introduction of acrylics. Custom painters have longed to use enamel, but until recently they have not registered widespread success with the medium. Then Joe Anderson found a way to mix and apply enamels in all the candy colors, and the rest is history. Although Joe discovered lace painting and cobwebbing quite by accident, he needed hundreds of experimental hours to perfect "candy" enamel.

Kits are ideal for the beginner; they're easy to use, and include the ten basic pearlescent candies, such as Gold, Tangerine, Blue, Lemon, Lavender, etc. Specially mixed kits are also available, but since they will be slightly different from the basic colors, extra paint should be ordered for spotting. A typical full kit (including enough paint to do a standard car) with have one gallon of undercoat color, one gallon of pearlescent and candy fade, strainers, tack rag, special wax, step-by-step instructions—all that's necessary to do the job. Price is around $50 for a full kit. Smaller kits are available. For instance, a motorcycle or T-bucket might require the intermediate kit (quarts instead of gallons), and the mini-kit has pints. There are even aerosol cans for dashes or touch-up.

The whole point is that custom painting can be easy. Another plus for pearl enamel is that there is no weather problem. It can be raining cats and dogs and enamel can be applied. In fact, this might be a blessing in disguise, since dust and dirt in the air are the only real enemy when applying enamel. Fish eye and wrinkle preventer are already added to the kits to eliminate the hazard of dampness.

Pearl enamel is applied as any enamel, usually over the synthetic enamel primer/surfacer. Because enamel flows much better than lacquer, it tends to cover minor scratches and nicks that lacquer would miss. Once the color coat is on, pearl highlighting can be sprayed on selected spots to emphasize the custom color. No color sanding or rubbing is required.

One of the greatest research programs carried on by the automotive industry and its myriad affiliates is being aimed at providing superior automotive finishes. This little-heralded search for better paints has led to many minute changes in the covering a car gets, but major, all-at-once changes are relatively unknown. Even the introduction of acrylic paints did not warrant banner TV commercials, although acrylic was designed to provide a sleek, long-lasting, minimal-maintenance covering.

The same kind of slow, word-of-mouth notoriety pervades the custom finish world also. When Joe Bailon introduced candy apple many years ago, only a handful of West Coast customizers picked up the idea, and very few enthusiasts knew what that "special show" paint was. In fact, it wasn't until almost ten years later that a pearl formula was finally printed in an enthusiast magazine. Not so with Metalflake.

For many years, special car enthusiasts have wanted to find a distinctive "metallic" substance that would have that extra bit of reflective quality. There are many restrictions on the use of metallics in paint, and thousands of experiments have been carried on by companies and individuals alike trying to find the right metallic. Light and coarse metallics, pearls over metallic, glitters, even exotic fish scales from the ocean, and ground glass have been used. The basic metallics aren't new, but making them really come alive has been a difficult project.

Metalflake, which is now produced by Metalflake Inc., Haverhill, Massachusetts, is a highly reflective paint base. Interestingly, the flakes were almost an afterthought of a manufacturing process designed to make metallic threads for upholstery fabrics. Spools of the thread that inadvertently fell from the machines were useless. It was found that such thread could be cut in rather large chunks and dropped into vinyl floor tiles to give them an unusual effect.

At first there were only two cuts. That has been modified now, with three cuts available; 1/64 for an extra brilliant effect (much like ground glass and very coarse), Micro 1 for a medium sparkle, and Micro 2 for a fine sparkle. The coarse flake particles are approximately one-quarter the size of a small, straight pinhead. The smaller flakes are really tiny, approximately 385 million particles in a pound.

Metalflake comes in red, green, blue, bronze, gold, silver, burgundy, and violet and may be mixed in any number of interesting combinations. While toner can be used to get a desired appearance over a specific base, less paint will be required if colored flake is used. The following is a sample of the colors available (send to Metalflake, P.O. Box 950, Haverhill, Massachusetts, for a color chart and application instructions):

Antique Blue	Embers	Maroon
Apricot	Fantasy	Meteor Red
Aqua	Fire Brand	Nile Green
Blue Indigo	Flame	Peacock
Bouquet	Green Apple	Royal Blue
Bright Red	Gunmetal	Sapphire Blue
Bronze	Kelly Green	Shamrock
Burgundy	Lake Blue	Silver
Chartreuse	Lavender	Sky Blue
Copper	Lemon & Lime	Sovereign
Deep Gold	Light Gold	Sunset
Desert Sand	Marigold	Violet

Metalflake should be applied over a primer/surfacer of the same general tint, which will reduce color spotting. The flake is mixed with thinned acrylic clear (the clear should be mixed 1½:1 with thinner), to about 12 ounces of flake per gallon of reduced clear. As the flake is heavy, it will rapidly settle to the bottom of the mixing container and must be thoroughly agitated before being poured into the gun cup. The same settling occurs in the spray gun, although there are two methods of keeping the flake in suspension. One is to place marbles or bolts in the cup and agitate the gun well after several strokes have been made. The other is to hold a rag over the nozzle, forcing air back into the cup. This will "burble" the mixture and keep the flake suspended.

Spray on a couple of heavy coats of flake, at least enough to get 90 percent coverage over the undercoat. Always spray flake and metallics very wet, as this allows the individual flakes to lie down. Allow about five minutes' setup time between coats. Remember to agitate the gun often to keep the flake in suspension, and spray away from the car until the flake mixture is coming from the nozzle.

Flake is sprayed at a rather low pressure, between 25 and 30 pounds. A general utility spray-gun nozzle and cap should be used, such as the DeVilbiss 043, 30, or 306. Binks guns have equivalent nozzle/cap combinations. It is important to spray flake with an even pattern at low pressure, to avoid "heavy" streaking. This, in conjunction with the wet application, will tend to flow the flakes smoothly, cutting down on the amount of clear required for a smooth finish.

After at least thirty minutes' drying time, blow off the loose flake. Rub the surface by hand while blowing to smooth off rough edges that might be standing up. One custom painter uses a long steel tube over a broom handle (like a cake dough roller) and rolls the surface flat. Do not sand!

Apply approximately seven full coats of clear acrylic and allow each coat to set up from five to ten minutes. After the seventh coat, let the paint air-dry overnight, then apply seven more coats of clear. If a color toner is to be used, it must be sprayed during the initial coats of clear, as the toner should be well below the surface, immune to final sanding. Fourteen coats of clear seems a lot, but this is the recommendation from Metalflake. Professional painters may not spray as many coats, but will usually put on more clear per coat than the beginner.

Clear paint has a tendency to break down after a year or so, and the more that is applied the more susceptible it will be to checking. The key, of course, is to keep the clear well protected with a quality wax.

While it is possible to sand the final coats of clear after they have thoroughly air-dried, it is recommended that the car not be sanded for three to four weeks. This allows the paint to harden really well. Block sand the finish with 220-grit wet followed by 340-grit wet until the clear is perfectly smooth. It won't take much clear if the flake has been prepared as directed. Do not sand through to either toner or flake! Wash and wipe the finish dry, tack off, and apply a light coat of thinner with 15 percent clear added. When this final coat has dried, apply rubbing compound to the car with a machine buffer.

It is best to shoot flake with acrylic, since the acrylic stays wet long enough for the flake to lie down, and it also has excellent lasting qualities. Lacquer can be used, but lacquer clear tends to turn amber and will break up sooner than acrylic. It must be remembered that acrylic is a form of "plastic," and this is where a very special hint from Joe Anderson comes in.

Since clears will tend to break up with exposure to the elements, some method of reasonable repairs were needed, yet something short of actually repainting the car. Joe found that acrylic clear could literally be "melted" back together, that is, the cracks could be flowed shut. Just spraying more clear over the surface will not do the trick. Instead, fog on several coats of wet thinner. This will cause the surface to flow together again, making the clear as good as new. It is this very plastic, or vinyl, look that makes acrylic Metalflake so popular.

There is still much to be learned about Metalflake, but it is undoubtedly one of the most striking automotive finishes to appear in decades. Flake is used widely in the fiberglass business, since it can be sprayed in the mold jell coat, giving an indestructible finish which is actually impregnated in the glass.

Other techniques for custom painting are in wide use, and are really not too difficult to master. Flame painting is coming back; it's really nothing more than a pattern fogged over the basic paint color. Surrealistic painting has always been around, as well as panel painting. Panel painting is again gaining in popularity, since it can be combined with edge definition fogging to highlight the natural body lines of any car. Variations on a particular theme are limitless with custom painting, but the true paint artist must learn to be subtle. It is easy to be garish, much more difficult to make those small jewel-like changes.

While variations on a basic theme are common, there are two really unusual new custom techniques that bear close inspection. Interestingly, both were discovered by mistake, and both by Anderson. The first is "cobwebbing," a rather nebulous name given to a strange bit of painting now gaining a wide following among new car owners. Anderson discovered this technique one day when he started to spray a car with unthinned acrylic (the thinner had been forgotten). The paint just sort of puffed out of the gun in a most haphazard fashion, with a result so striking that it deserved further experimentation.

Cobwebbing can be made to look like anything, from an honest cobweb to a sort of surrealistic, never-ending string. From initial experiments, Anderson decided the effect was not unlike antique marble, and indeed many hot rod-type body styles accept this antiquing quite well. While cobwebbing can be thick or thin, heavy or fine, harsh or subtle, the painter should definitely spray a number of practice panels before attempting to paint a car.

For cobwebbing, acrylic paint is sprayed very thick, and that means unthinned. There is a difference in the thickness of acrylics, but it is possible to thicken a can by leaving it uncapped for a while. It is essential that the paint be strained into the gun uncut. Straining will take some time but eventually the acrylic will make it through.

The type of spray gun used is not too vital, although a large nozzle/air cap combination should be included. Binks made up a combination gun for one painter that has worked well. This is a remote-cup unit using a Number 7 gun equipped with a 36 fluid nozzle, 36 SD air nozzle, and a 7357 air adjusting valve. All this sounds quite fancy, but any paint equipment sales store will know what is required when informed that the paint must be sprayed very thick and at low pressures.

Low pressure means, usually, between 15 to 20 pounds at the regulator. The amount of air pressure depends entirely upon the effect desired and the area to be covered. If the area is very big, the pressure can be increased slightly to increase the fan coverage. At higher pressures, though, the particles of paint tend to break up, until at a very high pressure the effect is more like Zolotone. The haphazard, but seemingly connected, long stringers of paint are lost.

Now comes the difficult part. When cobwebbing, everything must progress at a well-organized pace. Before starting the webbing, the gun must be ready and waiting, since the speed of the application is vital. With the base coat ready, apply a final clear base coat with a slow thinner or even a retarder. This coat must remain wet while the webbing is applied; that's why speed is of the essence.

While the base coat is wet, spray on the webbing. Previous

experiments will have shown exactly what type of pattern is most desirable. It will have been found that just moving the gun in a particular pattern will cause different types of webbing; overlapping will give another, etc.

Finally, let the webbing dry thoroughly before adding the top coats of clear. This is essential, as wet webbing will smear and run when clear is added. The quickest way to define a really good web job is to see how sharp the paint "strings" are. Build the finish with clear acrylic as with Metalflake and do the final finishing in the same manner.

The effect of cobwebbing can be determined by any number of variables. It can be applied over Metalflake or pearl or an ordinary color. It can be applied over a base undercoat and then toner can be added to the clear. Just about anything can be done with it. It can even be sprayed as a thick line, with the painter actually drawing a continuous line on the panel. The possibilities are limitless.

A little more limited, perhaps, is the latest painting technique called "lacing." Lace painting hit the West Coast about a year ago, again quite by accident. Anderson was in the process of mixing and testing a batch of paint one day when he accidentally sprayed over some lace which happened to be lying on the paint bench. When the lace was moved, a rather exotic pattern showed on the wood beneath—an effect worth following up.

Joe found that large sheets of lace in varying patterns could be purchased at the five-and-dime store, sheets big enough to cover an entire hood, or top, or deck lid. It was also found that the patterns varied from minuscule flowers to rather large designs, a factor that must be considered when selecting the pattern for any particular car. A Cadillac will call for a subtle, sophisticated pattern while a hot rod might do well with a flamboyant, strong design.

To make a lace pattern, the area to be painted is masked off (lace makes a very effective panel highlight). The lace is then stretched taut over the panel and masked in place. The lace must be in direct contact with the surface at all points, otherwise the paint will blow beneath the lace, causing a softening of the pattern edges.

Once the pattern is in place, any color may be sprayed on the car. If the car is a dark color, the tone of the pattern spray may be lighter, and vice versa. It is also possible to spray the pattern over a toner or Metalflake, or to put a toner in the pattern spray. You can even spray over the pattern with a toner if desired. The combinations are many and varied.

If an entire top is pattern painted, the natural body lines and moldings make a break. But if a panel is painted, it is desirable to stripe around the pattern. Also, it is possible to spray on a pattern with enamel paint. Then when the lace is removed, if you don't like the pattern, you can merely wash it off with thinner and start again. Of all the custom painting techniques that will set a stock car apart, lace painting is the best for the beginner.

If there is any supreme test of an automobile paint, it surely comes during the course of a normal racing season. Oval track and sporty car racers subject hard-charging hunks of metal and fiberglass to punishment that the average automobile will never know in a lifetime. Dragsters try to burn the color off with heat and exotic fuels. Even diminutive karts treat paint like poor relations. Trying to find a good paint for racing cars has been a project of custom painters for a long time.

Dean Jeffries has been involved in custom race car painting for many years, during which he experimented with several finishes before finally settling on acrylic as his particular answer. Dean paints a large number of oval-track race cars, including a host of top Indianapolis runners. When his first A. J. Foyt creation hit the brickyard it started a run on candy colors, a popularity that doesn't seem about to diminish.

Jeffries prefers to stick with acrylics because they allow the touring race car owners to have their cars fixed up anywhere, should body damage warrant paint repair.

The real breakthrough in race car paint has been the epoxy mixture, because of its tremendous wearing quality, a factor that has been carefully watched during the past few years.

Epoxy paints actually consist of two parts—and are really a form of liquid plastic. A typical epoxy will include a quantity of basic color and a smaller amount of catalyst which is added just before spraying. The catalyst works in the same manner as if it were being mixed with a fiberglass filler. The idea is to cause the paint to actually "kick" into a hard, very durable finish.

Epoxy paint has become almost standard for heavy-duty industrial applications such as gas stations, oil field equipment, fleet trucks, school busses—wherever a super-hard finish is required. The only reason factories have not utilized it more in automotive finishes is the narrow range of colors available from the manufacturers. Custom painters, on the other hand, have worked with many colors.

When epoxy is used (such as on an aluminum car) it is first sprayed with special primer. Zinc chromate should not be used as a base beneath epoxies, as fuel-proof epoxy will not adhere to standard-type paints. Epoxy must be applied over epoxy!

This special primer is noted for its super flow-out characteristics which makes it especially attractive if the car body is not perfectly prepared. The "long flow" allows the primer to fill sanding scratches, and because it is a plastic, it does not shrink with drying or age.

Epoxy primer is applied over aluminum as if it were enamel. An ordinary enamel-type spray gun is used and the only precaution is to keep the material from sagging. The primer need not be sanded unless a really super-smooth job is desired. In this case, mix the paint and catalyst and allow it to set for two days (pot life). During this time it will begin to activate; then when the car is sprayed it will only take one day before the primer hardens. After the primer is hard, water sand as in normal painting.

It is possible for the professional to apply the color coat over primer that has not hardened, but the amateur is cautioned to follow the manufacturer's directions to the letter. Epoxy primer dries to a wet look, and can even be toned toward the pearl colors.

If pearl is to be included in the paint scheme, it goes over the color coat while the color is still wet. A coat of clear follows—and the car is ready for the elements.

Epoxy can be applied over regular paint if a few precautions are followed. A special primer/sealer must be sprayed over the original paint, but this sealer must not be touched with sandpaper. The car should be prepared as though the primer/sealer were really the final coat of color. If the sealer is sanded, chances are that some spots will be sanded through to original paint, and the epoxy will not stick to that spot! This particular sealer dries in three hours and the color can be sprayed directly over the sealer.

Although epoxy flows so well that extra-special preparation is not necessary to obtain a porcelain-like appearance, and although it will not scratch or nick and lasts indefinitely, it still can use the protection of wax. If you wish, rub it out with compound after the first three or four weeks. In essence, epoxy will wear away rather than chip or break as do normal paints.

Epoxy is an especially attractive medium for Metalflake, since its smooth flowing characteristics (when wet) make all the sprayed flake go on the car and lie flat. When flake is sprayed with ordinary paints, much of the medium is lost as dry over-spray. One pound of flake in epoxy will do what three pounds will in normal paint. Another plus for epoxy is that when a flake job is applied with normal paints, so much clear is required to get a smooth finish that excessive shrinkage is bound to occur with time and environment. Not so with this type of plastic.

Old wives' tales to the contrary, epoxies can be spotted if necessary. The area is sanded in the normal fashion, then sealed, and painted with more epoxy. It can even be spotted with acrylics, with the acrylic merely washed off later and a more permanent repair made.

The business of "washing" epoxy is an interesting feature. As an example, Don Garlits had his dragster painted orange, but the name painted on the side was wrong. Rather than sand away the name, the painter just washed it away with acetone and painted on a new name. The epoxy was not disturbed in any way. This ability to withstand tough abuse is the real value of epoxy. It isn't easy to remove once it has been applied, but that's the idea behind race car paints, something that becomes like the metal itself.

Obviously, epoxy is impervious to hot, nitromethane-type fuels, one reason for its popularity among drag racers. Even with all its advantages, epoxy doesn't cost much more than a regular pro job, because so little preparation is required. Epoxy paint costs a bit more, but it is worth every dime. Especially for a race car.

11

The Electric Car

There is much being written currently about the possibilities of *an* electric car, and practically nothing about *the* electric car. While it is nice that engineers somewhere are trying to conceive a method of using electrical energy for automotive propulsion, the hot rodder must content himself with working out the evils of contemporary automobile electrics. Evils, because at first glance the electrical system of any car seems nothing less than a gigantic bag of snakes. It need not be so bewildering, but the rodder (beginner and old-hand alike) must understand some basic principles first.

A word always heard when electricity is discussed is voltage. This is nothing more than a measure of pressure, much as inches are a measurement of length. Another electrical term is amps, or amperes. This is a measurement of current flow through the wire circuit. Last of all is resistance to current flow, measured in ohms.

By way of a simple explanation, consider water flowing through a pipe as similar to electricity through wire. The amperes, or current flow, can be compared to the flow of water in a pipe. The water cannot move unless it is pushed; this can be accomplished by a pump or some kind of physical pressure. The electrons in a wire cannot move unless they are pushed also; this is accomplished by a generator or battery. The voltage is a pressure exerted upon the electrons in the wire forcing them to move; thus we have amps, or current flow.

When water is being pumped through a pipe, just so much will come out the various taps. If more water is desired from a specific tap, we must either raise the water pressure, or close some of the other taps. The resistance to current flow may be likened to the restriction of water flow determined by the size of the water pipe.

If too many things are powered from a certain wire, none will receive all the current it needs to function properly. The wire must be large enough to carry all the current to supply all the items in the particular circuit. For example, if a car has a 3-amp radio, a 2-amp windshield wiper motor, and 7-amp lighting, it will take at least a 12-amp wire to carry the current. Otherwise the wire will get hot and possibly burn the insulation and/or short out. Wire larger than necessary may always be used; that's why a 12-volt system can be run through 6-volt wiring. But never run a 6-volt system through 12-volt wiring. Yes, we know it sounds strange but there is an easy explanation. Leaving aside the actual math involved, wattage or energy is what does the work. Watts are the product of amperes times volts; the higher the voltage, the lower the amps needed to produce the watts that do the work. Thus, in a 6-volt system the amperage is increased and the wiring must be heavier than is necessary for the 12-volt system. Following is a table of wire sizes for both voltage systems for easy reference.

AMPERES	WIRE SIZE	AMPERES	WIRE SIZE
35A	8–9	7A	16–17
25A	10–11	5A	18–19
20A	12–13	3A	20–22
15A	14–15		

Color coding is included in all automobile wiring as a convenient method of tracing. If all the wires to the generator were the same color, or those to the taillights, confusion would become chaos. In 16-gauge wire there are at least 18 different colors available commercially; in 12-gauge there are 10 colors. Variations are infinite, with alternating stripes, checks, and numbers. As a rule, all ground wires are black, all hot wires are red, and so on.

The heart of the electrical system of any car is the battery. This is usually 6- or 12-volt, depending upon the year and make of car. The battery itself is nothing more than a storehouse for electrons. The scientific theory is that the current flows from positive pole of the battery to the negative pole. This flow is measured in terms of amperes on a device called an ampere meter, or just plain ammeter. In your car, the ammeter shows the amount of current flow into the battery during charge, or out of the battery during discharge.

Fortunately, unless the rodder is doing a "ground-up" car, wiring will usually fall into the engine-swap variety. That is, lengthening or shortening wires to fit (rerouting), or changing voltage (6 to 12 volts). Most swaps are easy, but some turn into nightmares for the amateur. Patience, and a good wiring diagram, are allies here. The very first problem of swap wiring is that of soldering.

Take the soldered connection for example. Soldering is a very important part of any wiring job, no matter how small. And surprisingly, there is a right way and a wrong way to do it. Always use a good soldering iron of approximately 100–150 watts. Select a good rosin core 50-50 solder. Do not use acid core solder as it will tend to eat up the wire over a period of time. During soldering, keep the iron tip clean by wiping it frequently on a damp rag. The solder should ensure a good electrical connection—not take mechanical strain.

Strip the wire ends and knot, twist or somehow get them together. Lay the solder directly on the joint and then lay the solder-ing iron on the solder. When the solder flows, remove the iron.

One of the most frequent wiring jobs in a transplant is splicing wires together. One method is to strip the wires and solder as above, then tape the bare spot. A second is to strip the wire and install pin ends that connect via a plug. A third choice is the solderless crimp type of splicer where bare wire ends are insterted into the insulated splicer and the splicer is then crimped with a tool available through all parts houses. If the splice is made where the wires need to be separated often (headlights, generator, igni-tion) the pin and plug are best.

If the car is not old, or was made since 1950, it is possible to locate an entire new wiring harness in some local dealerships. Best way to determine whether new wiring is needed is merely by bending the wire double. If the insulation breaks, the harness is in trouble. For most Ford products and some Chevy years, con-tact either Antique Auto at 9113 East Garvey Boulevard, Rose-mead, California; Ford Parts Obsolete, 1320 West Willow, Long Beach, California; or Chevy Parts Obsolete, 506 West Warron, Nashville, Georgia. These firms carry a comprehensive line of specialized wiring for these particular cars.

If you are not sure how the wiring should be completed, it is advisable to consult the wiring diagrams of both the basic vehicle and the vehicle from which the engine came. These illustrations are available in the shop manual for the specific year concerned.

Dropping a 6-volt engine into a 6-volt chassis is easy as far as the electrical system is concerned. The same is true for the 12-volt combinations. The only possible problem that might crop up would be in the 6-volt combos where the polarity might vary. In some cars the system is positive grounded, in others it is nega-tive grounded. The engine starter and generator will work equally well on either polarity, but generator regulators and some ignition coils are polarity sensitive. The regulator must have the same polarity as the engine electrical system and as the car system. Polarity of ignition coils is easily changed by switching the battery and coil leads on their primary terminal posts.

Some of the cars that had 12-volt electrical systems in 1953–55 had positive ground systems, but most of the systems were negative ground. All cars built after 1955 have negative ground. It is important, therefore, to follow the same polarity precautions decribed above when working with the 1953–55 model.

There are three ways to mate the 12-volt engine to the 6-volt chassis. One is to convert the engine accessories to 6 volts; another is to convert the car system to 12 volts; and the third is to utilize a combination 6-volt/12-volt system. The first is hardly advisable, the second is best, the third is the most practical. However, in the remote instance when a 6-volt engine is placed in a 12-volt chassis, the only possible route is number one.

The main problem of converting an engine from 12 to 6 volts is in finding a 6-volt starter that will fit. Even then a different flywheel might have to be installed. For this kind of conversion it is necessary to replace the generator (use a pulley with the correct diameter and width) and ignition coil also. The 12-volt coil is designed to operate on 9-volts (through a resistor), so it wouldn't cut the mustard with only 6 volts.

Converting the car system from 6 volts to 12 volts is much harder than it may seem, especially if all the stock instruments are to be retained. Such a conversion means changing all the lights, gauges, radio, heater, etc. Changing the light bulbs and sealed-beam headlamps is easy—everything swaps—but the sheer mass of everything else makes this impractical.

It's possible to use original 6-volt electrical equipment with 12-volt current by placing a resistor of the correct capacity between each of the components and the battery. It is important that each component have its own resistor if it is to function correctly. However, there are several things against the use of resistors for this purpose. A battery, regardless of its voltage, has a certain "ampere-hour" capacity. This is the number of amperes the battery can deliver for a certain period of time. It is the measure of a battery's capacity to handle electrical power requirements.

The 12-volt batteries now in use in passenger cars have an ampere-hour rating approximately half that of 6-volt batteries; however, they are capable of doing as much work as 6-volt batteries because they push the amperes they deliver with twice the force, electrical accessories designed for 12 volts require only half the number of amperes consumed by equivalent 6-volt accessories.

The difference between 6-volt and 12-volt battery capacities and the amperage requirements of 6-volt and 12-volt components is of little interest to a rodder until he becomes involved with resistors.

Resistors used for most automotive applications are of the "wire-wound" type. They consist of a piece of wire, which is their conductor, supported in some manner by a member that is a nonconductor of electricity. At each end of the wire is a terminal post by which the resistor can be connected to an electrical circuit. Wires used in resistors vary in length, cross-sectional diameter, and material. By careful engineering of these factors it is possible to obtain the desired resistance for specific applications.

The purpose of resistors, as used for automobile applications, is to reduce the voltage delivered by a battery or generator to a lower voltage required by an electrical accessory. The best-known resistor in modern automobile electrical circuits is the one used with 12-volt ignition coils. This resistor reduces 12-volt current to approximately 9 volts before the current reaches the coil. One of the reasons coils that operate on a full 12 volts aren't used for ignition systems is that their action is too sluggish at the high cycling rates necessary for high engine speeds. A 9-volt coil can create a considerably greater secondary voltage output than a 6-volt unit, and its cycling ability is adequate for the crankshaft speed any modern engine is capable of turning.

To perform its function of reducing voltage, a resistor must consume a certain amount of electrical power. Also, a 6-volt accessory fitted with a resistor so that it can be operated by a 12-volt current still requires as many amperes as it did when its source of electrical power was a 6-volt battery. Therefore, a radio that requires 6 amperes from a 6-volt battery will also require 6 amperes from a 12-volt battery and resistor instead of the three amperes that would be required by an equivalent 12-volt radio. This double amperage requirement applies to any 6-volt electrical system component that is fitted with a resistor and used with 12-volt current. This means that the drain created on a car's electrical system by 6-volt accessories and resistors is approximately twice what it would be with 12-volt components. Because of a 12-volt battery's lower amperage-hour rating the battery would be able to operate the components only half as long as a 6-volt battery before it became discharged to the point where it would be unable to start the engine. However, this greater drain becomes important only when the battery is supplying the current, as when the engine is idling or not running. When the engine is running at speeds slightly above idle the generator is supplying at least part or all of the electrical power required. At normal engine cruising speeds the generator is supplying all the power.

A characteristic of resistors is that the voltage at the output side increases as the amperage in their circuit decreases. For the voltage to remain constant, the amperage flow must remain constant. It is because of this characteristic that resistors are made in many capacities for different applications.

At first glance one might think that a single resistor inserted in a 12-volt electrical system could be used to supply the demands of all a car's 6-volt electrical components. Actually, this could be done but the results would be far from satisfactory. As the amperage flow through the resistor increased or decreased when different components were switched on or off, the voltage in the circuits would decrease or increase. As the various components are designed for a certain range of voltage input, their reaction would not be normal when the voltage was higher or lower than the limits of this range. Voltage higher than the upper limit would result in short life of the components, and voltage lower than the lower limit would result in subnormal performance, such as dim lights.

Resistors, even when used individually, are not recommended for electrically activated gauges. These gauges function on the principle of variable amperage flow. The sending unit in the engine or fuel tank or wherever it might be controls the rate at which amperage flows through the indicating unit on the car's instrument panel. If a resistor were used to control the voltage in a gauge's circuit the voltage would rise and fall as the amperage flow varied. The gauge would work but it wouldn't be accurate.

Another method of handling the 12-volt engine, 6-volt chassis problem is to convert the electrical system to a mixed-voltage system. This would involve a 12-volt system for the engine and possibly the lighting circuits and a 6-volt system for the rest of the circuits. For simplicity and practicability, this is probably the best of the three possible solutions to the perplexing problem.

A mixed-voltage electrical system requires sources of both 12-volt and 6-volt electrical current. There are two ways to provide these. One is to use a 12-volt battery as both sources. Twelve-volt current is taken from the battery's posts in a normal manner and 6-volt current is obtained from a "tap" installed in the battery's middle cell strap. The tap allows current to be taken from only 3 of the battery's 6 cells. The second method is to install two 6-volt batteries in the car and connect them in series. The combined output of the two batteries will be 12 volts and the output of one of them can be used as the source of 6-volt current.

Of the two possible methods of obtaining the different voltages for a mixed-voltage system, the one that utilizes two 6-volt batteries is superior by far to the one that utilizes a 12-volt battery. The reason is that the 6-volt capacity provided by three of a 12-volt battery's cells is so limited compared to that of a standard 6-volt battery. It is possible that under certain conditions the three cells used for 6-volt current could be well on the way to a discharged condition while the other three cells were fully charged. That isn't a healthy condition for a battery. The battery used for 6-volt current with two 6-volt batteries would maintain a much higher charge while supplying the same amount of current because of its greater capacity.

Another advantage provided by two 6-volt batteries would be their nearly double ampere-hour capacity over that provided by a 12-volt unit. This would be of primary importance to the starting motor, as the starter could be operating approximately twice as long before the batteries became discharged. At those times when difficulty is encountered in getting an engine started for some reason or other, this greater store of power could be invaluable.

To install a 6-volt tap in a 12-volt battery, carefully drill through the battery's correct cell strap with a ¼-inch drill, taking care not to drill through the top of the cell, and then thread the hole with a ⁵⁄₁₆-inch, 20-thread tap. Make a stud about 1¼ inches long from a ⁵⁄₁₆-inch copper bolt with threads that match those in the strap with a flat washer and a nut run down snugly against the washer. Don't tighten the nut too tightly because it might pull the stud out of the strap. All 6-volt current for the electrical system will originate at this post.

A mixed-voltage system based on two 6-volt batteries requires the installation of an additional battery somewhere in the car. It isn't necessary that the batteries be close together. In fact, one of them can be in the engine compartment and the other in the trunk compartment. The trunk is an ideal location for one or both batteries because it is usually cooler than the engine compartment. Regardless of where they are located, each battery must be securely mounted to prevent its moving about. Standard battery boxes and hold-down equipment are ideal for this. Mount the boxes so that the batteries will be level.

When batteries to be used together are separated by distance or are located away from the engine, the conductor in the cable that connects them must be large enough to carry the current that will flow through it without creating excessive resistance. Cable in bulk lengths can be purchased from auto parts stores. Terminals that can be clamped or soldered to the ends of a cable's conductor—to enable the cable to be connected to the battery posts or to the terminal posts on starting motor solenoids— are also available. Cable of one gauge should have a conductor large enough for the length a cable would have to be for any 12-volt automotive installation. As the cable is not on the grounded side of the battery, it must be of the insulated type so that its conductor cannot touch the metal parts of he car's body or frame.

Installation of an individual 6-volt battery wouldn't be any more expensive than replacing the existing 6-volt battery with a 12-volt unit. It would take a little time to install the additional battery box and make and install the cable to connect the two batteries but this would be a one-shot deal. Subsequent battery replacement would be no more difficult than replacing any other battery.

After two 6-volt batteries have been mounted in a car it is a simple matter to connect them for 12 volts and to provide a 6-volt source. Assuming the electrical system is to be negative-grounded to conform with the components on most 12-volt engines, the negative post of the battery farthest from the engine is grounded.

This is done by connecting the post to either the engine or the car's frame with a ground cable of the correct length. If a cable not over approximately 30 inches long will reach the engine, use the engine as the ground; otherwise, connect the cable to the frame. The cable can be of the usual flat braided type because it doesn't need to be insulated; however, an insulated cable can be used if this is more convenient. With an insulated cable of suitable length, connect the grounded battery's positive post with the second battery's negative post. The second battery's positive post is then connected to the engine starting motor solenoid with an insulated cable of suitable length.

For the 6-volt portion of the system connect a length of 8-gauge insulated wire that has a suitable terminal on one end of its conductor to one end of the cable that connects the 2 batteries. The end of the cable to use would be the one closest to the firewall. In other words, the 6-volt lead should be as short as possible to reduce to the practical minimum the resistance it presents to the flow of current. It wouldn't make sense to run the wire all the way back to the end of the cable in the trunk compartment if it could be connected to the end in the engine compartment. The 6-volt current will come from the battery in the trunk compartment regardless of where the wire is connected, because that is the battery grounded; but the cable between the batteries—rather than an equivalent length of 8-gauge wire—will conduct the current the distance equal to that between the batteries. Clamp the wire terminal to the cable terminal with the nut affixed to the cable terminal's clamp bolt.

For the sake of convenience the free end of the 6-volt lead from one battery of a two 6-volt combination—or from the 6-volt tap in a 12-volt battery—should be connected to a terminal post or junction block mounted on the passenger side of the car's firewall. Junction blocks for this sort of installation are available at many surplus stores. They have several terminal posts that are connected to a common source of current, are well insulated, and have mounting holes that make them easy to install. Connect the 6-volt lead to the common connection for the posts and then connect the various components that require 6-volt current to the posts.

If it isn't possible to find a suitable junction block that can be used as the 6-volt source, a single post securely mounted so that it is insulated from the car's metal structure can be used instead. Secure the 6-volt lead to this post with suitable nuts and washers and then connect the 6-volt circuits to the same post as above.

Sources of 12-volt current from either two 6-volt batteries or a 12-volt battery are the starting motor solenoid post to which the cable from the battery is connected, or one of the ammeter's posts, just as in a standard electrical system. The ammeter post to use is the one to which the lead from the generator regulator is connected.

The instant the battery installation has been completed by connecting the positive post to the starting motor's solenoid, all of the electrical circuits will be exposed to 12-volt current. Therefore, before this is done it is necessary to separate the circuits to eliminate the possibility of the components that will use 6-volt current being damaged by excessive voltage. If the car is wired in the conventional manner it will be found when this is done that circuits for the instruments, radio, heater, and possibly other components originate at the "accessory" post on the ignition switch. Remove the wires for these circuits from the switch post but tie them together so they won't become separated and confused with the many other wires behind the instrument panel. If the car has an ammeter it's possible that the circuits for its lights and other components will originate at one of the ammeter's terminals. As the ammeter will not be part of the 12-volt system because current from the generator will pass through it, remove the wires for these circuits and tie them together. However, if the lights are to be converted to 12-volts—which is recommended because it isn't difficult to do, isn't expensive, and will result in more efficient road lighting—then the wire for the lights can be left on the ammeter post.

The circuits that originated at the ignition switch must be controlled in such a manner that they will receive current only when the ignition switch is on. The easiest way to do this is to use a relay controlled by the ignition switch to complete the circuit between the source of 6-volt current and the components. Twelve-volt current from the switch will actuate the relay but the relay will conduct 6-volt current. Many relays, including headlight and universal types, that can be used for this purpose are available from auto parts stores. These have two circuits, one to complete the other. The relay used for this installation should preferably be designed for 12-volt current but a 6-volt type could be used satisfactorily in most instances.

Mount the relay at some convenient location behind the instrument panel where the wires that were on the "accessory" post of the ignition switch will reach its "load" post. Exactly how a relay's terminal posts will be marked depends on the relay but the directions with the relay will explain how it is to be wired. The relay "switch" post is then connected to the "accessory" post on the ignition switch with a suitable length of 16-gauge wire. If the relay has a "ground" post, run another wire from this post to the firewall or some other metal part to ground the relay windings.

Connect the "battery" terminal on the relay to the 6-volt junction block or post with a length of 10-gauge wire fitted with terminals of the correct size. This wire must be at least 10-gauge to carry the amperage demands.

The wires that were removed from the ammeter should be connected directly to the 6-volt junction block or post. If the wires aren't long enough for this, make an extension for them from a piece of 10-gauge wire and suitable terminals. Connect the wires to the extension with a machine bolt and nut of the correct size, and then cover the joint and all exposed parts of the terminals with plastic tape to prevent their contacting any grounded metal surfaces under the instrument panel.

With the different wiring circuits connected as described, the ignition switch will control the ignition circuit directly and, through the relay, the instruments, radio, heater, overdrive control, electric fuel pump, etc., just as it did originally. The extension from the 6-volt source will supply current to the lights, unless they are converted to 12 volts and left connected to the ammeter, and the clock, if it has one. Other things, such as a cigarette lighter, and the horn, should receive current directly from the 6-volt source. A convertible top motor will also have to be connected to the 6-volt source because its amperage requirements are too great for the relay.

Circuits for window and seat motors are wired differently in different makes of cars. Some of them receive current only when the ignition switch is on but others receive current all the time. Circuits that receive current only when the ignition switch is on usually have their own relay that is actuated by current from the accessory post of the ignition switch. The switch terminal of a relay of this type should be connected to the load post of the 6-volt source with 10-gauge wire. If the circuit receives current at all times, connect it directly to the 6-volt source.

The correct way to wire the starting motor control circuit will depend on the type of starter switch on the instrument panel and the design of the solenoid required by the new engine starting motor. Solenoids of some types are wound so that they are actuated by being grounded, but others must receive current to be actuated. The switch on the instrument panel can be designed to ground the circuit through the solenoid or to allow current to flow to the solenoid.

An instrument panel switch that matches the solenoid on the new engine starting motor can be connected to the solenoid and be used without making any changes in the circuit. If the switch and solenoid do not match, another arrangement will have to be made.

The switch-solenoid combination that will appear to be the most hopeless is a switch for a solenoid that must be grounded and a solenoid that must receive current from the instrument panel switch. With this combination leave the original solenoid and switch as they were but connect the cable from the battery to the battery post on the new solenoid. Run a wire of at least 10-gauge from the battery post on the new solenoid to the original solenoid's battery post; another wire from the starter switch post on the new solenoid to the original solenoid battery post; and another wire from the starter switch post on the new solenoid to the old solenoid's starter cable post. Now, when the original solenoid is actuated with the switch on the instrument panel, current will flow from the battery post on the new solenoid, through the original solenoid, to the switch post on the new solenoid, causing the new solenoid to be actuated and close the circuit between battery post and the starter.

When changing the wiring for different circuits, there are certain precautions that must be taken if the circuits are to function correctly and if wires are to escape damage. If wires for any of the circuits must be lengthened, use wire the same size or larger than the original. Always use wire that has a conductor large enough to handle the circuit's amperage load. Wire that is too small will create a resistance that can have a bad effect on the operation of the accessories in the circuit. When in doubt as to the correct wire size, be on the safe side by using a larger wire.

Wires must be carefully routed and taped or clamped in position to prevent their contacting hot or moving parts in the engine compartment. A burned or worn spot in wire insulation can allow the conductor to touch a ground.

Most modern engine swaps always include the new alternator

in preference to a generator. If the new engine has been designed for an alternator, this choice is obvious, but if the switch has been made arbitrarily, it has usually been because of space. It is easier to make up a mounting bracket for an alternator than for a generator. However, the consideration of cost set aside, the alternator is a much better unit for the electrical system.

Alternators have been used on new cars since 1962–63, with some significant advantages over the generator. An alternator is a far simpler unit: two soldered connections compared to twenty-eight in the generator motor, one wire winding in the rotor compared to fourteen in the generator, etc. The alternator is lighter, shorter, runs cooler, keeps the battery charged even at low engine speeds, and generally lasts longer between overhauls. But for the engine swap, it can present some problems.

When an alternator is installed on a car not previously equipped with such a unit, it is necessary to change the initial wiring somewhat. Check the wiring diagrams supplied by the alternator manufacturer. If the car was originally equipped with an alternator, retain the original unit on the new engine to ease growing pains.

Compared to some of the other problems inherent in the average engine swap, the wiring dilema is relatively minor. To modify the wiring system on a car, even when an alternator is included, will take about two hours. The only criterion should be careful workmanship and thoughtful routing of the wires for all systems.

12

Racing Your Rod

Now that you have that gleaming hulk of mechanical sculpture completed, what's next? For some, it will be daily trips as ordinary transportation. For others, it is the American version of Europe's sports car, ideal for weekend cruises with similar vehicles. For still others, the hot rod is the epitome of individual participation in automotive competition. Organized racing, with attendant stiff safety regulations, becomes "proof of the pudding."

Since there is really no specific definition of hot rodding that seems to pinpoint the sport's limits, most enthusiasts have grown to consider practically everyone a hot rodder who works with cars. True, some become successful professionals, but the designation bears merit. Thus, the modern hot rod competitor may be racing his low budget stocker at the local drag strip or tooling a $100,000 racer around the Indianapolis 500 track. Hot rodders compete in a variety of events, from boats to karts to NASCAR stock cars.

Still, the bulk of the sport concentrates on drag racing—that special American phenomenon that has spread to many foreign lands. Drag racing is a relatively simple proof of an individual's ability. If he has built a strong engine, and if he has coupled it with a good chassis, he can expect results as good as, or better than, the experts.

It is interesting that although drag racing rules are the result of nearly two decades of experience, they have changed very little from the first mimeographed sheets to the current multipage books. The stress is still on building a safe vehicle and a competitive class for competition. While some individual drag strips have particular rules that might vary slightly, any builder who uses the National Hot Rod Association rule book as a guide will find technical inspection anywhere quite esay. At the same time, someone wishing to run a car at the Bonneville Salt Flats can use drag racing rules as a beginning. Even the rules for off-road racing are similar. There are specifics that apply to each type of competition, of course. For this reason, the enthusiast should write one of the following organizations for specific information:

National Hot Rod Association (Drag Racing)
  3418 West First Street
  Los Angeles, California 90004
American Hot Rod Association (Drag Racing)
  1820 West 91st Place
  Kansas City, Missouri 64114
Southern California Timing Association (Dry Lakes and Bonneville)
  3245 Idaho Lane
  Costa Mesa, California 93626
National Modified Midget Association (Oval Tracks)
  3215 Norstrom Way
  Sacramento, California 95833
American Motorcycle Association (Motorcycles)
  P. O. Box 231
  Worthington, Ohio 43085
International Kart Federation (Karts)
  529 South Second Avenue
  Covina, California

NASCAR (Stock Cars)
    1801 Valusia Avenue
    Daytona Beach, Florida
National Midget Racing Association (Oval Tracks)
    6132 McKnight Drive
    Lakewood, California
USAC (Indianapolis Cars)
    Indianapolis, Indiana
National Off-Road Racing Association (Off-Road Events)
    19730 Ventura Boulevard
    Woodland Hills, California 91364
National Drag Boat Association (Boats)
    P. O. Box 398
    Bellflower, California 90706

There are specific rules for each category of NHRA drag racing vehicles (stocker, dragster, altered, etc.), but all are required to meet definite safety regulations. These rules are in effect at all NHRA sanctioned events and are easy to comply with. On the subject of competition safety, *do not take a shortcut!* Technical inspectors can spot cheating or noncompliance with rules a mile away. Following are current NHRA safety regulations for drag racing. Running changes may have been made, however, so the enthusiast is directed to NHRA headquarters for an up-to-date rulebook (one dollar per copy).

INSPECTION: Each car, regardless of class, must complete and satisfactorily pass the inspection of the technical committee before being allowed to make a trial run or participate in any NHRA sanctioned event. All nuts, bolts, and component parts on each car's suspension system, chassis, and running gear must be secured with either lock nuts, lock washers, or cotter keys, and must have at least one full thread showing through nut.

AIR FOILS: Air foils, wings, and spoilers other than original factory equipment will only be allowed in open-bodied class cars (i.e. dragster, altered, and competition).

ALIGNMENT: Each car in competition, regardless of class, must have sufficient positive caster incorporated into the front-end alignment to ensure proper handling of the car at all speeds.

APPEARANCE: Vehicles participating in drag racing events must be presentable in appearance at all times. Ones that are considered improperly prepared may be rejected by the technical committee at any sanctioned event. The appearance of personnel attending contestant vehicles is equally important, and should be subject to the same consideration.

BALLAST: Any material used for the purpose of adding to a car's total weight must be permanently attached as a part of the car's structure, and must not extend behind the rear of the car's body or above the height of the rear tires. No liquid or loose ballast permitted (i.e., water, sandbags, rocks, metal weights, etc.). Any liquid other than engine fuel located behind the front firewall is considered ballast and is not permitted. To permit "making a class" due to the difference in scale calibration, a maximum removable weight of 100 pounds is permitted.* Removable weight must be securely mounted to the frame, or frame structure, by at least two ½-inch minimum diameter steel bolts; however, the use of railroad track, cylinder heads, or other bulky items is not permitted. Recommended forms of ballast are: heavier gauge steel floors—i.e., 16 or 18 gauge, etc. Heavier gauge and/or plate steel not permitted—frame reinforcing cross members, or the addition of safety equipment such as roll bars, flywheel covers, etc.

BATTERIES: All wet-cell batteries must be located outside of the driver or passenger compartments and must be securely mounted. A maximum of two (2) automobile batteries is permitted of 150 pounds combined maximum weight.

BRAKES: Brakes on each car, regardless of class, are tested for pedal "feel." Brakes must be in good working order with two-

---

* Where the maximum is 200 pounds, it must not be in one piece of weight, but in no less than two separate units.

wheel hydraulic brakes (rear wheels only) as a minmum requirement; four-wheel hydraulic brakes are required on cars competing
in Stock Eliminator class cars, or as noted under class requirements. Lightening backing plates, brake drums, and/or brake
shoes by cutting or trimming metal is not permitted. Lightening
or cooling holes must be drilled in such a manner that they do not
weaken the unit. If a hand brake is used, the brake handle must
be inside car's body, or driver's compartment. Brake lines must
be routed outside the frame rail or enclosed in a 16-inch length
of ⅛-inch minimum-wall-thickness steel tubing securely mounted
where line(s) pass the flywheel bell housing area.

CLUTCH: Each car in competition, except ones using automatic
transmissions, must be equipped with a foot-operated clutch.

CREDENTIALS: Each driver of a vehicle entered in any NHRA
sanctioned event must have a valid driver's license, subject to
inspection by officials at time of classification or at any other time
deemed necessary by the technical committee. Drivers in all fuel
classes and all cars equipped with superchargers (except stock)
are required to have valid NHRA Competition License. Female
drivers are eligible to compete in Super Stock and Stock classes
only, unless they have applied for, and been approved for, higher
class competition by an NHRA Division Director. (Application
forms are available from your respective NHRA Division Director.) In addition to an NHRA Competition License, all drivers
and owners of AA/F and AA/D cars are required to have a valid
F.I.A. Drag Racing License for competition at any event designated by NHRA as an F.I.A.-sanctioned event. (Application
forms are available from NHRA headquarters in Los Angeles.)

DRIVE LINES: On any car in which the driver sits over or in back
of the rear end center section,* a suitable protective shield of

---

* All such cars, using an open or Hotchkiss-type drive line, must have radius
arms, traction bars, or some suitable pinion support to prevent rear end housing
rotation. It is highly recommended that a torque tube—⅛-inch-minimum steel
wall thickness—be used to enclose all drive lines.

.120-inch minimum-thickness steel plate must be installed for those units with universal joints securely mounted to the rear end center section and the bellhousing adaptor. Couplers are highly recommended in place of U-joints wherever possible. For these units with straight couplers, the minimum requirement is .063-inch aluminum which must contain an inspection cover, for removal and inspection of the coupler, securely mounted to the rear end center section and the bellhousing adaptor or as noted in Class Requirements. In place of a cross member in the vicinity of the front universal joint, all competition cars—except Stock and Super Stock—using open drive shafts must have a retainer loop, 360 degrees, and of ¼-inch minimum-thickness steel, 2 inches wide, securely mounted and located within 6 inches of the front universal joint to support the driveshaft in event of U-joint failure. Open drive lines passing any part of the driver's body must be completely enclosed in ⅛-inch minimum-thickness steel plate securely mounted to the frame or frame structure.

DRIVER CONDUCT: Any driver who refuses to voluntarily reduce speed, or stop, if the car he is driving does not handle properly (i.e., excessive drifting of the car toward the center or edge of the track), or any driver whose car fishtails or weaves without due regard for the safety of himself, spectators, or other, faces immediate termination of participation. If during eliminations, the race is automatically forfeited to the offending driver's opponent. Any drver and/or pit crew member found to be under the influence of alcoholic beverages, or drugs, regardless of amount, will be ejected from the event, and such a condition is cause for suspension and/or revocation of competition privileges.

ENGINE: Crankshaft centerlines must not exceed 24 inches from the ground in any class. All competition cars with pressed-on front pulleys must have such pulleys installed to insure against accidental removal (drilled).

EXHAUST: Each car, regardless of class, must be equipped with exhaust collectors or stacks installed to direct the exhaust gasses out of the car body to the rear of the car, away from the driver and fuel tank. Exhaust stacks must incorporate a metal connecting strap to prevent loss of one or more stacks during competition. No flexible pipe permitted on any car in competition.

FIRE EXTINGUISHERS AND BLANKETS: Although each drag strip is required to provide adequate fire protection equipment, it is recommended that each contestant and/or his crew have a loaded serviceable fire extinguisher and a fire blanket in his possession—carried in the push car or otherwise available for immediate use. Dry chemical or CO_2 type extinguishers (2½ pounds minimum size) are recommended. Blankets may be fireproofed by immersing in a solution of 9 ounces of Borax, 4 ounces of boric acid to each gallon of water. Hand-wring, hang to dry. Repeat after each laundering.

FIREWALLS: Each car in competition must be equipped with a flameproof and fuel-proof firewall—including fiberglass—extending from side to side of the body and from the top of the engine compartment upper seal (hood, cowl, or deck) to the bottom of the floor and/or bellypan. Firewall must be constructed to provide a bulkhead between the engine and driver's compartment. All hoes or openings must be sealed with metal or other flameproof material.

FLASH SHIELD: Injector tubes may extend through individual holes in the hood, carburetors must not be openly exposed or uncovered. In place of a hood, carburetors must be equipped with a metal flash shield or velocity stacks which cover the top, back, and sides to prevent gas from being siphoned into the airstream or blown into the driver's face.

FLOOR: All cars without floors must be equipped with floor pans made of steel or aluminum which must extend the full length and width of the driver's compartment to the rear of the driver's seat. Cars equipped with floors or bellypans made of fiberglass or other breakable material must have metal subfloors. Bellypans and sub-floors enclosing engine or driver's compartment must contain suit-able drain holes throughout so that liquids and foreign matter cannot collect and thus create a fire hazard.

FLYWHEEL/CLUTCH: The use of stock type cast-iron flywheels and/or pressure plates is prohibited. See Class Requirements, Stock. Explosion-resistant units meeting SEMA Specs 1-1 are re-quired.

FLYWHEEL SHIELDS: Stick Shift. All cars in competition must be equipped with a suitable shield made of ¼-inch-minimum steel plate,* securely mounted to the frame or frame structure and com-pletely surrounding the bell housing (360 degrees) to protect frame, driver, and bystanders from fragments in case of clutch or flywheel disintegration. All cars in competition where flywheel shields are required must have an NHRA "accepted" adaptor shield meeting SEMA Specs 6-1. Fabricated units of ¼-inch-mini-mum steel plate will not be acceptable. All cars in Top Fuel, Top Gas, Funny Car and Competition Eliminator categories must use an NHRA "accepted" shield meeting SEMA Specs 6-1. Shields must not be bolted to the bell housing. Flywheel shields must be so constructed that they cover the top, sides, and rear of the bell housing, completely shielding the transmission bell or mounting

---

* Except NHRA "accepted" adaptor-shield: NHRA "accepted" full-coverage engine-to-transmission adaptors and similar units constructed of ¼-inch minimum-thickness steel plate are accepted without additional scattershield protection, only if the transmission bell and flywheel areas are completely covered. Fabricated steel housings must be so constructed that material and material thickness can be quickly determined by the technical committee. Flywheel shields manufactured of a material other than steel must be NHRA "accepted." It is highly recommended that these units be of one-piece construction. It is also highly recommended that a .250-inch steel shield be used in place of, or in addition to, the existing shield or housing and in all cases where a shield is required a motor plate should be used. All shields, flywheels, pressure plates, etc., should be attached with Grade 8 bolts. A brace or other device must be installed that will prevent the "can" or adaptor shield from being blown back into the driver's compartment in the event of flywheel or clutch explosion. Direct drive adaptor/shields may be externally vented in the noncritical back side area by means of a vent hole or holes not to exceed a total of four square inches. All venting must extend outside of the driver's cockpit area. Refer to shield manufacturer for specific details.

flange to stop fragments from entering driver's compartment. Shield must extend forward to a point at least 1 inch ahead of the flywheel and 1 inch to the rear of the clutch and pressure plate.

FLYWHEEL/TRANSMISSION SHIELD: With the exception of those cars competing in Super Stock and Stock classes, all cars in competition using any automatic transmission or any nonautomotive production stick-shift transmission must be equipped with a ¼-inch steel shield covering the unit. Use same requirements as listed under Flywheel Shields; Automatic Transmissions in the Allowance of the shields meeting SEMA Specs 4-1.

FLYWHEEL SHIELDS: Automatic Transmissions. Automatic transmissions must be equipped with a suitable shield made of ¼-inch minimum steel plate,* securely mounted to the frame or frame structure and completely surrounding the transmission section (360 degrees). Shield must start from a point 6 inches behind the engine block and be no less than 11 inches long.

FRAMES: All butt-welds must have visible reinforcement. Excessive grinding of welds not permitted.

FUEL SYSTEMS: Wherever possible, fuel tanks and fuel lines should be located ahead of the engine. Fuel blocks, if used, must be mounted at least 6 inches forward of the flywheel bellhousing area and must be enclosed in a 16-inch length of steel tubing, ⅛-inch-minimum wall thickness, securely mounted as a protection against fuel lines being severed. In the event fuel lines pass supercharger drive areas, it is highly recommended that they be encased in protective steel tubing. Fuel tanks located in front of the grille and out of the protective areas of the body, frame, and wheels must be protected against collision damage by some means of encasement (i.e., steel nerf bars, etc.). Cars with altered fuel systems (other than electric fuel pumps) must have a quick-action

---

* In place of ¼-inch steel plate will be the use of ⅜-inch minimum heat-treated aluminum—6061-T4 or T6—with a valid heat-treat certificate. Transmission shields manufactured of a material other than outlined in this Section must be NHRA "accepted" and meet SEMA Specs 4-1.

fuel shut-off valve within easy reach of the driver and located in the main fuel line between the fuel tank and the carburetor and/ or injectors. It is recommended that injector pumps be located away from the flywheel area wherever possible. Under no conditions are any fuel tanks, lines, or other units containing fuel permitted in the driver's compartment. All tanks must be completely isolated from the driver's compartment by a firewall, completely sealed to prevent any gasoline from entering the driver's compartment.

GASOLINE: Service station pump gasoline as sold to the general public through retail automotive service stations must be used. This gasoline, as sold, must have a specific gravity between 0.700 and 0.750. Aviation gasoline or additives of any type to increase gravity, octane rating, etc., will not be permitted except as noted under class requirements in each section.

HEAD PROTECTOR: A padded head protector must be installed at the back of the driver's head and constructed to prevent whiplash upon impact.

HELMETS & GOGGLES: All drivers in all classes (except stock cars *) and all motorcyclists must wear an NHRA "accepted" safety helmet while in competition on the strip. A list of "accepted" helmets may be obtained from the NHRA Technical Committee. Wind-proof, shatter-proof goggles must be worn by drivers of all vehicles not having windshields, and by all motorcyclists while on the strip.

IGNITION: Each car in competition must have a positive action on/off switch in good working order, located within easy reach of the driver, and on the same side of the car as the fuel shut-off control and hand brake. Magneto "kill-button" type switches are not permitted. It is recommended in all competition classes that the switch be mounted on either the hand brake or steering wheel

---

* Required on ALL Pro Stock, Super Stock, and Stock classes A through I stick and automatic. Highly recommended in all other stock classes.

(not required in this location on cars competing in Sections V or VI).

JACK AND JACK STANDS: No work may be done under any car in the pit area while the car is supported by only one jack. Additional safety devices such as jack stands are required to ensure safety in the event of jack failure. Disregard or failure to observe this rule is grounds for immediate disqualification.

LIQUID OVERFLOW: All cars in competition with any type of liquid overflow capable of dumping or spilling liquid must have a "catch-can" to accumulate the excess liquids and prevent them from being discharged on the strip. Minimum "catch-can" capacity: 1 pint.

MAGNAFLUX CERTIFICATES: Each car owner should voluntarily obtain a magnaflux inspection certificate on all altered or welded parts as protection against insecure welds, cracks or defects. Magnaflux certificates may be required by the technical committee on any altered or welded parts.

OCCUPANTS: No more than one person is permitted in any car during any run. All occupants of push cars must be inside of car or pickup cab in a seated position while push car is in operation.

PARACHUTES: All cars competing in classes where the NHRA speed record is in excess of 150 mph are required to have as standard equipment a breaking chute supplied by a recognized drag racing chute manufacturer. Tech inspectors should observe the proper operation of the chute and also inspect same for worn or frayed shroud lines, ripped or dirty canopies, and worn or ragged pilot chutes. Parachute cable housings should be mounted solidly to frame tube or other suitable member, no farther back than 1 inch from the "D" ring or release lever. Parachutes should be returned to the manufacturer every three months for complete inspection and repair. A parachute inspection date should be evident. Drag chutes must have their own independent mounting bracket and must not be mounted to the same bracket as the shoulder harness.

PROTECTIVE CLOTHING: Drivers of all fuel cars, and all cars equipped with superchargers (except Stock cars), and any car where an automatic transmission is in the driver's compartment are required to wear a reflective, heat-resistant, and flame-proof driving suit that meets SEMA Specs 3-1. Suits are to include, face mask, goggles, gloves, and reflective fire boots. In all other cars in competition, except Pro Stock, Super Stock, Stock and Modified Production classes, a leather (or fire-proof) jacket and/or fire-proof clothing is required. It is strongly recommended that fire-suits be worn in all open-bodied cars.

PUSH BARS: Tow starts are not permitted. Each car in competition must be equipped with a suitable bumper-height pushing attachment to facilitate starting and/or emergency pushing.

ROLL BAR AND ROLL CAGE: All cars in competition having any body modifications (i.e., chopped, channeled, gutted, or sectioned) must be equipped with a roll bar or cage roll structure. Minimum requirements are 1½-inch inside diameter steel tubing, with ⅛-inch wall thickness (1¾-inch outside diameter). All roll bars must be within 6 inches of the rear or side of the driver's head extending in height at least 3 inches above the driver's helmet, with driver in normal driving position and at least as wide as the driver's shoulders, adequately supported or cross-braced to prevent forward or lateral collapse of roll bar in case of spin-out, collision, or upset. Minimum requirements for cage-type roll structure are 1⅝-inch outside diameter steel tubing with ⅛-inch minimum wall thickness, securely mounted, gusseted, and braced. Low carbon (mild) steel tubing is recommended for all types of roll bar construction. Braces must be of the same diameter and wall thickness as the roll bar or cage-type structure, and intersect with the roll bar at a point not more than 5 inches from the top of the roll bar. All cage-type structures must be designed to protect the driver from any angle (360°). Threaded pipe, pipe fittings, lapweld pipe, magnesium or aluminum not permitted. Square corners must be properly gusseted. Flush-grinding welds not permitted.

SAFETY BELTS: All cars in competition must be equipped with an approved quick-release type driver safety belt in good condition. Belts must be securely fastened to the frame, cross member, or suitable reinforced mounting in such a manner that all fittings are in a direct line with the direction of pull. Steel castings, of the type recommended by FAA, or U-bolt type mounts are recommended. Flat steel plates, if used for installation, must be a minimum of ¼-inch thickness and have rounded edges to prevent cutting safety belts. Under no circumstances are bolts inserted through belt webbing accepted for mounting.

SAFETY HUBS: All cars in competition (except stock and some street class cars) must be equipped with satisfactory hubs. Stock bearing retainers are not accepted as safety hubs. A minimum of ⅛-inch steel plate reinforcement for stock bearing retainers is required. Wherever possible, internal safety hubs are recommended. In lieu of internal-type safety hubs a minimum of four hooks per driving wheel, each attached to the backing plate with not less than 2¼-inch-minimum bolts, required. Hooks must be made of ¼-inch minimum-thickness steel plate at least 1 inch wide, firmly mounted to retain the drum hub and wheel in the event of axle failure.

SHOCK ABSORBERS: Each car in competition must be equipped with one operative shock absorber for each sprung wheel. Shock absorbers must be either hydraulic or friction type, securely mounted and in good working order.

SHOULDER HARNESSES: A quick-release shoulder harness (aircraft type) is mandatory on all cars in competition whenever a roll bar or cage has been installed. All safety belt/shoulder harness installations must be of compatible nature and originally designed to be used with each other. Installations where the harness is sewed, fastened, or where safety belt is fed through loops in the harness is not permitted. Only those units that release all four attach points in one motion will be accepted. Shoulder harnesses must be securely mounted to the frame, cross member, or suitable reinforced mounting, and installed in such a manner that they will limit driver's body travel both upward and forward. Quick-release arm restraints are recommended. Upper torso restraining straps are highly recommended in all other cars. It is highly recommended that all seats be mounted vertically and incorporate a compatible crotch strap.

Each car's steering system will be inspected to determine its condition. Steering must be considered safe by the technical committee. Steering wheel "play" must be at a minimum. Drag link and tie-rod ends must be secured and keyed. All altered or modified steering systems will be closely checked for insecure welds and faulty parts. All welded parts must have additional visible reinforcement. Only conventional automotive steering systems are permitted. All rod ends (Heim, etc.) where used must be a minimum of ⅜-inch shank diameter and must be installed with flat washers to prevent bearing pull-out. Hollow rod ends are prohibited. All steering boxes, sectors and shafts must be mounted to the frame or suitable cross member and cannot be mounted in any case to the bell housing and/or bell housing adaptor shield, motor plate, or firewall. It is highly recommended that they be mounted to the rear of same.

STRESS: Any car having stress that is concentrated at a central point, on chassis by the location of rear-engine mount, engine support straps, roll bars, roll bar braces, or rear-end assembly, is required to have a reinforcing strap or truss-type brace to distribute the stress over at least a 3-foot area to relieve critical stress buildup or chassis fatigue at such points of component intersection.

SUPERCHARGERS: All cars equipped with a Rootes-type supercharger must have a shield or suitable chain guard, or belt guard, made of ⅛-inch minimum thickness steel plate, securely mounted to the engine or frame structure to contain belts or chains in the event of breakage. Gilmer belt drives may use $\frac{1}{16}$-inch steel plate or equivalent. Where Gilmer belt drive systems are completely covered by hood and side panels, and all fuel lines passing drive area are encased in a minimum of 16 inches of ⅛-inch-thickness steel tubing, drive covers may be omitted. Supercharger Gilmer belt-drive shields may also be omitted if fuel lines in the belt-drive area are manufactured from braided steel and/or protected with steel tubing armor at least ⅛ inch thick and securely fastened to the car's frame and/or engine. It is however highly recommended that an additional device be installed to protect the fuel lines in the case of a blower drive failure. A blower cover or shield is also highly recommended.

SUPPORT STRAP: An engine support strap made of steel plate or aircraft cable (chain not accepted), or some other means of supporting the rear of the engine in case of clutch or flywheel disintegration, is required on all competition cars. Some means must be used other than the engine motor plate.

SUSPENSION: All cars must have a full suspension system of the type produced by an automotive manufacturer (i.e., springs, torsion bars, etc.). Rigid-mount front axles are prohibited. Rigid mount rear axles are permitted when so indicated under section's Class Requirements. All rod ends (Heim, etc.) where used must be a minimum of ⅜-inch shank diameter and must be installed with flat washers to prevent bearing pull-out. Hollow rod ends are prohibited. Three-wheel vehicles are not eligible for any competition class. "C" type lift-kits are not permitted in any class of competition.

THROTTLE: Each car, regardless of class, must have a foot throttle incorporating a positive-acting return spring attached directly to the carburetor throttle-arm and must register a minimum pull of 2 pounds. A positive stop or over-ride prevention must be used to keep linkage from passing over center and sticking in an open position. Some means of manually returning the throttle to a closed position by use of the foot must be installed on all altered linkage systems, in addition to return springs (except hydraulically operated systems). Commercially available cable throttle systems are permitted. Choke cables, brazed or welded fittings on steel cable are not allowed. Licensed hand controls are permitted in stock classes.

UPHOLSTERY/SEATS: The driver's seat in any car in competition must be so constructed, braced, mounted, and upholstered that it will give full back and shoulder protection to the driver in the event of car upset, spin-out, or collision. The driver's seat must be supported on the bottom and back by the frame or cross member. All seats must be upholstered. Properly braced, supported and constructed seats of aluminum or fiberglass—accessory seats—are acceptable; however, plastic "kitchen-chair-type" seats are not allowed in any car. All accessory seats must have a minimum 24-inch-high seat back. Seats of bare metal or fiberglass are prohibited in any car in any class.

WEIGHT: In addition to weight-to-cubic-inch classification ratios, the following minimum total car weights (per engine[s] used) are in effect and must be observed, regardless of competition class, except those chassis which are constructed to meet or exceed the specifications set forth in the Specialty Equipment Manufacturers Association (SEMA) suggested standards. All cars so constructed must have attached to the chassis the label "Meets SEMA Suggested Specifications." Chassis of all vehicles in AA/D and all fuel dragsters are required to be labeled "Meets SEMA Specifications." All labels MUST be attached to the car's structure for identification. All AA/D and all Fuel Dragsters must be labeled "Meets SEMA Suggested Specifications 2-2."

WEIGHT DISTRIBUTION: Each car in competition must have an

adequate percentage of its weight carried on the front wheels to ensure proper handling ability at all times. Additional front-end weight will be required by the technical committee on cars experiencing wheel stands or carrying the front wheels during acceleration.

WHEELS AND TIRES: Hubcaps must be removed for inspectors, who will check for loose lugs, cracked wheels, worn or oversize lug holes, spindles, axle nuts, cotter pins, etc. Snap-on hubcaps are not permitted on any class car during competition. Tires will be visually checked for condition, pressure, etc., and must be considered safe by the technical committee prior to any runs by the car. Implement tires are prohibited. All street tires must have a minimum of $\frac{1}{16}$-inch tread depth. Each car in competition must be equipped with automotive type wheels with a minimum 12-inch diameter, unless class requirements stipulate otherwise. Motorcycle wheels or lightweight automotive wire wheels must be equipped with .100-inch minimum diameter steel spokes, properly cross-laced to provide maximum strength. All spoke holes in rim and hub must be laced. Omissions to lighten wheels are not permitted.

WINDSCREENS: On open-bodied cars, or any other class car permitted to enter competition without a windshield, a metal or other fire-proof deflector must be installed. The deflector should be so constructed that it will divert wind, liquids, foreign matter, etc., over the driver's head, be securely mounted, and installed in such a manner that it does not in any way obstruct the driver's frontal view.

WINDSHIELD AND WINDOWS: Windshields, and/or windows on all competition cars, when listed under Class Requirements, must be of shatter-proof material, safety glass or Plexiglass. Windshields and/or windows must be clear without tinting or coloring except factory tinted safety glass. Product identification decals will not be allowed on the front windows and/or windshields.

Following is a list of NHRA district personnel:

NORTHEAST DIVISION—1

Maine, Vermont, New Hampshire, Rhode Island, Connecticut, Massachusetts, New York, Pennsylvania, New Jersey, Maryland, West Virginia, Delaware, District of Columbia; Quebec, Nova Scotia, New Brunswick, and Eastern Ontario, Canada.

Division Director	*Division Tech Director*
Darwin Doll	Greg Xakellis
P. O. Box 306	321 Groff Avenue
York, Pennsylvania 17405	Lancaster, Pennsylvania 17602

SOUTHEAST DIVISION—2

South Carolina, Alabama, Georgia, Florida, Mississippi, Tennessee, North Carolina, Virginia.

Division Director	*Division Tech Director*
Buster Couch	Darrell Davis
3620 Sherrydale Lane	11406 Vera Drive
Decatur, Georgia 30032	Jacksonville, Florida 32218

NORTH-CENTRAL DIVISION—3

Michigan, Missouri, Ohio, Indiana, Kentucky, Illinois, Wisconsin; Central and Western Ontario, Canada.

Division Director	*Division Tech Director*
Bob Daniels	Marty Barratt
P. O. Box 24257	P. O. Box 24257
Speedway, Indiana 46224	Speedway, Indiana 46224

SOUTH-CENTRAL DIVISION—4

New Mexico, Texas, Oklahoma, Arkansas, Louisiana.

Division Director	*Division Tech Director*
Dale Ham	Chuck Nelson
2207 Lipscomb Street	513 Birchwood Drive
Amarillo, Texas 79109	Garland, Texas 75040

WEST-CENTRAL DIVISION—5

Wyoming, Colorado, Kansas, Nebraska, North Dakota, South Dakota, Iowa, Minnesota; Manitoba, Canada.

Division Director
Darrell Zimmerman
P. O. Box 43
Julesburg, Colorado 80737

Division Tech Director
Kenneth Arnold
Box 138
Julesburg, Colorado 80737

NORTHWEST DIVISION—6

Washington, Oregon, Idaho, Montana, Alaska; Alberta, Saskatchewan, and British Columbia, Canada.

Division Director
Bruce Bowler
7320 Northeast 70th Street
Vancouver, Washington 98662

Division Tech Director
Jack Shannon
6115 Magnolia
Everett, Washington 98201

SOUTHWEST DIVISION—7

California, Nevada, Arizona, Hawaii, Utah.

Division Director
Bernie Partridge
P. O. Box 1118
Ridgecrest, California 93555

Division Tech Director
Jim Dale
9082 Helena Avenue
Montclair, California 91763

Hot rod competition will take many forms, but in all cases it will prove a significant involvement for the enthusiast. The sport has many facets, all exciting, all fresh with the ingenuity of hundreds of thousands of men and women who just happen to enjoy things mechanical. As a hobby, hot rodding has no superior.

Index

Index